The Innovation Paradox

The Innovation Paradox

Developing-Country Capabilities and the Unrealized Promise of Technological Catch-Up

Xavier Cirera and William F. Maloney

WORLD BANK GROUP

ISBN (print): 978-1-4648-1160-9
ISBN (electronic): 978-1-4648-1184-5
DOI: 10.1596/978-1-4648-1160-9

Cover art: La Creación de las Aves, (The Creation of Birds) by Remedios Varo. Used with the permission of INBA; further permission required for reuse. Reproducción autorizada por el Instituto Nacional de Bellas Artes y Literatura, 2017 (Reproduction authorized by INBA, 2017).
Cover design: Bill Pragluski, Critical Stages, LLC.

Library of Congress Cataloging-in-Publication Data
Names: Cirera, Xavier, author. | Maloney, William F. (William Francis), 1959–author.
Title: The innovation paradox : developing–country capabilities and the unrealized promise of technological catch-up / Xavier Cirera and William F. Maloney.
Description: Washington, D.C. : World Bank, [2017] | Includes bibliographical references and index.
Identifiers: LCCN 2017036854| ISBN 9781464811609 (print) | ISBN 9781464811845 (electronic)
Subjects: LCSH: Technological innovations—Developing countries. | Information technology—Developing countries—Management.| Organizational change—Developing countries.
Classification: LCC HC59.72.T4 C57 2017 | DDC 338.9/26091724—dc23
LC record available at https://lccn.loc.gov/2017036854

Contents

Boxes

Figures

Tables

Foreword

Productivity growth is critical for accelerating development. Poverty across the globe cannot fall unless poorer countries raise their per capita incomes. Some of this income growth will come from investing in better physical and human capital. However, we know that a significant share of income growth derives from productivity growth, and specifically from innovations that render physical and human capital more productive.

Understanding how innovations arise and are adopted, and which policies can support them, is important for development policy design. It is now even more important, given the new wave of digitalization and automation that is rapidly altering economies around the world. One of the key findings of the research presented here is that the observed low level of technological adoption in developing countries is a rational response of firms to a range of conditions they face: barriers to accumulating physical and human capital, low firm capabilities, and weak government capacity. Unlocking the enormous growth potential of moving countries closer to the technological frontier however is not as simple as, say, providing additional incentives for research and development. Moving countries closer to the frontier will require far-reaching policy changes that tackle multiple constraints to technological adoption.

The research presented here is part of a larger research project on productivity, led by the Office of the Chief Economist of the World Bank's Equitable Growth, Finance, and Institutions Vice Presidency. We are confident that researchers and development practitioners alike will highly value the new findings on innovation patterns and the directions for development policies it contains.

Jan Walliser
Vice President
Equitable Growth, Finance, and Institutions
World Bank Group

Preface

Productivity accounts for half of the differences in GDP per capita across countries. Identifying policies to stimulate it is thus critical to alleviating poverty and fulfilling the rising aspirations of global citizens. Yet, productivity growth has slowed globally over recent decades, and the lagging productivity performance in developing countries constitutes a major barrier to convergence with advanced-country levels of income.

The World Bank Productivity Project seeks to bring frontier thinking on the measurement and determinants of productivity, grounded in the developing-country context, to global policy makers. Each volume in the series explores a different aspect of the topic through dialogue with academics and policy makers, and through sponsored empirical work in our client countries. The Productivity Project is an initiative of the Vice Presidency for Equitable Growth, Finance and Institutions.

The present volume focuses on the roughly half of overall productivity growth that is driven by firms adopting new technologies, products, and processes. In particular, it examines a heretofore under-researched "innovation paradox": Returns on technological adoption are thought to be extremely high, yet countries appear to invest little, implying that this critical channel of productivity growth is underexploited. The analysis sheds light on how to redress this paradox and leads to rethinking many aspects of innovation-related productivity policies.

William F. Maloney
Chief Economist
Equitable Growth, Finance and Institutions
World Bank Group

Acknowledgments

This report was written by Xavier Cirera (Senior Economist, World Bank's Trade and Competitiveness Global Practice) and William F. Maloney (Chief Economist, World Bank's Equitable Growth, Finance, and Institutions [EFI] cluster). The authors thank Jan Walliser (Vice President, Equitable Growth, Finance, and Institutions), Anabel González (Senior Director, Trade and Competitiveness Global Practice), and Klaus Tilmes (Director, Trade and Competitiveness Global Practice) for their support as well as Esperanza Lasagabaster, Paulo Correa, and Ganesh Rasagam, successive managers in the Innovation and Entrepreneurship unit of the World Bank.

The work builds on a combination of analytical work by the authors and inputs from a series of background papers carried out under the umbrella of the project and related to earlier initiatives. The authors specifically thank Patricio Aroca (Universidad Adolfo Ibáñez, Chile), Mariano Bosch (Inter-American Development Bank), Edwin Goñi (Inter-American Development Bank), Carlos Molina Guerra (University of Chicago), Albert Link (University of North Carolina), Vladimir López-Bassols (Independent Consultant), Asier Mariscal (Carlos III University), Andres Rodriguez-Clare (University of California, Berkeley), Leonard Sabetti (CERDI, Université d'Auvergne), Mauricio Sarrias (Catholic University of the North, Chile), John Scott (Dartmouth University), and Felipe Valencia (Bonn University) for their contributions, as well as Oscar Calvo-González, Leonardo Iacovone, Daniel Lederman, David McKenzie, Silvia Muzi, Mariana Pereira-López, and Daria Taglioni at the World Bank.

The authors are especially grateful to Nick Bloom (Stanford University), Renata Lemos (World Bank), Rafaella Sadun (Harvard Business School), John Van Reenen (Massachusetts Institute of Technology), and Daniela Scur (Oxford University) for their support with the World Management Survey and for ongoing discussions on managerial practices. We acknowledge invaluable comments from José Miguel Benavente (Inter-American Development Bank), Laura Chioda (EFI, World Bank), Charles Edquist (Centre for Innovation, Research, and Competence in the Learning Economy, Sweden), Keun Lee (Seoul National University), Bengt-Åke Lundvall (Aalborg University, Denmark), Juan Rogers (Georgia Technological University), and Luis Servén (Development Research Group, World Bank) for their work on the national innovation system.

The policy chapters partially draw from the work on innovation policy by the World Bank Trade and Competitiveness Global Practice and the Innovation and Entrepreneurship unit in particular, as well as from various other innovation policy activities at the World Bank, with specific inputs from Anwar Aridi, Jaime Frias, Justin Hill, Natasha Kapil, and Juan Rogers (Georgia Technological University). It also benefited from the work on the Public Expenditure Reviews in Science, Technology, and Innovation that was piloted in Colombia and later implemented in Chile and Ukraine.

The research on management and technology extension systems, benefited from joint World Bank–Government of Colombia work developing their technological program, and we thank Paula Toro and Rafael Puyana (Departamento Nacional de Planeacion, Colombia), Martha Lucia Perlaza and the team at the National Productivity Center (Cali, Colombia), as well as Eduardo Bitrán (Production Development Corporation *CORFO*, Chile), and Xavier Duran (University of the Andes, Colombia) for extended conversations on the topic. In Asia, we benefited from interviews with Junichiro Mimaki and Junko Motozawa (Small and Medium Enterprise Agency, METI), Akihiro Takagi and Takenori Nasu (Japanese International Cooperation Agency), and Kenji Fujita (Japanese Productivity Center). In Singapore, the authors thank Audrey Lok and Mohamed Sirajuddin Jaleel (SPRING), and Guan Wei Lee (Research and Enterprise Division, Ministry of Trade and Industry).

For their careful review of the entire document, we thank Martin Bell (SPRU, University of Sussex), Nick Bloom (Stanford University), Paulo Correa (World Bank), Paulo Figueiredo (FGV, Brazil), David McKenzie (World Bank), Carlo Pietrobelli (UN-MERIT), Sudhir Shetty (World Bank), John Sutton (London School of Economics), and Mary Hallward-Driemeier and Denis Medvedev at the World Bank. The report also benefited from the comments from World Bank colleagues Ali Abukumail, Maja Andjelkovic, James Brumby (Director, Governance Global Practice), Cesar Calderon, Ana Cusolito, Mark Dutz, John Gabriel Goddard, Naoto Kanehira, Smita Kuriakose, John Panzer (Director, Macro and Fiscal Management Global Practice), Samuel Pienknagura, Jean-Louis Racine, Mariam Semeda, Siddharth Sharma, Michael Wong, and Michael Woolcock.

The authors also thank Diletta Doretti and Susana Rey, as well as Bill Shaw and Nora Mara, who edited the report. Rumit Pancholi, Susan Graham, and Patricia Katayama provided production and acquisitions support.

Finally, the authors thank the financial support from the European Union; the African, Caribbean and Pacific Group of States Secretariat; and the governments of Austria, Norway, and Switzerland through the Competitive Industries and Innovation Program trust fund.

Abbreviations

ATP	Advanced Technology Program
BDS	Business development services
BvD	Bureau van Dijk
CDG	Capability and Development Grant
EDB	Economic Development Board
ES	Enterprise Survey
EU	European Union
FDI	Foreign direct investment
GDP	Gross domestic product
GII	Global Innovation Index
GRI	Government Research Institute
GVC	Global value chains
ICV	Innovation and capability voucher
JIS	Japanese Industrial Standards
LEAD	Local Enterprise and Association Development
LEFS	Local Enterprise Finance Scheme
LETAS	Local Enterprise Technical Assistance Scheme
LIUP	Local Industry Upgrading Program
M&E	Monitoring and evaluation
MEP	Manufacturing extension partnership
MNE	Multinational enterprise
MITI	Ministry of International Trade and Industry
MOPS	Management and Organizational Practices Survey
NBER	National Bureau of Economic Research
NIC	Newly industrialized countries
NIS	National Innovation Systems
NIST	National Institute of Standards and Technology
NPB	National Productivity Board
NQI	National quality infrastructure
OECD	Organisation for Economic Co-Operation and Development
OTR	Operational and technology roadmapping

PACT	Partnership for Capability Transformation
PDIA	Problem-driven iterative adaptation
PER	Public expenditure review
PIC	Productivity and Innovation Credit
PPP	Purchasing power parity
PRI	Public research institutions
QC	Quality control
R&D	Research and development
RCT	Randomized control trials
SDF	Skills Development Fund
SDP	Supplier Development Program
SERC	Science and Engineering Research Council
SHRM	Strategic human resource management
SIBS	Survey of Innovation and Business Strategy
SME	Small and medium enterprises
STEM	Science, technology, engineering, and mathematics
STI	Science, technology, and innovation
TAC	Trade associations and chambers of commerce
TAP	Technology Adoption Program
TFP	Total factor productivity
TPM	Total productive maintenance
UNESCO	United Nations Educational, Scientific, and Cultural Organization
WMS	World Management Survey
WVS	World Value Survey

Executive Summary

The Innovation Paradox

The centrality of innovation to the rise of advanced economies was captured by David Landes' (1969) classic metaphor of *The Unbound Prometheus*, referring to the Greek god who released the power of fire to mankind. Defined as the introduction of new products, technologies, business processes, and ideas in the market, as well as the invention of new ideas, *innovation* drives Schumpeter's creative destruction process (Schumpeter [1942] 2008), underlies modern growth theory, and is the critical ingredient in historical accounts of how countries achieve prosperity.

In turn, the gains from Schumpeterian catch-up afforded to follower countries—arising from the radiation of ideas, products, and technologies to developing countries—represents an externality of truly historic proportions that should rise with increased distance from the technological frontier. Yet Prometheus remains bound in developing countries. This study documents that, despite the vast potential returns to innovation, developing countries invest far less, measured along a variety of dimensions, than advanced countries. Firms and governments appear to be leaving billions of dollars on the table in forgone productivity growth and lost competitiveness. Indeed, policy advice to move into production baskets thought to be more growth-friendly misses the critical point that countries unable to innovate in their present industries are unlikely to do so in new industries.

To explain this *innovation paradox* the report focuses on three central determinants of innovation performance: (1) the critical complements to innovation investment needed to realize the high potential returns; (2) the range of firm capabilities required to undertake innovation and take it to market; and (3) the required government capabilities for implementing effective innovation policies. The analysis draws on two important traditions, the neoclassical and the National Innovation Systems (NIS) literatures, highlighting the common ground between them, with the ultimate goal of contributing to more coherent and effective policy making in developing countries.

The Nature of Innovation in Developing Countries

The first part of the report describes firm innovation in developing countries and provides a resolution to the *innovation paradox*. Chapter 2 draws on several new sources of firm data to generate stylized facts about the nature of innovation investments undertaken across the development process. The analysis shows that firms report innovation across the income spectrum and in all sectors, but that innovation often consists of marginal improvements in process or products, rather than significant technology adoption or new product imitation, and it very infrequently involves frontier research. The coexistence of the extraordinarily low levels of innovation-related investment in poor countries with the dramatically high returns thought to accompany technological adoption and Schumpeterian catch-up, particularly far from the frontier, define the innovation paradox.

More important, investments in innovation-related inputs increase with income per capita. The paucity of high-level investment is suggestive that the appropriate policy model to support innovation in developing countries will differ from that of advanced countries, where policy often centers on research and development. More generally, the co-movement with the development of a wide variety of innovation inputs suggests a high degree of complementarity among different factors of production in the innovation function.

Explaining the Innovation Policy Paradox: The Importance of Complementarities

Chapter 3 offers a resolution to the innovation paradox. The new data sources analyzed show that the higher returns to innovation predicted by Schumpeterian catch-up are far from being realized. The returns to innovation are often positive and high but, below a certain level of development, decrease with distance from the frontier and may even become negative. The chapter proposes that this decline is driven by the absence of a broad set of complementarities, such as physical and human capital, which becomes more acute with distance from the frontier and more than offsets the gains from Schumpeterian catch-up. If a firm (country) invests in innovation but cannot also import the necessary machines, contract trained workers and engineers, or draw on new organizational techniques, the returns to that investment will be low. In turn, the underlying conditions that impede the accumulation of any of these types of capital— such as the cost of doing business, trade regime, competitiveness framework, or capital markets, as well as those seen as particular to innovation, such as intellectual property rights protection or market failures that disincentivize the accumulation of knowledge— affect the returns and hence the quantity of innovation investment.

This insight has two implications for innovation policy and evaluation. First, it suggests that the policy maker's conception of the NIS must go beyond the usual institutions and policies to offset widely recognized innovation-related market failures, to include these broader complementary factors and supporting institutions. Second, conventional measures of benchmarking innovation performance, such as comparing raw levels of gross domestic expenditure on R&D (GERD), are likely to be misleading if they do not take into account the stock of other complementary factors: countries with low levels of physical or human capital probably should not try to target advanced country levels of R&D.

Managerial Practices As a Key Input for Innovation

Chapter 4 focuses on describing a key input and complementary factor for innovation: managerial and organizational practices. An ample literature in the NIS tradition argues that, in order to innovate and manage innovation projects effectively, firms need to acquire a range of capabilities. Teece and Pisano (1994)—and, more in the mainstream, Sutton (2012), Sutton and Trefler (2016), or Hallak (2006), among others—have also stressed the acquisition of these capabilities as fundamental to both productivity and quality upgrading. Accounts of the East Asian miracles in the NIS tradition place primary emphasis on the process of learning and raising the capabilities for innovation of firms, rather than on the particular sectors they were in (see Kim 1997; Hobday 2000; Dodgson 2000; Lee 2013).

The recent introduction of the World Management Survey (WMS), initiated by Bloom and Van Reenen (2007, 2010), has permitted a quantum leap in the comparative quantitative analysis of management practices and their implications for productivity and innovation. In particular, the WMS has documented that developing country firms are indeed lagging in a wide range of capabilities that are critical to the Schumpeterian catch-up process. Average scores in monitoring, employment of just-in-time processes, internal feedback mechanisms, long-run planning and goal stretching, and human resource policies in poor country firms are well below those in frontier countries. Firms that lack the capabilities required to respond to market conditions, identify new technological opportunities, develop a plan to exploit them, and then cultivate the necessary human resources will find it difficult to innovate.

Using several new data sources, chapter 4 confirms the importance of advanced managerial and organizational practices for innovation. Empirical analysis shows their direct impact on innovation. Even after controlling for the usual inputs such as R&D, managerial and organizational practices are important predictors of innovation and productivity across countries, firm size, and country income levels, and can partly explain the lower returns to R&D found in poorer countries.

In sum, developing these capabilities is of paramount importance for innovation policy, especially in countries and firms that are more distant from the technological frontier.

What Drives Managerial Capabilities?

The above findings beg the question of why managerial capabilities are so weak in developing countries. Chapter 5 shows that scores are of lower quality than those in the frontier (the United States) across the entire distribution, which implies that convergence to the frontier requires not only the exit of badly run firms but also upgrading of the best firms. Several factors emerge as affecting managerial quality. More educated managers tend to be better. Limits on competition can impair managerial capabilities, either by enabling the most inefficient firms to survive or by failing to provide adequate incentives for firms to upgrade. Firms with diffuse ownership tend to be among the best, whereas government-owned companies and family-owned firms are weaker, the ubiquity of the latter in developing countries partly due to weak rule of law.

Chapter 5 also explores several sources of learning and upgrading capabilities. One critical source is related to participation in international trade. Openness to trade provides incentives to upgrade and exposure to new ideas. Imports can increase access to technology and its embedded know-how, and exporting enables firms to learn about more sophisticated and contested markets. Foreign direct investment (FDI) can also provide important learning opportunities: Firms with foreign ownership tend to be better managed and are more likely to perform R&D and to introduce product innovations. Exposure to multinational enterprises (MNEs) and participation in global value chains (GVCs) can also be important sources of knowledge spillovers, although in many cases spillovers do not occur because domestic firms lack the complementary capabilities that would allow them to accumulate knowledge.

The Innovation Policy Dilemma

The second part of the report focuses on how governments can better support innovation and in particular the accumulation of innovation capabilities. This requires confronting what we label the *innovation policy dilemma*: For developing countries, the greater magnitude of the market failures to be resolved and the multiplicity of missing complementary factors and institutions increase the complexity of innovation policy; at the same time, governments' capabilities to design, implement, and coordinate an effective policy mix to manage it are weaker.

Weak Government Capabilities

Governments in many developing countries lack the human resources and organizational efficiency to design and implement policies that could redress market and system failures and hence foment innovation. This weakness constitutes another key to the innovation paradox, yet the role that public servants, ministries, and agencies play in ensuring or undermining the effectiveness of innovation policy is generally absent in academic and policy discussions. Chapter 6 offers an overall view of the necessary policy capabilities and how to improve them.

Governments require capabilities for policy making across four key dimensions:

1. *Policy design* requires the ability to identify market failures, design the appropriate policies to redress them, and establish clear metrics for success. Many failed experiments in developing countries result from simply importing

from advanced countries institutional models and best practices that may not address the true failures or be politically viable. Many agencies, such as public research institutions, lack a clearly defined mission and incentives that would align them with identified clients and goals and shield them from capture.

2. *Efficacy of implementation* requires strong public management practices, as well as processes for evaluating, adapting, and modifying or terminating policies when needed.

3. *Coherence of policy* across the NIS requires the ability to take an overview of the overall system and effectively coordinate across ministries and agencies. In practice, policy is often balkanized by ministry or administrative level, and there is little alignment between the stated goals of policies and actual budgets and impact.

4. *Policy consistency and predictability* require systems that cultivate innovation policies and institutions over time, overcoming fluctuations in political economy and guaranteeing a predictable environment for long-run innovation investing. Instead, there is often limited national consensus on the importance of the innovation agenda and high-level political commitment, and policy is subject to weak backing and frequent reversals.

None of these capabilities is easy to generate or maintain.

Supporting the "Capabilities Escalator"

The final step in addressing the innovation policy dilemma requires choosing the appropriate combination of innovation policy instruments—*the policy mix*—in the context of scarce government capabilities. Chapter 7 offers a heuristic framework, the "capabilities escalator," where policies to support firm upgrading are prioritized consonant with the level of capabilities of the private sector, and of policy makers and institutions, and ratchet up through progressively higher stages of sophistication:

1. Stage 1 primarily supports production and management capabilities
2. Stage 2 increases the focus on supporting technological capabilities
3. Stage 3 expands the support to invention and technology-generation capabilities

Given the heterogeneity of firms found even in relatively poor countries, the framework is not meant to be deterministic but rather to highlight overlooked policy considerations. For example, as the report shows, and despite the absence of such policies in most developing country growth strategies, many advanced countries such as Italy, Japan, Singapore, and the United States have invested and continue to invest heavily and profitably in the first stage of the escalator. Chapter 7 discusses some of the key policy instruments in the transition toward more sophisticated technological and invention capabilities such as technology centers, public research institutions, and other R&D instruments. Developing stage 3 capabilities is an agenda of decades that must be started concomitantly with efforts in the earlier stages, but it cannot be considered a substitute for the policies to support stage 1 capabilities—firms need to walk before they can run.

Rethinking Innovation Policies

To conclude, the report shows that the low innovation activity observed in developing countries is not due to some irrationality on the part of firms and governments. Nor is it simply a question of remedying the commonly articulated knowledge-related market failures. Rather, innovation in the developing world faces barriers that are orders of magnitude more challenging than those found in the advanced world. Thus, fostering innovation requires a rethinking of innovation policies along three key dimensions.

First, the importance of a wide range of innovation complementarities implies that the scope of the NIS that policy makers must keep in mind is much larger than in advanced countries and must include everything that affects the accumulation of all types of capital—physical, human, and knowledge—and their supporting markets. What looks like an innovation problem, such as a low rate of investment in R&D, may reflect barriers to accumulating other factors, including physical and human capital.

Second, firm managerial and technological capabilities are a central complementarity to narrowly defined innovation expenditures, and their cultivation is critical to fomenting a continual process of technological adaptation and quality upgrading. This implies a rebalancing of policy priorities toward management and technology extension instruments and away from a focus mostly or exclusively on promoting R&D. Although R&D is an important input for innovation, it requires a set of capabilities that are unlikely to be prevalent in developing countries and its promotion cannot be at the expense of the other investments in the capabilities escalator.

Finally, the complexity and problems in constructing a functional NIS and building private sector capability are greater in developing countries, whereas government capabilities to manage them are weaker. Innovation policy thus needs an honest balancing of capabilities with tasks, which requires working on a selective set of issues rather than trying to import a full set of institutions and policies from elsewhere.

The analytical work here brings to light important shortcomings in the way statistical agencies collect and interpret data, and the report implicitly makes a plea for more accurate measurement to help policy makers understand innovation in their economies and to better benchmark performance of firms and the NIS.

Both better data and better analytical frameworks are necessary as developing countries face the dramatic and unpredictable evolution of the world economy. The rate of technological change is accelerating, and we cannot know with assurance which sectors or industries will offer rapid routes to prosperity, or what technologies will drive them. However, Pasteur's counsel that "fortune favors the prepared mind" remains as vitally relevant for countries as for people, and this report provides a map of areas where policy makers need to ensure they are ready. Raising the capabilities of firms to manage this uncertainty and chart their way forward, ensuring that the innovation system provides necessary complementary inputs and flows of knowledge, and strengthening government capabilities to manage a large and expanding set of challenges, are all keys to resolving the innovation paradox and preparing countries for the opportunities ahead.

References

Bloom, Nicholas, and John Van Reenen. 2007. "Measuring and Explaining Management Practices across Firms and Countries." *Quarterly Journal of Economics* 122 (4): 1351–1408.

———. 2010. "Why Do Management Practices Differ across Firms and Countries?" *Journal of Economic Perspectives* 24 (1): 203–24.

Dodgson, Mark. 2000. "Strategic Research Partnerships: Their Role, and Some Issues of Measuring their Extent and Outcomes—Experiences from Europe and Asia." Paper presented to the Workshop on Strategic Research Partnerships sponsored by the National Science Foundation and convened at SRI International, Washington, DC, October 13.

Hallak, Juan Carlos. 2006. "Product Quality and the Direction of Trade." *Journal of International Economics* 68 (1): 238–65.

Hobday, Michael. 2000. "East versus Southeast Asian Innovation Systems: Comparing OEM- and TNC-Led Growth in Electronics." In *Technology, Learning, and Economic Development: Experiences of Newly Industrializing Economies*, edited by Linsu Kim and Richard R. Nelson, 129–60. Cambridge, UK: Cambridge University Press.

Kim, Linsu. 1997. *Imitation to Innovation: The Dynamics of Korea's Technological Learning*. Boston, MA: Harvard Business School Press.

Landes, David S. 1969. *The Unbound Prometheus: Technical Change and Industrial Development in Western Europe from 1750 to the Present*. Cambridge, U.K.: Cambridge University Press.

Lee, Keun. 2013. *Schumpeterian Analysis of Economic Catch-up: Knowledge, Path-Creation, and the Middle-Income Trap* . Cambridge, UK: Cambridge University Press.

Schumpeter, Joseph. 2008. *Capitalism, Socialism and Democracy*. Harper Collins. (Original work published 1942)

Sutton, John. 2012. *Competing in Capabilities: The Globalization Process*. Oxford, U.K.: Oxford University Press.

Sutton, John, and Daniel Trefler. 2016. "Capabilities, Wealth, and Trade." *Journal of Political Economy* 124 (3): 826–78.

Teece, David, and Gary Pisano. 1994. "*The Dynamic Capabilities of Firms: An Introduction*." *Industrial and Corporate Change* 3 (3): 537–56.

1. The Innovation Paradox

Introduction: The Innovation Imperative

The centrality of innovation to the rise of advanced economies was captured by David Landes's (1969) classic metaphor of *The Unbound Prometheus*, referring to the Greek god who released the power of fire to mankind. Defined as the introduction of new products, technologies, business processes, and ideas in the market, as well as the invention of new ideas; *innovation* drives Schumpeter's creative destruction process (Schumpeter 2008, originally published in 1942) underlies modern growth theory, and is the critical ingredient in historical accounts of how countries achieve prosperity.[1]

In turn, the radiation of ideas, products, and technologies to developing countries represents an externality of truly historic proportions. In the long run, productivity improvements can account for half of gross domestic product (GDP) growth (Easterly and Levine 2001), with adoption of technologies making up a sizable share of those. This implies that the wealth transfers from North to South are hundreds of billions of U.S. dollars per year, dwarfing international aid flows. Although recent estimates of the returns to research and development (R&D) for the United States and Spain put them at a striking 40–60 percent annually, Griffith, Redding, and Van Reenen (2004) argue from Organisation for Economic Co-operation and Development (OECD 2005) data that the returns rise much higher (potentially in the triple digits) with increased distance from the technological frontier, reflecting the gains from Schumpeterian catch-up afforded to follower countries. Even prominent observers more concerned with equity and how the fruits of prosperity are shared, such as Piketty (2017, p. 21), concur: "Knowledge and skill diffusion is the key to overall productivity growth as well as the reduction of inequality both within and between countries." Moreover, the benefits from innovation go beyond income alone: the unmeasured welfare gains from improvements in health and longevity are thought to be almost as large as those measured by GDP per capita.[2]

The Innovation Paradox

Despite the vast potential returns to innovation, this study documents that developing countries do far *less* innovation, measured along a variety of dimensions, than advanced countries. This we term the "Innovation Paradox." Developing country firms and

The Concept of Innovation

One important problem in the study of innovation is the lack of clarity and consensus on what "innovation" means. Innovation means different things to different people. In this report, we adopt a broad, Schumpeterian view of innovation, which is more useful to understand the growth process of countries.

Innovation can be defined as the ability to use knowledge to develop and apply new ideas that result in changes in the production and organizational structure of the firm. Schumpeter (1934) defined several of these applications that qualify as innovation:

- Introduction of a new product or modifications to an existing product
- A new process or technology in an industry
- The discovery of a new market
- Development of new sources of supply of inputs and raw materials
- Changes in industrial organization

Innovation is, therefore, broader than invention. It includes commercial applications of new technology, new material, or new methods and processes. It primarily involves the process of adoption of existing technologies, the process of copying or imitating attributes from other products, or the adoption of new managerial and organizational practices or business models from other companies.

Innovation also includes the invention of new technologies and disruptive business models. Although important, these are a small part of the innovation process, especially in those countries farther away from the technological frontier. The popular view of innovation that understands innovation primarily as invention, patenting, or the generation of disruptive technologies misses the larger part of the innovation process—the more incremental implementation of ideas and knowledge to improve the firm—which, as discussed extensively in the report, lies at the heart of the "growth miracle" in East Asia.

An implication of this broader view of innovation is the fact that firms accumulate knowledge to apply these new ideas in different ways. These include not only R&D activities but also other knowledge accumulation activities, often informal or through collaboration with other firms, through learning from clients, or by participating in global value chains or international markets.

Although chapter 2 defines in more detail firm-level innovation, the reader should keep in mind this broader definition of innovation throughout the report.

governments appear to be leaving billions of dollars on the table, uncollected. Indeed, Pritchett (1997), among others, documents a "Great Divergence" of the last two centuries where, instead of poor countries catching up, with few exceptions rich countries continue to pull ahead. Comin and colleagues (Comin and Hobijn 2004; Comin and Ferrer 2013) argue that it is precisely the differences in the rate of adoption of new technologies that drives the magnitude of the Great Divergence.[3]

In figure 1.1, Maloney and Valencia Caicedo (2017) suggest that the ability to identify, absorb, and adapt technologies, as represented by the number of engineers per capita, is indeed a key part of the divergence story. In 1900, countries such as Argentina, Chile, Denmark, Sweden, and the southern United States had similar levels of income but vastly differing capacities to innovate. These differences, in turn, predict well today's differences in income: the Nordic countries and U.S. states sped ahead while Latin America lost ground. By contrast, in the 20th century, the growth miracles of Japan and the Asian Tigers reflected their capacity to innovate and shorter technological adoption lags (Comin and Hobijn 2010).

Analogously, box 1.2 offers historical examples of how identical industries experienced both faster growth and greater diversification in countries better able to manage new technologies than in countries with less capacity. Hence, policy advice to move into production baskets thought to be more growth friendly misses a critical point: countries that have been unable to innovate and apply technological advances to their present industries are unlikely to do so in new industries. Hence, innovation capacity appears as the more critical policy priority for economic development.

FIGURE 1.1   The Capability to Innovate in 1900 Drives Income Levels Today

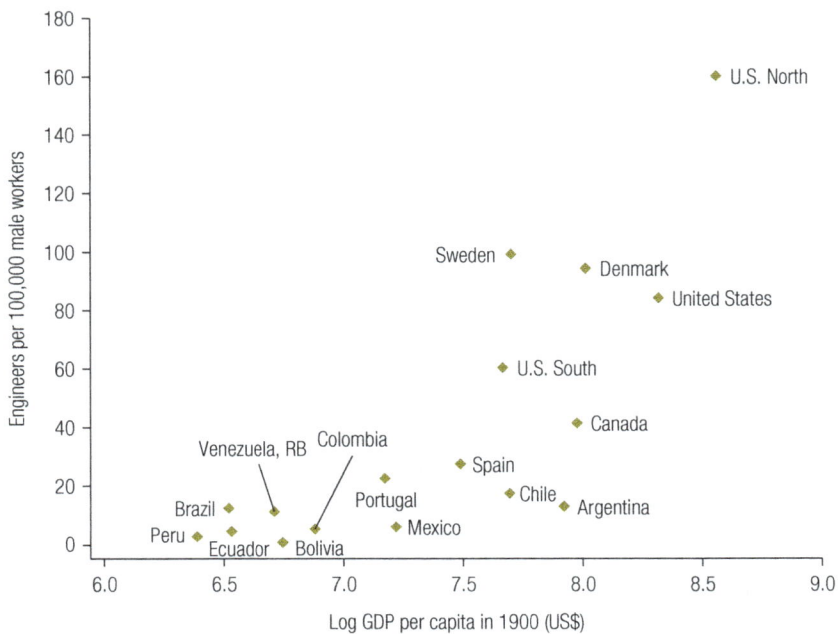

Source: Maloney and Valencia Caicedo 2017.

Innovation and Development Outcomes

History offers numerous examples of countries losing competitiveness or missing opportunities to diversify while other countries succeeded. Wright (1986) documents the difficulties the U.S. South faced in absorbing the knowledge required to replicate the North's steel industries: despite having all the necessary raw materials, the Birmingham Steel Company was unable to adapt production technologies to local ores. The same lackluster performance occurred in the southern textile industry. By contrast, Japan was able to take the same extant textile technologies and modify them for a local context, eventually establishing its first leading manufacturing industry. In the face of foreign competition in the early 20th century, Brazil experienced retrogression in its long-established iron industry until it made a deliberate push midcentury to upgrade technologically. Similarly, Spain and Chile became uncompetitive in copper in the 19th century because they could not identify and adopt new advances in mining and metallurgy, and eventually had to sell out to foreigners who could. By contrast, the United States leveraged its copper into a stock of high-level technical human capital and a network of universities and laboratories that pushed the frontiers of metallurgy and chemistry and laid the foundations for many of its subsequent industries.

Likewise, in Asia, Japan was a major exporter of copper and relied on the industry as a mainstay of its economy until the end of World War II. As in the United States, Japan's technological upgrading in the Meiji period (1868–1912) gave rise to major companies like Sumitomo, which began in the 17th century as a traditional mining company but later diversified into the machinery, chemicals, electric cables, metals, and the banking conglomerate that it is today. Development based on an extractive natural resource had radically different outcomes in Latin America than in the United States and Japan. We see the same dynamic at work today: Norway has leveraged its oil and gas deposits into a diversified economy with a dynamic high-tech sector whereas, for instance, Nigeria has not. In each case, the difference is clearly not in *what* is being produced, but rather *how*. Innovation is a critical part of that how (see Lederman and Maloney 2012; Maloney and Valencia Caicedo 2017).

The Still-Bound Prometheus

The paradox of low investment in innovation despite vast potential gains in efficiency, quality, and diversification, and the lack of effective policies to facilitate these returns, suggest the existence of barriers to the flow of knowledge and effective governance. Prometheus somehow remains fettered in the developing world.

This report examines three such barriers: (1) weak firm capabilities to undertake meaningful innovation, (2) the general absence of critical innovation complementarities, and (3) weak government capabilities to manage the increased complexity and breadth of the innovation policies implied by the previous two.

In exploring these three barriers, the report explicitly seeks common ground between two analytical traditions that often find themselves at odds in both the conceptual and the policy spheres. The first is the standard neoclassical tradition that, to oversimplify, sees innovation policy as largely remedying market failures particular to innovation.

A commonly invoked failure is that, because knowledge can be used by many, a person making the investment in research or identifying new technologies to bring to a country will not be able to recoup the full benefit of the investment—others can profit from the investment at no cost to themselves. Redressing this failure has given rise to a variety of policy tools such as R&D subsidies or tax incentives, matching grants, and the creation of nonmarket institutions such as public research institutes or universities.

On the other hand, policy discussions in the National Innovation System (NIS) literature focus more on the interactions among the various actors and nonmarket institutions necessary for knowledge creation and diffusion—the innovation *system*—and the nonlinear nature of knowledge creation.[4] For instance, Triple Helix models stress the dynamic interactions between university, industry, and government.[5] Governments, therefore, have a role in cultivating the necessary institutions, overseeing the interactive process, and intervening to redress systemic failures where necessary. In particular, the NIS literature has been very critical of the neoclassical conception of the firm, of the market failure approach as adequate to guide policy, and more generally of the minimalist state approach to growth policy.

However, recent evolution on both sides of the divide, we argue, leaves a broad area of common ground.[6] To begin, both traditions put the firm, not universities or think tanks, as the central generator of value added and the driver of growth; both broadly accept the market as the primary allocator of factors of production, albeit with different views of what can be said about the optimality of the outcome; and both are doubtful that the composition of the production basket is the primary barrier to growth.[7] In addition, the neoclassical tradition has seen an increased focus on the role of institutions in supporting the market, which makes it potentially more open to the kind of systemic concerns of the NIS tradition. Perhaps of greatest importance, the emergence of systematic measures of management capabilities has opened the door to a potential consensus view of the bounded rational firm and the corresponding innovation policy.

In developing our analysis of the three barriers to innovation, we will both draw on and seek to highlight the common ground between the two traditions, with the goal of contributing to more coherent and effective policy making.

Firm Capabilities

In the neoclassical simplification, the firm is a fully rational, forward-looking actor cruising with perfect foresight to the technological frontier, impeded only by a set of well-understood market failures. We take advantage of new sources of cross-country data to confirm that, however useful in many analytical contexts, this is not an adequate characterization of the average developing country enterprise. Such firms may lack capabilities ranging from basic bookkeeping and plant layout skills, to the tools to plan over a multiyear horizon, to the ability to identify a relevant technological advance and then cultivate the human resources needed to adopt it. They may have neither a clear idea of the technological frontier nor the abilities to approach it—that is, how to innovate. In this context, the standard battery of policies to redress the garden-variety market failures in the advanced world—R&D tax credits, matching grants, public research institutes—will not find able partners in the private sector and will be ineffective. Accounts of the East Asian miracles in the NIS tradition place primary emphasis on the process of learning and raising the capabilities for innovation of firms, rather than on their particular sectors (see Kim 1997; Hobday 2000; Dodgson 2000; Dutrénit et. al 2013; Lee 2013).

The report reviews the recent evidence on firm capabilities; presents original research showing that basic managerial skills are central to the introduction of new processes, technologies, and products as well as to patenting; and documents that these capabilities are sorely lacking in developing countries. Few firms can articulate a long-run strategic plan of any kind, let alone an innovation project per se; and, unsurprisingly, few have human resource strategies that would support such a project. We introduce the "capabilities escalator" where firms advance from basic production capabilities to the ability to adopt and adapt technologies and then invent (figure 1.2). We offer evidence on what appears to drive differences in the level of capabilities across firms and countries, and the final chapter presents evidence on the kinds of policies that appear successful in moving them up the escalator. Why firms do not naturally move themselves up the escalator, despite proven high returns to investing in business support services, remains an open question; but the literature offers substantial evidence of severe market failures in the form of information asymmetries—firms do not know what they do not know—that appear to be exacerbated in developing countries, as well as about the efficacy of the available support services.

A central message of this report is that equating innovation policy to frontier science and technology policy will lead to frustration and waste if the firm dimension is neglected. This is not to say that developing countries shouldn't lay the foundations for

FIGURE 1.2 **The Capabilities Escalator**

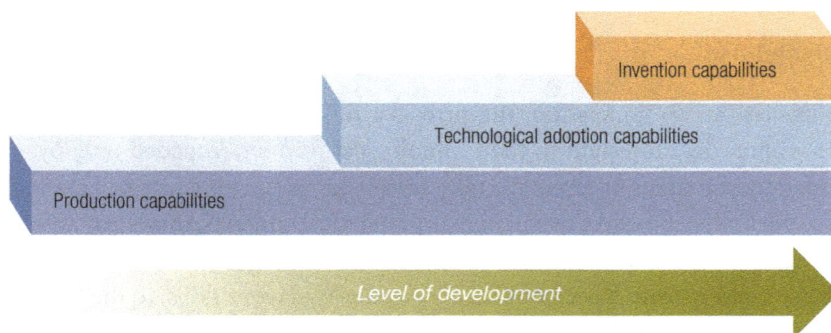

the emergence of world-class universities and think tanks that can push the technological frontier; this is an agenda of generations and needs to be started now. However, without a corps of capable firms to take these ideas to market, these investments will yield little in terms of growth.

Missing Complementarities

Firm capabilities are only one complementary factor essential to the innovation process that is scarce in developing economies. Conceptually, innovation can be thought of as the accumulation by firms of knowledge capital. It is thus subject to the impediments to the accumulation of any type of capital—for instance, thin financial markets, macroeconomic volatility, or obstructive business climates—in addition to those barriers specific to innovation. Furthermore, this accumulation of knowledge capital is not a free-floating activity, but rather occurs in a "production function" that also incorporates the accumulation of physical, human, and managerial capital. Advanced countries may count on well-functioning education systems and business climates to ensure the accumulation of these complementary factors of production, but developing countries cannot. This implies that what is called the National Innovation System or Innovation Ecosystem in developing countries must extend beyond the concerns generally identified in discussions of Triple Helixes and the like to a much broader set of business environment issues.

More profoundly, however, the focus on complementary factors provides one of the keys to the innovation paradox: while the potential gains from Schumpeterian catch-up increase with distance from the technological frontier, the quantity and quality of complementary factors decrease. As a result, if a government were to offer grants to undertake innovation projects or R&D activities, scarce human capital may produce products of limited quality, poor links with the private sector may limit the potential for marketability, weak firm capabilities may mean that managers neither see the profit potential in the idea nor are able to organize production, barriers to capital imports or weak financial markets may prohibit investing in the needed material to operationalize the idea, or the local education system may not provide adequately trained workers to productively run new technologies adopted. In sum, the absence of these critical complementarities means that the actual returns to innovation are far less than promised by the catch-up effect. The innovation paradox, then, is a direct analogue to Lucas's (1990) classic query about "why capital doesn't flow from rich to poor countries" given that its scarcity should guarantee a higher return in the latter.

This, in turn, has implications for how we benchmark innovation performance. A low level of R&D relative to the Republic of Korea or the United States may say nothing at all about innovation-related market failures but rather reflect more generic factors affecting all accumulation or the accumulation of complementary factors. Hence, the standard raw comparisons of gross domestic expenditure on

R&D can mislead policy making, emphasizing increases in R&D spending without digging sufficiently deeply into why the returns are not leading to such investment happening naturally.

Weak Government Capabilities: The Innovation Policy Dilemma

Finally, on the other side of the capabilities ledger, governments need to be able to generate an informed overview of the broader innovation system and identify failures, design coherent multi-instrument responses, implement them effectively and consistently over time, and then evaluate their effectiveness. Furthermore, as figure 1.2 suggests, the policy mix or combination of instruments and institutions to support innovation needs to evolve, becoming progressively more sophisticated and dense with development.

Here we find another key to the innovation paradox: for developing countries, the greater magnitude of the market failures to be resolved—for instance, in upgrading firm capabilities—and the multiplicity of missing complementary factors and institutions increase the complexity of innovation policy, at the same time that government capabilities to manage it are weaker. Hence, the report attempts to shed light on the implementation challenges inherent in innovation policy making in developing countries.

On the design front, weak capabilities can lead to defaulting to *isomorphic mimicry* (Andrews, Pritchett, and Woolcock 2012)—importing organograms and practices that may not address the local failures and that do not generate corresponding functionality. Logical frameworks that would discipline policy by first identifying the market failures critical to the local context, then engaging in cycles of experimentation and evaluation to generate the greatest local functionality, tend to be the exception rather than the rule.

Effective implementation of these policies requires developing the appropriate tools for execution and strengthened management quality in an administrative context where policy instruments are deployed in a coherent manner, and consistently over time. However, in much of the developing world, policy is balkanized by ministry or administrative level, and in many cases there is little alignment between the stated goals of policies and actual budgets and impact. Furthermore, even though cultivating a functional NIS, including high-quality firms and knowledge institutions, requires decades of sustained effort, high-level commitment is frequently lacking and there is often little policy continuity across political cycles. Finally, the institutions established to execute policy often lack a clearly defined mission and corresponding incentives that would align them with these goals.

As with weaknesses in firm capabilities, these government capability deficits constrain and shape innovation. Redressing both is a long-term development priority; in the short to medium term, they need to be considered in both the ambitiousness and the design of innovation policy.

The Plan of the Report

The narrative of the report is structured in two main parts; the first largely empirical and analytical and the second policy focused. Throughout, we draw on new sources of innovation and management data, and analysis that enable us to place the discussion on firmer empirical foundations than was previously possible. The focus of these data leads the report to disproportionately discuss formal firms in the manufacturing and service sectors. This in no way implies a lesser importance of the issues for micro and informal firms, agricultural enterprises, or start-up innovative ventures: the processes of capabilities accumulation, barriers to innovation, or policy instruments described in the report also apply to them. We highlight these where the literature and data permit.

In part I, chapter 2 exploits several new sources of data and empirical approaches to explore the patterns of innovation effort in developing countries, establishing the apparent complementarities across a range of factors of production. Chapter 3 introduces the Innovation Paradox, finds its roots in innovation complementarities, and develops the implications of this both for how we conceive of the NIS and for the resulting difficulties in benchmarking innovation performance. Chapter 4 goes deeper into describing the importance of one particular input for innovation—managerial capabilities—and chapter 5 describes some of the process of accumulation and learning of these capabilities.

In part II on policies, chapter 6 takes up the problem of developing government capabilities and the challenge of implementing innovation policy more effectively. Specifically, the chapter focuses on three key issues for innovation policy: (1) identifying the failure that constrains innovation investments, (2) strengthening government capabilities for innovation policy making, and (3) the design of the agencies that implement these policies. Chapter 7 discusses the instruments available to increase firm capabilities for innovation, and how the policy mix or combination of instruments that form innovation policy may vary as national innovation systems become more mature. The last chapter concludes.

Notes

1. See, for example, Romer (1990); Aghion and Howitt (1992); Aghion, Akcigit, and Howitt (2013) for endogenous growth theory; and Mokyr (1992,1998), Rosenberg (2000), and Nelson (2005) for historical accounts.
2. Nordhaus (2002) estimates that the economic value of increases in longevity over the 20th century approximates the value of measured growth in nonhealth goods and services, and hence GDP very incompletely measures the true "output" of the health sector. Becker et al. (2005) calculate a "full" measure of income incorporating an economic value of longevity for 96 countries from 1960 to 2000; they find that 1.7 percentage points of the 4.1 percent full growth rate for the poorest 50 percent of countries are due to increases in longevity arising from reduction in disease. Lichtenberg (2014) documents a large impact of foreign drug research on life expectancy. Hence, the ability to transfer and adapt health advances developed elsewhere with

modest amounts of innovative effort may potentially generate much larger social returns for poorer countries.

3. Likewise, Howitt and Mayer-Foulkes (2005) and Feyrer (2008) argue that Quah's (1996) finding that countries converge to "twin peaks" arises from diverging productivity as opposed to diverging physical capital or human capital accumulation, pointing again to knowledge-related barriers preventing catch-up. Numerous models (Aghion and Howitt 1992; Howitt and Mayer-Foulkes 2005) postulate situations in which countries enter a "stagnation equilibrium" far from the technological frontier because they are unable to incorporate new technologies.

4. See among others Freeman (1987), Lundvall (1992, 1997), Nelson (1993), Soete, Verspagen, and Ter Weel (2010) and Edquist (2011). Also, Freeman (1995) and Lundvall et al. (2002) discuss the origins of the term. Freeman states that the concept of a National Innovation System originated with Friedrich List's ([1841] 1909) discussion of the system of institutions and policies most related to learning about new technology and applying it to Germany's catch-up with England. See also Smits, Kuhlman, and Shapira (2010) for a recent review, as well as Lee (2013) in the context of leapfrogging in Asia and Latin America.

5. See Etzkowitz (2001) and Etzkowitz and Leydesdorff (1995). Firms increasingly engage in higher levels of training and knowledge sharing. Government acts as a public entrepreneur and venture capitalist, in addition to its traditional regulatory role in setting the rules of the game. Universities combine discrete pieces of intellectual property and jointly exploit them. Innovation has expanded from an internal process within and even among firms to an activity that involves institutions not traditionally thought of as having a direct role in innovation, such as universities. Edquist (2011) similarly stresses that there is no linear path from basic research to applied research and then to the implementation of new processes and products but rather that innovation is characterized by complicated feedback mechanisms and interactive relations.

6. See Maloney (2017) for a detailed discussion.

7. See for example Dodgson (2000, 261) who notes, "An important policy question for less technologically developed nations, such as Malaysia and Indonesia, is whether the present emphasis on electronics is likely to produce any longer-term sustainable comparative advantages. One might justifiably ask whether emphasis could be better placed on more traditional and historical, but still potentially high technology, high value-added industries, such as tropical cash crops in Malaysia and textiles in Indonesia."

References

Aghion, Philippe, Ufuk Akcigit, and Peter Howitt. 2013. "What Do We Learn from Schumpeterian Growth Theory?" NBER Working Paper No. W18824, National Bureau of Economic Research, Cambridge, MA.

Aghion, Philippe, and Peter Howitt. 1992. "A Model of Growth through Creative Destruction." *Econometrica* 60 (2): 323–51.

Andrews, Matt, Lant Pritchett, and Michael Woolcock. 2012. "Escaping Capability Traps through Problem-Driven Iterative Adaptation (PDIA)." Working Paper 299, Center for Global Development, Washington, DC.

Becker, Gary S., Tomas J. Philipson, and Rodrigo R. Soares. 2005. "The Quantity and Quality of Life and the Evolution of World Inequality." *American Economic Review* 95 (1): 277–91.

Comin, Diego, and Martí Mestieri Ferrer. 2013. "If Technology Has Arrived Everywhere, Why Has Income Diverged?" NBER Working Paper No. 19010, National Bureau of Economic Research, Cambridge, MA.

Comin, Diego, and Bart Hobijn. 2004. "Cross-Country Technology Adoption: Making the Theories Face the Facts." *Journal of Monetary Economics* 51 (1): 39–83.

————. 2010. "An Exploration of Technology Diffusion. *American Economic Review* 100 (5): 2031–59.

Dodgson, Mark. 2000. "Strategic Research Partnerships: Their Role, and Some Issues of Measuring Their Extent and Outcomes—Experiences from Europe and Asia." Paper presented to the Workshop on Strategic Research Partnerships sponsored by the National Science Foundation and convened at SRI International, Washington, DC, October 13.

Dutrénit, G., K. Lee, R. Nelson, L. Soete, and A. Vera-Cruz, eds. 2013. *The Palgrave Macmillan Learning, Capability Building and Innovation for Development.* Basingstoke, Hampshire (U.K.): Palgrave Macmillan.

Easterly, William, and Ross Levine. 2001. "What Have We Learned from a Decade of Empirical Research on Growth? It's Not Factor Accumulation: Stylized Facts and Growth Models." *The World Bank Economic Review* 15 (2): 177–219.

Edquist, Charles. 2011. "Design of Innovation Policy through Diagnostic Analysis: Identification of Systemic Problems (or Failures)." *Industrial and Corporate Change* 20 (6): 1–29.

Etzkowitz, Henry. 2001. "The Second Academic Revolution and the Rise of Entrepreneurial Science." *IEEE Technology and Society Magazine* 20 (2): 18–29.

Etzkowitz, Henry, and Loet Leydesdorff. 1995. "The Triple Helix—University–Industry–Government Relations: A Laboratory for Knowledge-Based Economic Development." *EASST Review* 14 (1): 14–19.

Feyrer, James. 2008. "Aggregate Evidence on the Link between Age Structure and Productivity." *Population and Development Review* 34 (Suppl.): 78–99.

Freeman, Christopher. 1987. *Technology Policy and Economic Performance: Lessons from Japan.* London: Pinter.

————. 1995. "The 'National System of Innovation' in Historical Perspective." *Cambridge Journal of Economics* 19 (1): 5–24.

Griffith, Rachel, Stephen Redding, and John Van Reenen. 2004. "Mapping the Two Faces of R&D: Productivity Growth in a Panel of OECD Industries." *Review of Economics and Statistics* 86 (4): 883–95.

Hobday, Michael. 2000. "East versus Southeast Asian Innovation Systems: Comparing OEM- and TNC-Led Growth in Electronics." In *Technology, Learning, and Economic Development: Experiences of Newly Industrializing Economies*, edited by Linsu Kim and Richard R. Nelson, 129–60. Cambridge, UK: Cambridge University Press.

Howitt, Peter, and David Mayer-Foulkes. 2005. "R&D, Implementation and Stagnation: A Schumpeterian Theory of Convergence Clubs." *Journal of Money, Credit and Banking* 37 (1): 147–77.

Kim, Linsu. 1997. *Imitation to Innovation: The Dynamics of Korea's Technological Learning.* Cambridge, MA: Harvard Business School Press.

Landes, David S. 1969. *The Unbound Prometheus: Technical Change and Industrial Development in Western Europe from 1750 to the Present.* Cambridge, UK: Cambridge University Press.

Lederman, Daniel, and William F. Maloney. 2012. *Does What You Export Matter? In Search of Empirical Guidance for Industrial Policies.* Washington, DC: World Bank.

Lee, Keun. 2013. *Schumpeterian Analysis of Economic Catch-Up: Knowledge, Path-Creation, and the Middle-Income Trap.* Cambridge, UK: Cambridge University Press.

Lichtenberg, Frank R. 2014. "Pharmaceutical Innovation and Longevity Growth in 30 Developing and High-Income Countries, 2000–2009." *Health Policy and Technology* 3 (1): 36–58.

List, Friedrich. 1909. *The National System of Political Economy.* London: Longmans, Green and Co. (Original work published 1841).

Lucas, Robert E. 1990. "Why Doesn't Capital Flow from Rich to Poor Countries?" *American Economics Review* 80 (2): 92–96.

Lundvall, Bengt-Åke, ed. 1992. *National Systems of Innovation: Towards a Theory of Innovation and Interactive Learning.* London: Pinter.

———. 1997. "Development Strategies in the Learning Economy." Paper submitted at STEPI's 10th Anniversary Conference, Seoul, Republic of Korea, May 26–29.

Lundvall, Bengt-Åke, Björn Johnson, Esben Sloth Andersen, and Bent Dalum. 2002. "National Systems of Production, Innovation and Competence Building." *Research policy* 31 (2): 213–31.

Maloney, William. 2017. "Revisiting the National Innovation System in Developing Countries." World Bank, Washington, DC.

Maloney, William F., and Felipe Valencia Caicedo. 2017. "Engineering Growth: Innovative Capacity and Development in the Americas."

Mokyr, Joel. 1992. *The Lever of Riches: Technological Creativity and Economic Progress.* Oxford, UK: Oxford University Press.

———. 1998. "The Second Industrial Revolution, 1870–1914." Manuscript, Northwestern University, Evanston, IL.

Nelson, Richard R. 1993. *National Innovation Systems: A Comparative Analysis.* New York: Oxford University Press.

———. 2005. *Technology, Institutions, and Economic Growth.* Cambridge, MA: Harvard University Press.

Nordhaus, W. D. 2002. "The Health of Nations: The Contribution of Improved Health to Living Standards. NBER Working Paper No. 8818, National Bureau of Economic Research, Cambridge, MA.

OECD (Organisation for Economic Co-operation and Development). 2005. *Oslo Manual: Guidelines for Collecting and Interpreting Innovation Data*, 3rd ed. Paris: OECD Publishing.

Piketty, Thomas. 2017. *Capital in the Twenty-First Century.* Cambridge, MA: Harvard University Press.

Pritchett, Lant. 1997. "Divergence, Big Time." *Journal of Economic Perspectives* 11 (3, Summer): 3–17.

Quah, Danny. 1996. "Convergence Empirics across Economies with (Some) Capital Mobility." *Journal of Economic Growth* 1 (1): 95–124.

Romer, Paul. 1990. "Endogenous Technological Change." *Journal of Political Economy* 98 (5, pt. 2): S71–S102.

Rosenberg, Nathan. 2000. "Schumpeter and the Endogeneity of Technology." *Economic Journal* 111 (475, Features): F778–81.

Schumpeter, Joseph. 1934. *The Theory of Economic Development: An Inquiry into Profits, Capital, Credit, Interest and the Business Cycle.* Cambridge, MA: Harvard University Press.

———. 2008. *Capitalism, Socialism, and Democracy.* New York: HarperCollins. (Original work published 1942).

Smits, Ruud, Stefan Kuhlmann, and Philip Shapira, eds. 2010. *The Theory and Practice of Innovation Policy: An International Research Handbook.* Cheltenham, UK: Edward Elgar.

Soete, Luc, Bart Verspagen, and Bas Ter Weel. 2010. "Systems of Innovation." In *Handbook of the Economics of Innovation*, edited by Bronwyn H. Hall and Nathan Rosenberg, 1159–80. Amsterdam: Elsevier.

Wright, Gavin. 1986. *Old South, New South: Revolutions in Southern Economy since the Civil War.* New York: Basic Books.

PART I

Understanding Innovation in Developing Countries

2. The Nature of Innovation in Developing Countries

Introduction

How frequently do firms in developing countries innovate, and what types of innovation do they undertake? The literature on the advanced countries is extensive, especially around the topics of investment in research and development (R&D) and patenting. However, to date, the information on developing countries, both how much they innovate and the nature of that innovation, has been scarce. This chapter draws on several new sources of firm data to explore these patterns across the spectrum of countries and how they evolve over the development process. We document a great breadth of innovation-related investments, ranging from small process improvements to capital-embodied technology transfer to R&D. However, overall innovation inputs and outputs increase dramatically as countries get richer.

What Is Innovation?

Innovation has recently emerged as central to debates around how to rekindle productivity growth in both advanced and less advanced countries. Roughly, half of cross-country differences in income per capita across countries are thought to be due to differences in total factor productivity (TFP) (Klenow and Rodriguez-Clare 1997; Hall and Jones 1999; Jones 2016). In turn, although better allocation of factors of production emerges as an important factor in productivity growth (Hsieh and Klenow 2009; Restuccia and Rogerson 2008), a potentially larger contribution arises from improved efficiency and product quality *within* firms and among newly entering firms (see, for example, Collard-Wexler and De Loeker 2014 and Restuccia 2016). These gains reflect innovation in production technique, product design, and to some extent branding, all of which are driven by the ability to create, manage, and leverage new ideas.[1]

To date, we have had only limited information on the nature of innovation activities in developing countries, on how countries develop the capacity to innovate, how it evolves over time, and what the potential barriers to innovation are. Most work on innovation has been done through the advanced country lens, and innovation is commonly seen as the work of highly educated labor in R&D–intensive companies with strong ties to the scientific community. It has, therefore, been largely perceived as a "first world" activity.

However, innovation also includes attempts to try out new or improved products or processes, or experiment with alternate ways to do things (Bell and Pavitt 1993; Kline and Rosenberg 1986). Further, the notion of Schumpeterian catch-up is precisely one of technology adoption, imitation, and adaptation of existing nonfrontier technologies (Comin et al. 2008; Klinger and Lederman 2006), where firms adopt incremental (as opposed to radical) changes (Fagerberg, Srholec, and Verspagen 2010). It is also a process that requires the combination of different innovation inputs and outputs, such as product and processes, marketing or organizational innovations (Bell and Pavitt 1993).

This extended conception of innovation is captured in figure 2.1; a broad set of tangible and intangible assets with embedded knowledge, ranging from basic human and organizational capital to R&D, need to be accumulated and combined to yield innovation outcomes in the form of new or improved products and services, production and delivery processes, business organization, and patented intellectual property. These, in turn, can lead to greater productivity and associated social benefits such as better jobs, firm growth, and diversification.

Characterizing Innovation in Developing Countries: Some Stylized Facts

Generating measures of firm-level innovation has been difficult, especially for developing countries, because of the lack of comparable information. In this section, we draw on several new sources of data, the World Bank Enterprise Surveys (ES) (see annex 2A for a detailed explanation),[2] Bureau van Dijk (BvD) Orbis,[3] and the World Management Survey[4] to characterize the nature of innovation in these countries and how it evolves across the development process.

FIGURE 2.1   **The Innovation Function**

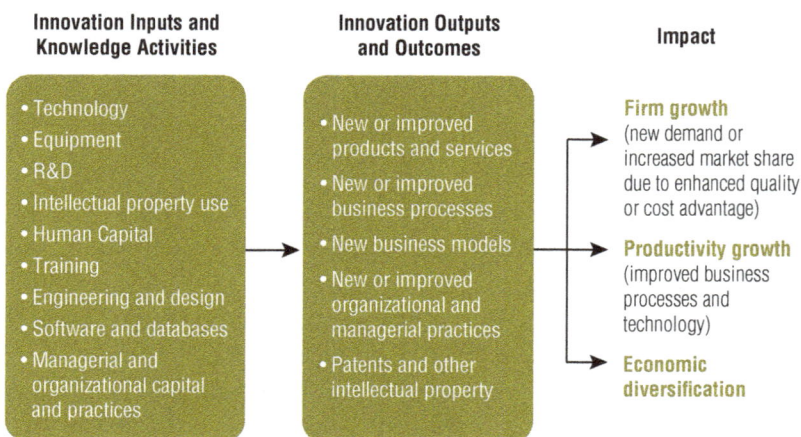

Defining Firm-Level Innovation

In chapter 1, the report emphasizes the broader and Schumpeterian view of innovation as the accumulation of knowledge and implementation of new ideas. Specifically, *innovation* is the implementation of a new or significantly improved product (good or service) or process, a new marketing method, or a new organizational method in business practices, workplace organization, or external relations (OECD 2005, Paragraph 146).

Several observations can be made regarding this definition, in particular:

- An innovation must be *novel* or a *significant improvement* (at least) to the firm (and possibly to the market or other higher levels) and must be *implemented* (that is, introduced inside the firm or commercialized). On the other hand, there is no requirement for the innovation to be *successful*.
- The general definition does not mention *intention* or *objective*, but it seems implicit that innovation aims at improving the firm's competitive position and is associated with uncertainty.
- There is no reference in the broad definition to technology, and the current definition (since the third edition of the *Oslo Manual* [OECD 2005]) explicitly considers "nontechnological" forms of innovation (marketing and organizational) that were not previously included, thereby encompassing a broader set of knowledge sources/types besides scientific/ technical ones.

The *Oslo Manual* defines the following four main subtypes of innovations:

1. A *product innovation* is the introduction of a good or service that is new or significantly improved with respect to its characteristics or intended uses. This includes significant improvements in technical specifications, components and materials, incorporated software, user friendliness, or other functional characteristics. In the context, traditional surveys have used three metrics to measure the complexity or novelty of the innovation:

   a. New products to the firm
   b. New products to the market
   c. New products to the international market

2. A *process innovation* is the implementation of a new or significantly improved production or delivery method. This includes significant changes in techniques, equipment, and/or software:

   a. Innovative methods for manufacturing products or offering services
   b. Innovative logistics, delivery, or distribution methods for inputs, products, or services
   c. Innovative supporting activity for processes, such as maintenance systems or operations for purchasing, accounting, or computing.[a]

3. A *marketing innovation* is the implementation of a new marketing method involving significant changes in product design or packaging, product placement, product promotion, or pricing. These aim at increasing the effectiveness and efficiency of marketing, to gain competitive advantage.

(Box continues on the following page.)

Innovation Outputs

Although we have data only on a few dimensions on the elements in the center of figure 2.1—product and process innovation, improved organization, and intellectual property creation—the description of the data is nonetheless revealing.

Product and Process Innovation

Figure 2.2 combines the two main innovation datasets for developing and developed economies; the United Nations Educational, Scientific, and Cultural Organization (UNESCO) data[5] (blue dots) and the ES[6] (green dots) to plot the share of manufacturing firms that report introducing either process or product innovation against national income. Given some important measurement challenges that are discussed in box 2.2, we include duplicate values for a few countries with information in both datasets, to compare differences in innovation rates.[7]

What is immediately clear is that firms in poor countries report substantial innovative activities using both surveys. Further, figure 2.3 shows that this is broadly true across sectors. The Enterprise Surveys suggest that professional services and manufacturing have the highest innovation rates (between 50 and 60 percent of firms reporting either product or process innovation), compared to about 24 percent in construction, 30 percent in hotels, 36 percent in transport, and 25 percent in wholesale and retail. However, the broader point remains that reported innovation is widespread throughout the economy, and hence policy should not restrict itself a priori to one sector.

FIGURE 2.2 **Innovation Levels Vary by Country Income (Share of Manufacturing Firms Reporting Product or Process Innovation)**

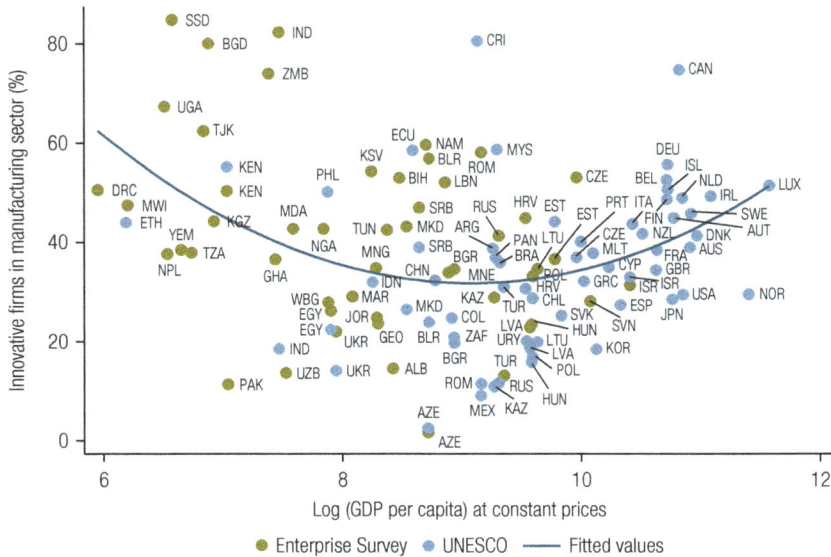

Source: Elaboration using Enterprise Survey data (www.enterprisesurveys.org) and United Nations Educational, Scientific, and Cultural Organization (UNESCO) data.
Note: GDP = gross domestic product.

BOX 2.2

Problems in Innovation Measurement

Several approaches to measuring innovation have been pursued, each focusing on different aspects of the innovation process. The first measurement efforts attempted to quantify specific inputs to innovation such as R&D, others have looked at outputs such as patents, or focused instead on proxies such as productivity. It is only more recently that attempts have been made to directly measure innovation activities and outputs within firms using so-called *innovation surveys*. Guidelines for conducting this type of survey were developed in the early 1990s and codified in the *Oslo Manual* (OECD 2005) to harmonize concepts and definitions for cross-country data collection. The most well-known example of these surveys is the Community Innovation Survey (CIS), a biennial survey carried out across the European Union. In the last two decades, the use of innovation surveys and statistics has grown across all regions, and about 100 countries have now carried out at least one innovation survey based on the *Oslo Manual* guidelines (Oslo-type) often modeled after the CIS.

In a review of existing frameworks, Cirera, López-Bassols, and Muzi (2017) identify two main gaps in the measurement of business innovation. First, existing approaches tend to be R&D–centric and do not fully recognize the importance of nontechnological innovation, which is more prevalent in developing countries. Frameworks that consider innovation capabilities more broadly can considerably enrich existing measurement models. Second, the current measurement of innovation outputs, primarily product and process, is problematic because it is highly subjective; it poorly identifies the extent of novelty of technological improvement; and it is incomplete, because important questions about the technology introduced or the degree of disruption are not measured.

(Box continues on the following page.)

Problems in Innovation Measurement *(continued)*

This has resulted in some volatility in innovation incidence rates. Experimental evidence has shown the difficulties in properly identifying innovation. For example, a recent study has shown that respondents in the United States are more likely to identify innovation with something new or unique and not to consider improvements as innovation; in Europe, on the contrary, people are more inclined to indicate both novelty and improvement as elements of innovation (Galindo-Rueda and Van Cruysen 2016). In addition, the way the questionnaires are framed matters. An experiment conducted by Statistics Norway shows that innovation rates are significantly different when captured by a stand-alone innovation survey than by a combined R&D and innovation survey (Wilhelmsen 2012). In Flanders, innovation rates were considerably and systematically higher when measured with a short questionnaire than when using a long questionnaire (Hoskens 2015). Although it is not clear which survey instrument is most accurate with respect to measured innovation rates, these results clearly suggest that survey methodology and design can greatly impact the results. Cirera and Muzi (2016) find for a sample of 11 countries in Sub-Saharan Africa and South Asia that responses to questions formulated identically to the same firm in two periods, one with a short module in a general firm survey and another in a longer dedicated innovation questionnaire, vary greatly within the same firm, even when the same person is interviewed. The authors find that the time elapsed between interviews or the quality of the interview play a more important role in explaining these differences than a lack of understanding about innovation concepts. This calls for the need to improve the way innovation questions are formulated with the objective of minimizing framework biases.

Finally, methodological issues can also affect the measurement of innovation across firms of different size. A recent study in Poland, which compares innovation rates across firms' size, shows higher innovation rates for micro firms as compared to small and medium firms (Rozkrut 2015). This counterintuitive result may be explained by the fact that micro firms may be more likely than larger firms to report improvements as innovation.

FIGURE 2.3 All Sectors Innovate, but Innovation Rates Vary by Sector

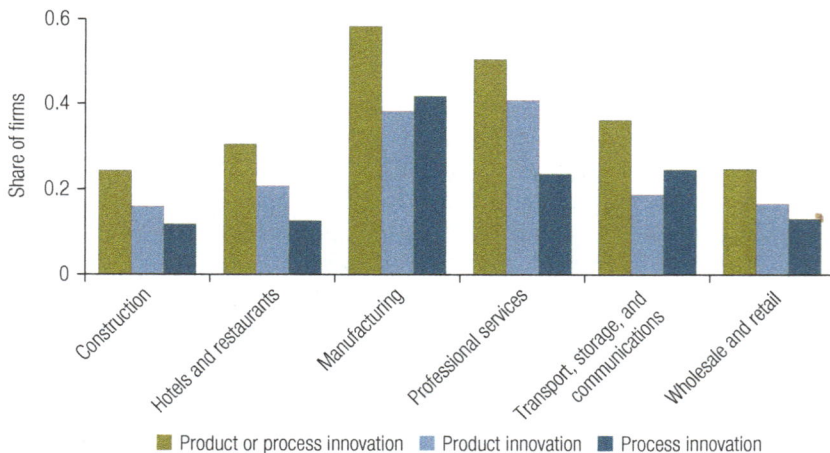

Source: Elaboration using Enterprise Survey data (www.enterprisesurveys.org).

The Innovation Paradox

Is There a U-Shaped Curve in Innovation or a Measurement Problem?

The U-shaped curve shown in figure 2.2 is somewhat surprising: very poor countries report higher levels of innovation than, for instance, China, Colombia, or South Africa; and the slope increases again as countries approach the technological frontier. The high level of variance among the low-income countries and often disparate values from different surveys for the same country point to significant measurement issues (see box 2.2). For example, the ES reports that 80 percent of manufacturing firms in India innovate, whereas the UNESCO data report only 20 percent (annex 2B). The overall correlation between the two sources is only .28, with the ES consistently showing higher values. This suggests that, because the ES comprises the bulk of the low-income sample, the U-shaped relationship is exaggerated. That said, some double-sampled countries, such as Kenya or Serbia, emerge with confirmed values higher than many Organisation for Economic Co-operation and Development (OECD) countries. Further, the U shape would emerge with either data set alone.

Though we cannot go deeply into what is driving this, two important sampling issues suggest themselves. First, there may be a compositional effect. For instance, in South Sudan, which shows the highest response in our sample, as in Africa in general, there are very few formal firms and, of these, many may be international importers; introducing new products to the domestic market may include exactly that—introducing a new import line, but with minimal level of technological transfer.

Second, careful examination of responses reveals systematic differences in what is reported as innovation across the income spectrum. Firms in poor countries report, for example, changing lighting fixtures as process innovation whereas this is less often the case in the advanced countries. In the Africa region, of those firms introducing a "product innovation," only 14 percent introduce a completely new product—half the share of the other regions. In Chile, Aroca and Stough (2015) examine in detail a random sample of 50 Chilean small and medium enterprises (SMEs) reporting considerable product and process innovations and find that only one in five of these firms produced true innovative outcomes and associated business growth. Annex 2A similarly finds a lower correlation of reported innovation with productivity enhancement as countries move farther from the frontier. Cirera and Sabetti (2016) find no impact of innovation on productivity in developing countries when this is defined as imitation, which is suggestive of very marginal changes that are reported as imitation.

Further, this intuition is further supported by examining some subcategories where innovations are more tightly and clearly defined, thereby allowing less discretion in response. Figure 2.4 suggests that the U pattern shown above is a survey response issue. For countries with a gross domestic product (GDP) per capita below US$40,000, the ES distinguishes between more radical product innovation, or products new to the country or the world, and simple adoption/imitation of existing products or processes,

FIGURE 2.4 **Innovations That Are New to the Market Increase with Income per Capita**

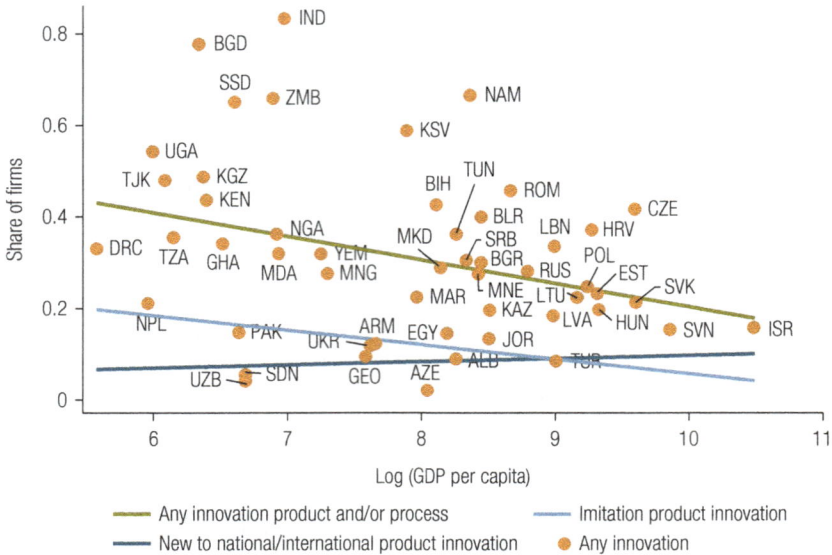

Source: Elaboration using Enterprise Survey data (www.enterprisesurveys.org).

which is less precisely defined. We see that high scoring and poor countries again impart something of a bowl shape to the overall relationship between innovation and income level (figure 2.4). However, the dark blue line showing the share of firms undertaking more radical product innovation increases with income, from roughly 3 to 10 percent.

In short, available surveys may not fully capture differences in both the nature and the quality of the innovation effort that respondents claim. Annex 2B provides some guidelines on how to improve innovation measurement in developing countries. Although it is clear from the evidence reviewed that many firms do innovate, the finding of an initial decline in innovation with development would likely disappear once accounting for the quality or novelty of the reported innovations.

Intellectual Property and Patenting

Creating codified intellectual property is another innovation output (see again figure 2.1) and offers an even more precise measure of innovative activity. Though patenting activity very incompletely captures the universe of relevant activity (see for example Moser 2013), patent applications in the U.S. Patent and Trademark Office (USPTO) or European Patent Office do provide a more standardized measure of a particular type of knowledge output.[8] Hence, the patterns shown in patent data are more reliable than the indicators discussed above for broader classes of innovation, though they are perhaps less relevant for developing countries.

The firm-level data from BvD Orbis enable us to disaggregate patenting activity into incidence (share of firms that patent) and intensity (patents per patenting firm). Although the Orbis data may not be collected in a fully uniform way across countries, figure 2.5 suggests some rough stylized facts.

FIGURE 2.5 **Patenting Activity Is Much Higher in the Richest Countries**

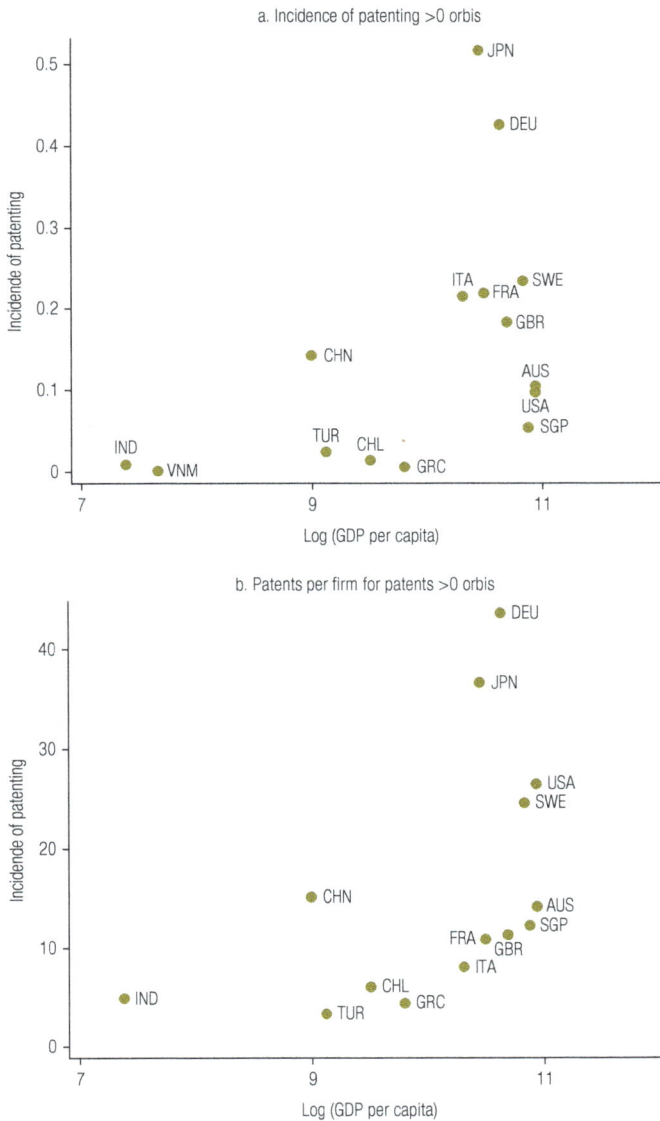

Source: Maloney and Sarrias 2017.

First, as expected, in most developing countries, with the plausible exception of China,[9] well below 5 percent of firms do any patenting; however, this ramps up as we approach the technological frontier, most dramatically in Japan and Germany where over 40 percent of firms in the sample report patenting. This finding is consistent with figure 2.4 above showing that a similarly low share of firms introduces any radically new products or processes. Even Australia, Singapore, and the United States appear in this data to have relatively few firms patenting.

It is also the case, however, that firms engaging in patenting increase the number of patents filed for across the development process. Again, for most countries up to the income level of Greece or Italy, the very few firms that patent, file for relatively few patents. Though the Orbis data cannot be taken as representative of the overall firm population, they do confirm the sharply increasing share of patents per inhabitant over the development process found using USPTO data (figure 2.5) and suggest it results from both incidence and intensity increasing. The data also confirm that more sophisticated innovation activities increase as well and that relatively few firms in lower-income countries engage in radical innovation, either by introducing new processes or products or by actually patenting.

Some Stylized Facts

Overall, the evidence suggests five stylized facts in relation to innovation outputs:

- A large fraction of firms report innovating in product and process across the entire income spectrum.
- Innovative activity occurs across the economy and is not just restricted to, for instance, the manufacturing sector.
- Imitation and adoption are the prevalent forms of innovation in low- and middle-income countries.
- Innovation increases with income. Though the subjective data on introducing new products or processes suggest more innovation among the very poor countries than the middle-income countries, controlling for the quality of these reported investments is not possible using current surveys. With tighter definitions of what constitutes an innovation, we find innovation positively correlated with income overall.
- The process of increasing innovation nationally includes both increasing the share of firms that undertake innovation as well as the intensity with which they do it.

Innovation Inputs

Figure 2.1 reflects a wide range of inputs into the innovation process, ranging from basic organizational capacity to R&D. Data limitations force us to focus on a narrow subset of these that have been collected on a consistent cross-country basis.

R&D

R&D spending is the most commonly discussed input into innovation, largely because it is one of the very few inputs measured with consistency across firms and countries. R&D is thought to facilitate both advances at the technological frontier and catch-up through building absorptive capacity (see, for instance, Cohen and Levinthal 1990) and most studies find it robustly related to innovation. Analysis with the ES data confirms this: R&D is an input into product and process innovation measured either by whether the country does R&D or by overall intensity. Cirera (2017) attempts to control more directly for causality and finds R&D significantly related to product innovation in particular.

Furthermore, numerous authors (Hausman, Hall, and Griliches 1984; Hall, Griliches, and Hausman 1986; Blundell, Griffith, and Van Reenen 1995; Blundell, Griffith, and Windmeijer 2002; Kortum and Lerner 2000) establish the existence of a knowledge production function at the micro level relating R&D and patenting activity. At the national level, Bosch, Lederman, and Maloney (2005) show that patenting increases with development and that an analogous aggregate global knowledge function exists (see figure 2.6).[10]

FIGURE 2.6   Patents and R&D Expenditures Are Closely Related and Rise with Income

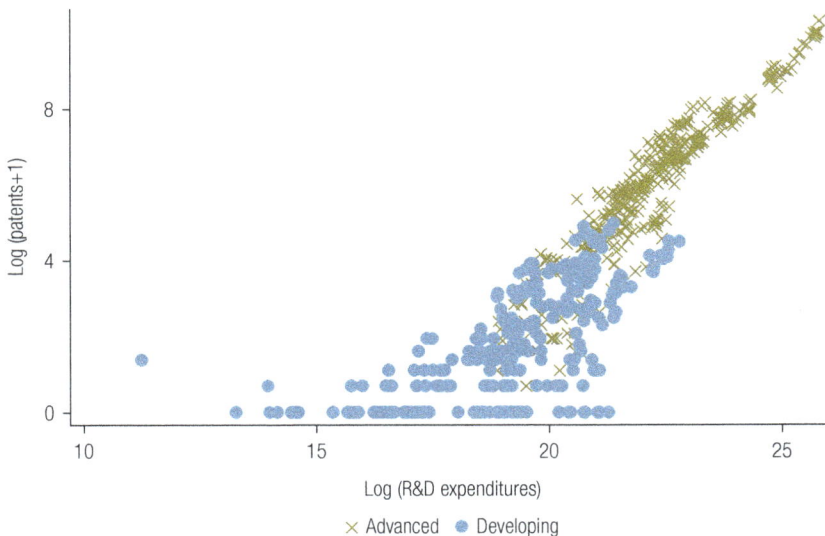

Source: Bosch, Lederman, and Maloney 2005.

Note: The figure shows the relationship between log (patents+1) and log (R&D expenditures) for the 1976–2000 period. The dots and crosses correspond to year–country observations. Patents = number of utility patents granted by the U.S. Patent and Trademark Office. R&D = real research and development expenditures collected by the United Nations Educational, Scientific, and Cultural Organization; the Organisation for Economic Co-operation and Development (OECD); the Ibero-American Science and Technology Indicators Network; and the Taiwan Statistical Data Book. Advanced countries correspond to the OECD group used in most previous studies, minus Mexico and Republic of Korea, but including Israel. Developing countries are the rest of countries.

Finally, an extensive literature documents a robust impact of R&D on productivity per se. Many micro studies using the Crépon–Duguet–Mairesse (CDM) model (Crépon, Duguet, and Mairesse 1998) (see box 3.1 in the next chapter) have documented a positive correlation between product innovation (driven partly by R&D) and productivity. (See Hall 2011 and Mohnen and Hall 2013 for a survey of a large sample of studies in the OECD.) A robust relationship with TFP also emerges in the literature. For example, Hall, Mairesse, and Mohnen (2010) find that the returns to R&D are positive across OECD countries, and higher than for capital investments. Though these studies generally do not cover developing countries, estimates using the ES data show that the average firm-level return to R&D, while varying across countries, is generally positive, regardless of income level. Furthermore, meta-analysis of agricultural R&D investment studies from a sample covering all regions of the world suggests consistently high rates of return to R&D (Alston et al. 2000).

Both the aggregate data from UNESCO and the firm-level data from the ES show that investment in R&D, as a share of GDP or per worker, increases sharply with development (figure 2.7). Moreover, this pattern holds regardless of the type of innovation novelty pursued—imitation or radical innovation (figure 2.8)—consistent with the "two faces of R&D spending" described by Cohen and Levinthal (1990). As with the patterns of patenting activity presented earlier (see figure 2.5), the ES data suggest that a large part of the increase with development is due to increased intensity in the firms that undertake it (figure 2.9, blue line). Roughly 10 percent of firms do any R&D up to the income level of Israel (incidence, red line). The ES data suggest that across countries and sectors these firms tend to be larger and to participate in international markets, in high-tech manufacturing, or in knowledge-intensive services sectors. The shallow bowl in incidence, again, is largely driven by a suspiciously high incidence in, for instance, Bangladesh, India, Kenya, and Uganda. However, the intensity of R&D in these countries is very low. The rise in national R&D intensity across figure 2.9 is largely driven by an increase in spending among firms doing R&D, which shows effectively a quintupling across the income span.

In sum, data on R&D capture important dimensions of the process of innovation because R&D drives both imitation and invention. R&D is conducted by few firms in developing countries, and the rise in R&D intensity over the development process is largely driven by increased spending by these firms. However, were we able to combine the ES and OECD data as we could with patents, we might expect the incidence to rise as well, matching the pattern of patenting.

Critically, the ES data show that a much larger share of firms report that they innovate than report formal R&D.[11] Fewer than half of sampled firms (in most countries less than 30 percent) that introduce a product or a process innovation do any formal R&D, which indicates that other innovation inputs are at play. Again, this suggests that developing country policy must look beyond R&D in seeking to promote innovation.

FIGURE 2.7 R&D Intensity Rises with Convergence to the Productivity Frontier

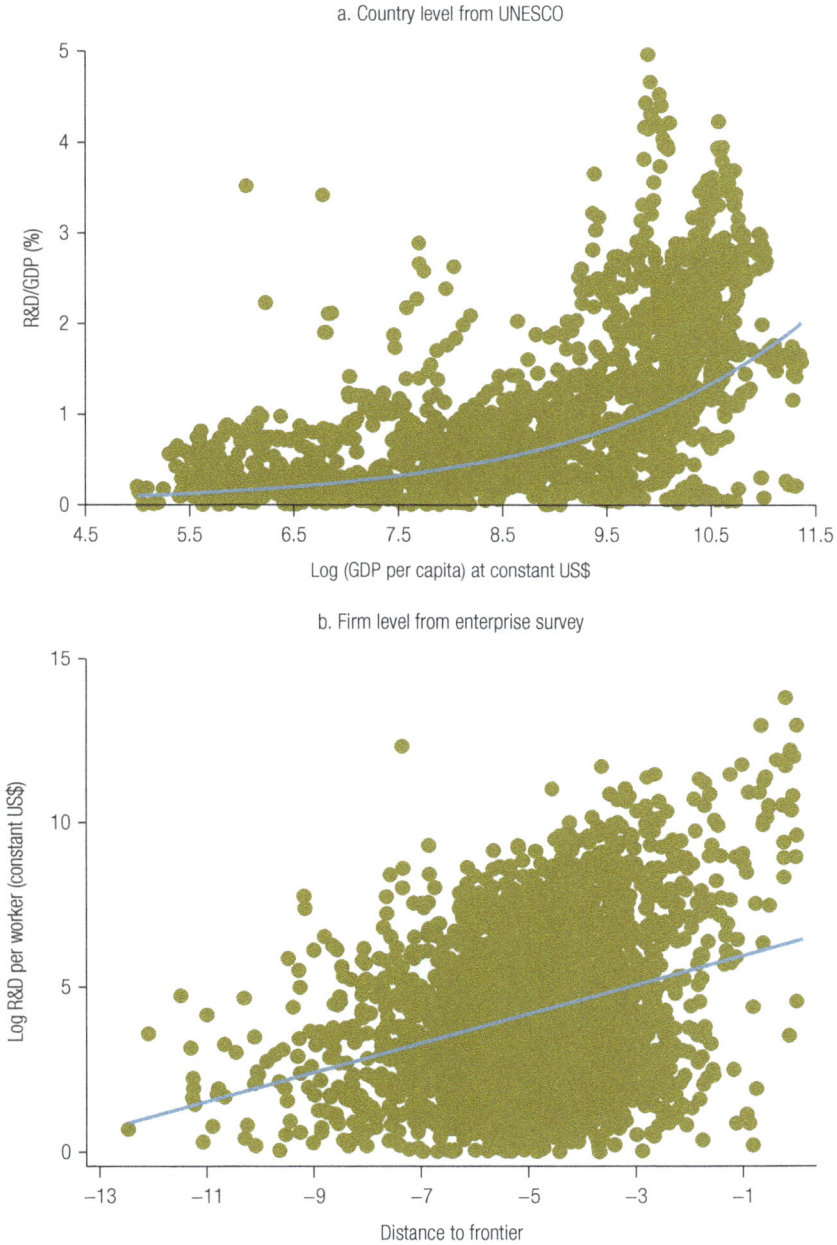

a. Country level from UNESCO

b. Firm level from enterprise survey

Source: Elaboration using Orbis and Enterprise Survey data (www.enterprisesurveys.org).

Note: In panel b distance to the frontier is calculated as the difference between the firms' log of sales per worker and the 95th percentile labor productivity in the sector for the entire dataset. We exclude extreme sales per worker values. The line represents smoothing linear fit. GDP = gross domestic product; R&D = research and development; UNESCO = United Nations Educational, Scientific, and Cultural Organization.

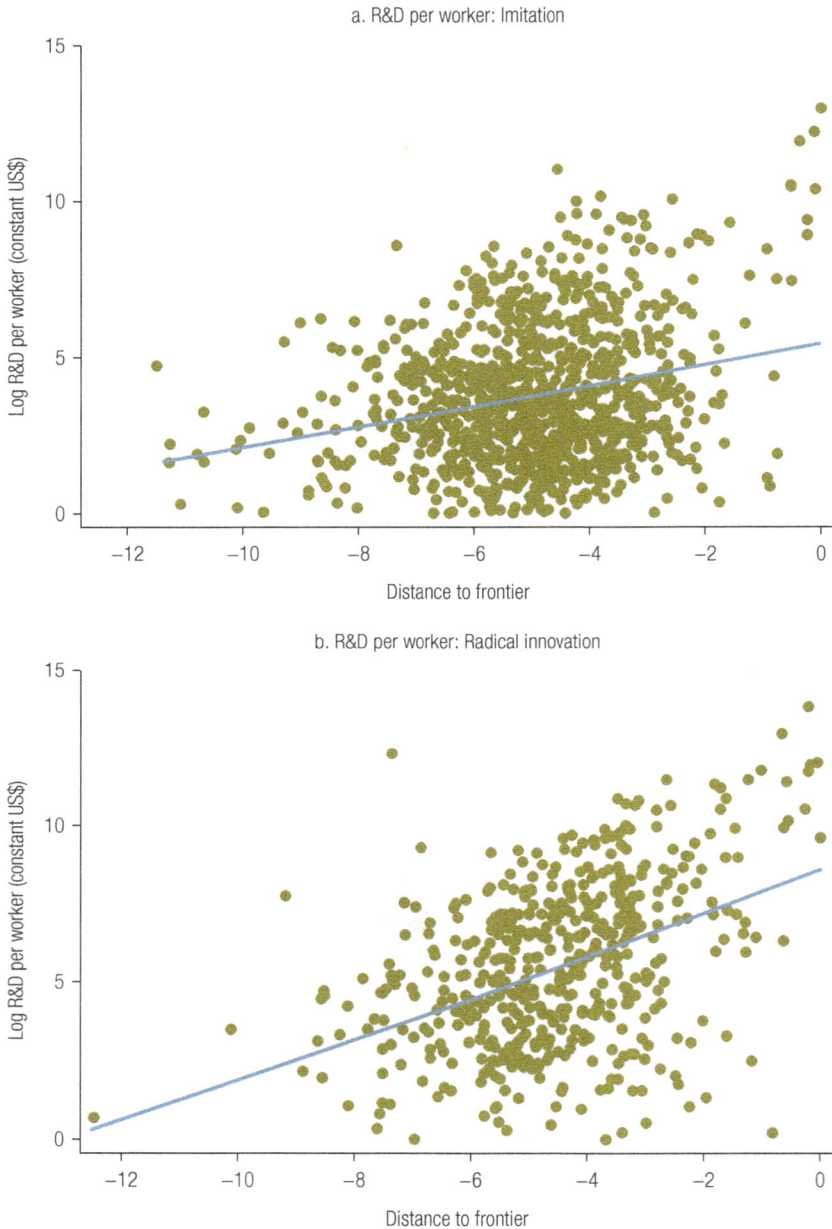

FIGURE 2.8 **R&D per Worker on Imitation and Radical Innovation Also Rises with Convergence to the Productivity Frontier**

a. R&D per worker: Imitation

b. R&D per worker: Radical innovation

Source: Elaboration using Enterprise Survey data (www.enterprisesurveys.org).

Note: Distance to the frontier is calculated as the difference between the firms' log of sales per worker and the 95th percentile labor productivity in the sector for the entire dataset. We exclude extreme sales per worker values. The g line represents smoothing linear fit. R&D = research and development.

FIGURE 2.9   R&D Intensity Rises with Income per Capita

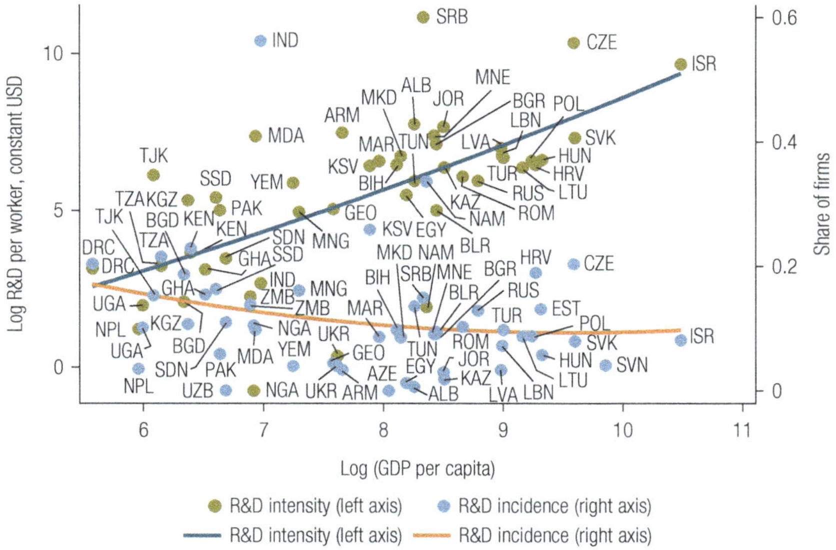

Source: Elaboration using Enterprise Survey data (www.enterprisesurveys.org).

Note: R&D (research and development) incidence is calculated as the share of firms doing R&D using sampling weights. R&D intensity is calculated as the average logarithm of R&D per worker in US$ using sampling weights.

Technology Licensing

Licensing is another important input into innovation activities, although to date the returns to such investments have not been estimated. ES data suggest that, even among relatively advanced countries like the Czech Republic, Israel, and Turkey, only 20 percent of firms engage in licensing (figure 2.10). Note, however, that licensing captures only the small segment of technological adoption from abroad where royalties are paid for the use of intellectual property. This share increases with development; hence, licensing appears complementary to the home country production of intellectual property (patenting).

Purchases of Equipment and Training

The purchase of equipment is one important form of absorbing (embedded knowledge) and thereby generating productivity catch-up or "off-the-frontier" innovation. For example, more than 75 percent of Turkish firms indicate that the purchase of machinery and equipment is their main mechanism for knowledge acquisition, as opposed to other possible sources of knowledge (World Bank 2005). The ES also collects data on other types of investment in knowledge accumulation activities for Africa and South Asia. For most countries, the purchase of equipment is reported to be the main other source of knowledge acquisition, with an average incidence of 45 percent of firms for Asia and 29 percent for Africa. Expenditures on equipment, and less so expenditures on training, broadly track expenditures on R&D, and the resources per worker spent on equipment broadly rise with income, proxied by the distance of the firms'

FIGURE 2.10 **Technology Licensing Is Lower in Less Developed Countries**

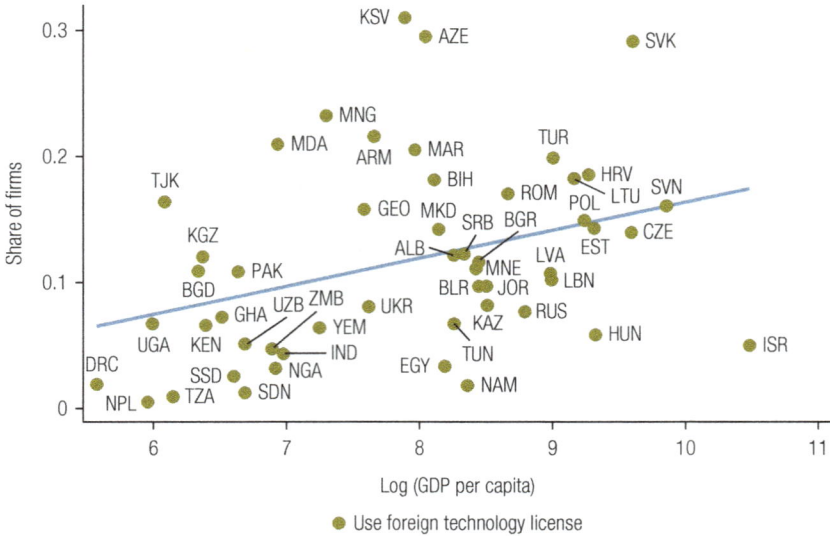

Source: Elaboration using Enterprise Survey data (www.enterprisesurveys.org).

labor productivity to the productivity frontier (measured by the largest decile productivity in the same sector for the whole sample) (figure 2.11).

Management Quality

The final category in figure 2.1 is investment in organizational/managerial capital. Bloom et al. (2014) argue that differing management practices contribute roughly 25 percent of the observed differences in productivity between countries and between firms in the United States. Though the next chapters will take up this subject in greater detail, here we present some stylized facts put forward in recent work by Bloom and Van Reenen (2007, 2010) and Bloom et al. (2016) quantifying management practices across the world.

The new availability of data has raised the profile of this issue in the economics profession, although the National Innovation System literature has long argued that managerial and organization competencies are critical inputs for innovation. For example, one reason why firms don't do more R&D or licensing may be that they lack managers with the ability to identify high-return potential projects, engage in the long-term planning required for their gestation, and then recruit, train, and motivate the talent to implement them. However, what is clear from figure 2.12 is that the quality of managerial practices is much higher in advanced countries than in developing countries.

FIGURE 2.11 **Like R&D, Expenditures on Equipment and Training Are Higher in Firms Closer to the Frontier**

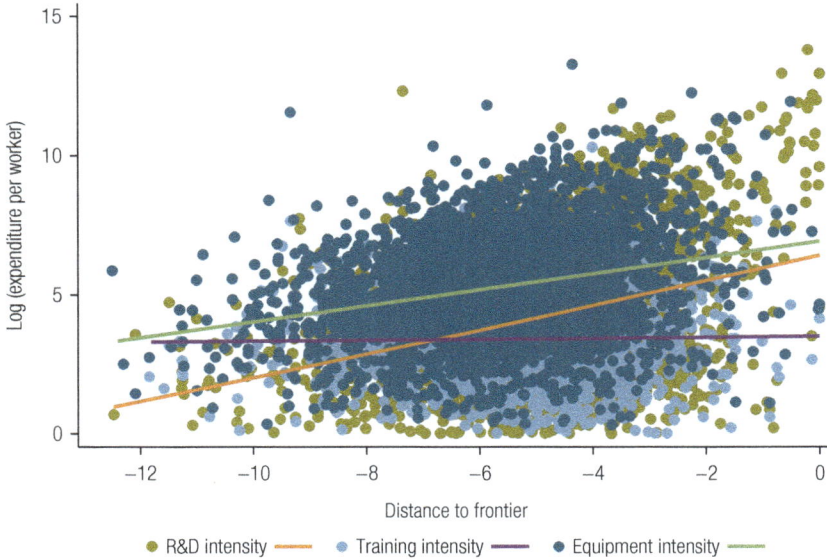

Source: Elaboration using Enterprise Survey data (www.enterprisesurveys.org).

Note: Distance to the frontier is calculated as the difference between the firms' log of sales per worker and the 95th percentile labor productivity in the sector for the entire dataset. We exclude extreme sales per worker values. The lines represent smoothing a linear fit. R&D = research and development.

FIGURE 2.12 **Managerial Practices Are Better in Richer Countries**

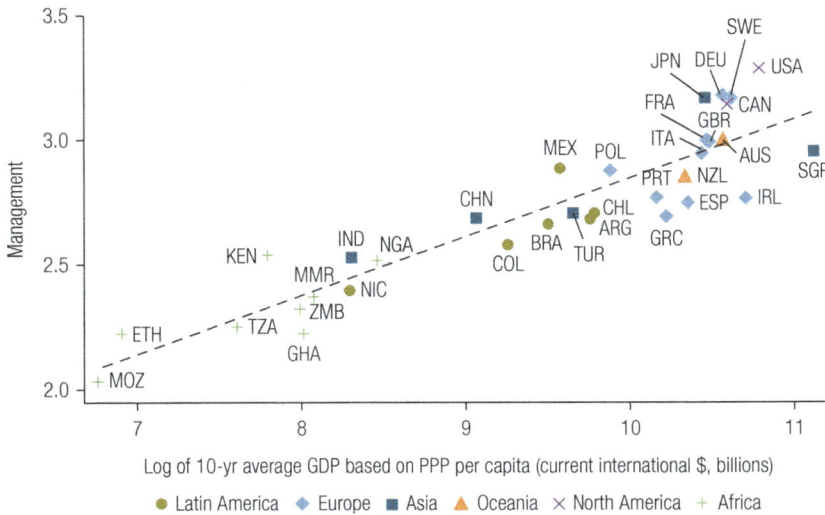

Source: World Management Survey 2012.

Note: Figure shows the management scores for the 15,454 interviews across the countries in the WMS survey. Management is scored on a 1 to 5 basis for 18 questions, with these country scores reflecting the average across all 18 questions across all firms in each country. Gross domestic product (GDP) data are on a purchasing power parity (PPP) basis for 2013 from the International Monetary Fund World Economic Outlook. Smaller and larger firms in China, Mozambique, and Nigeria have been restratified to balance the sampling frame.

The Nature of Innovation in Developing Countries

Some Stylized Facts

In sum, several additional stylized facts emerge from the analysis in relation to innovation inputs:

- As with innovation outputs, the intensity in the accumulation of innovation inputs rises with level of development.
- A large fraction of the firms reporting that they undertake product or process innovation do not undertake formal innovation, such as R&D or licensing. This suggests that policy needs to look beyond these commonly measured inputs when thinking about the determinants of innovation.
- All inputs examined—R&D, licensing, purchase of equipment, and training or management quality—increase with level of development, reflecting both an increased number of firms undertaking innovation and, more important, the intensity of innovation within those firms.

Concluding Remarks

The literature is clear that innovation, thought of as both the transfer of existing technologies and products and the invention of new ones, is fundamental for growth and economic development. This chapter has employed new sources of data to generate stylized facts about the nature of innovation investments undertaken across the development process. Three points merit highlighting in addition to the patterns discussed above.

First, across the income spectrum and in all sectors, firms report innovating. However, that innovation often consists of marginal improvements in process or products, rather than significant technology adoption or new product imitation and very infrequently involves frontier research. It is clear, therefore, that the policy model appropriate for developing countries will differ from that of advanced countries. This topic will be taken up in Part II of the report.

Second, investments in innovation-related inputs increase together with income per capita. This is suggestive of a high degree of complementarity among these "factors of production:" If a firm (country) is going to invest more in innovation, they are likely to need to invest in machines, trained people, and new organizational techniques as well. The implications of this basic insight for how we approach innovation policy and benchmark innovation performance insight are discussed in chapter 3 and are far reaching.

Third, that these investments rise together with development, and the fact that in developing countries only a small fraction of firms undertake significant investments in serious product or process upgrading, technology licensing, managerial practices, or R&D, may seem somehow reasonable, but upon reflection, it is not obviously so.

The coexistence of the extraordinarily low levels of innovation related investment in poor countries with the dramatically high returns thought to accompany technological adoption and Schumpeterian catch-up, particularly far from the frontier, poses a true "innovation paradox." The dimensions of this paradox and how the patterns of complementarity documented here may contribute to our understanding of it are explored in the next chapter.

Annex 2A The World Bank Enterprise Survey Innovation Data

This is the most comprehensive set of cross-country surveys on innovation information carried out to date. The survey implemented during the period 2013–15 used a stratified sampling strategy, where firms are stratified by industry, size, and location. Firm size levels are 5–19 (small), 20–99 (medium), and 100+ employees (large). Because in most economies most firms are small and medium sized, the ES oversamples large firms. One advantage of the survey is that it collects substantial balance sheet and other information regarding the investment climate, which enables analysts to link innovation efforts to firm performance. The standard ES questionnaire includes a large array of issues: firm characteristics, access to finance, annual sales, costs of inputs/labor, workforce composition, and other business climate and performance measures. The mode of data collection is face-to-face interviews.

The data are collected in two stages. In the first stage, the core enterprise survey questionnaire is implemented. Then, in the second stage, the innovation questionnaire is implemented in a large sample of firms surveyed by the core questionnaire. In some regions, such as the Middle East and North Africa and Europe and Central Asia, both surveys are implemented sequentially in the same interview. In other regions, such as Sub-Saharan Africa and South Asia, the innovation survey is implemented a few weeks after. In addition, the managerial quality module of the innovation questionnaire is implemented only in a subsample of firms, mainly medium and large firms, which reduces the sample considerably. In total, the original pooled sample with innovation questions is about 34,000 firms, but the sample of firms that answered the management module is reduced to about 10,000 observations. The countries with the largest representation in the sample are India (25 percent) and Egypt (11 percent). Whereas in the original sample most firms are concentrated in the manufacturing sector (50 percent) and wholesale and retail (29 percent), the management practices module concentrates mainly in manufacturing (86 percent). In addition, the size composition changes by construction because only medium (60 percent) and large (37 percent) firms were interviewed.

The innovation survey differentiates between two types of technological innovation outcomes, product and process, and two nontechnological innovations, marketing and organization. However, there is significant confusion in the identification of the different types of innovation outcomes by firms in the survey. For example, new marketing processes such as discounts, new packaging, or new client segments are sometimes misconstrued as process or product innovations. The fact that interviewees provide a recorded description of the product and process innovations enables us to verify the identified innovations, and reclassify wrongly attributed cases to their respective category or invalidate cases that do not constitute an innovation at all (see Cirera 2017 for a description of the methodology). Overall, the cleaning exercise results in a decrease in both product and process innovation rates due to cases of incorrect classifications of innovation or misclassifications of marketing as product or process innovations. Figures 2A.1 and 2A.2 show before and after cleaning unweighted means by country. The reduction in innovation rates due to cleaning is significantly large in the Africa region and Eastern Europe, and especially for product innovation. This suggests that using raw data from innovation outcomes could lead to biased interpretations, given their subjective nature and the lack of clarity in the definition of the different types of innovation. In order to mitigate some of this bias, in what follows we use the cleaned data on innovation outcomes.

Regarding management practices, we construct a measure of management quality as similar as possible to Bloom and Van Reenen (2007). In the management chapter of the innovation module, respondents of medium and large firms (more than 50 workers) describe management behavior covering four major themes: (1) operations, (2) monitoring, (3) targets, and (4) incentives. The operations management section focuses on the degree to which a firm acts upon encountering problems in the production process. The monitoring section focuses on the tracking of production performance indicators. The targets section covers the time horizon of production targets, and the incentives section deals with whether managers are offered performance incentives. Because the scaling of each question may vary, we convert the scores from each practice to z-scores by normalizing to mean zero and standard deviation one.

FIGURE 2A.1 Cleaned Data on Product Innovation Differ from Original Data

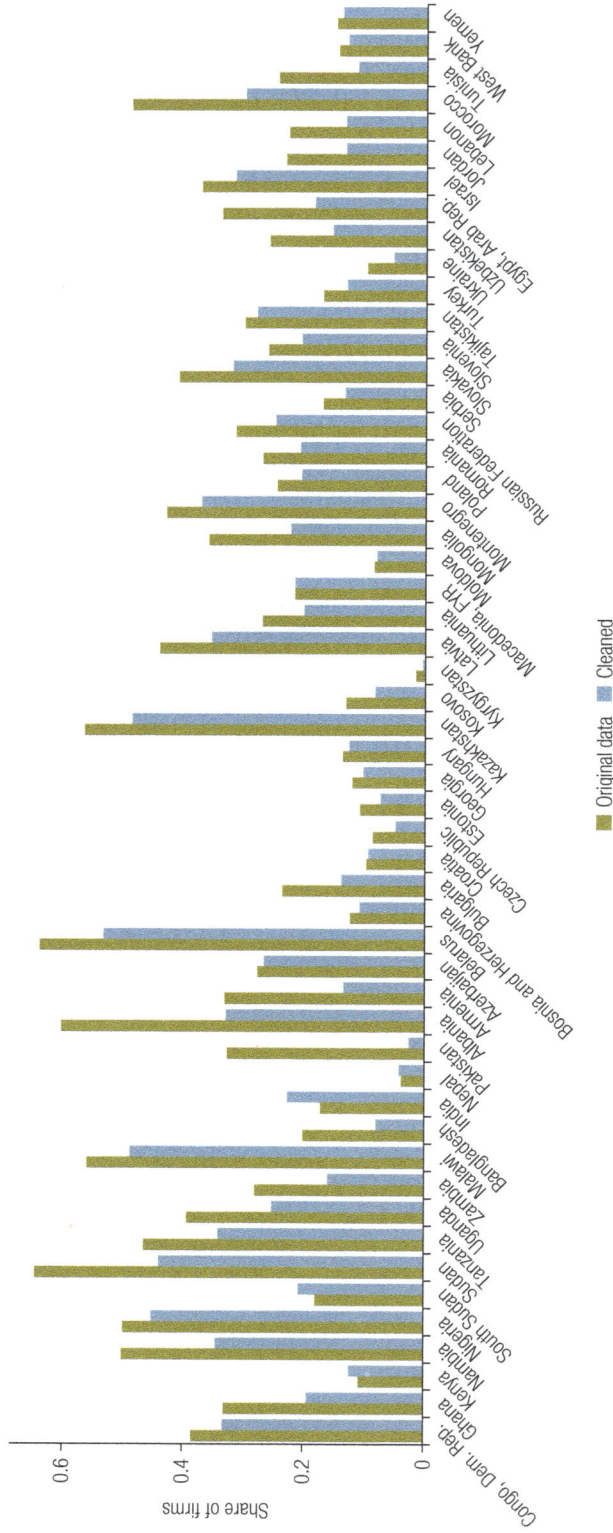

Source: Elaboration using Enterprise Survey data (www.enterprisesurveys.org).

FIGURE 2A.2   Cleaned Data on Process Innovation Differ from Original Data

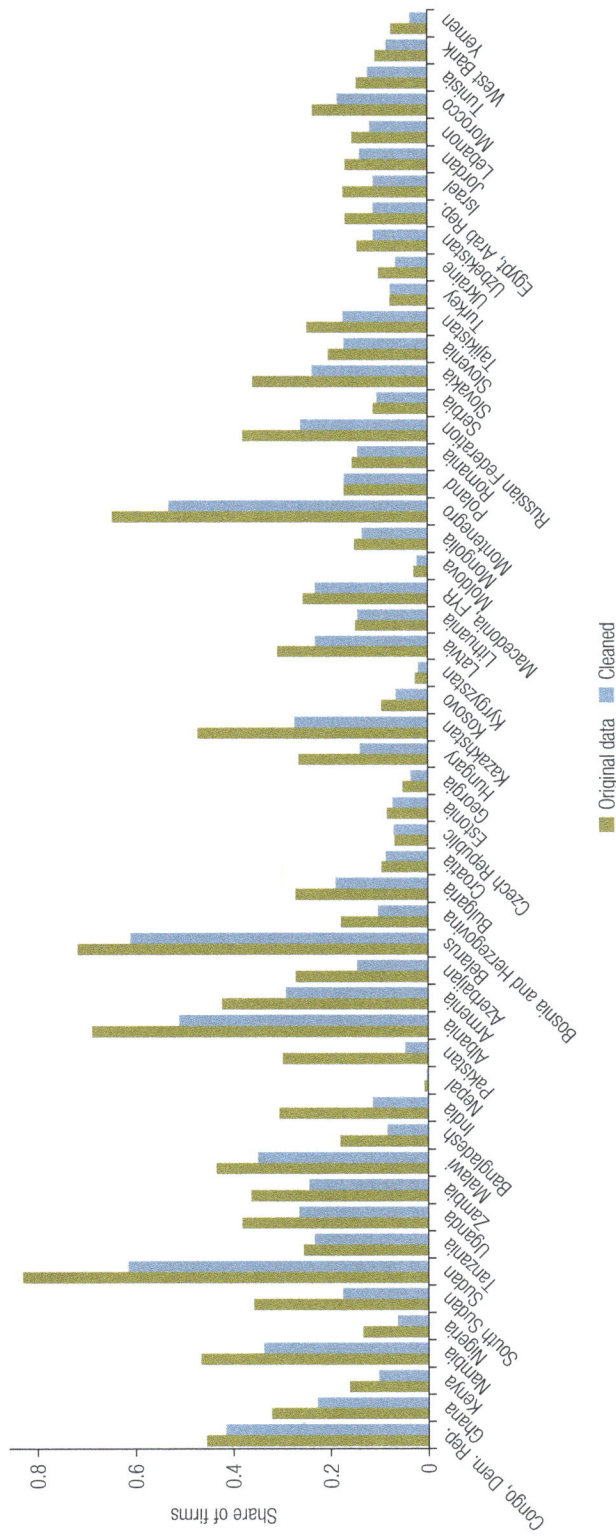

Source: Elaboration using Enterprise Survey data (www.enterprisesurveys.org).

Annex 2B Improving Innovation Measurement in Developing Countries

As box 2.2 discusses, there are significant problems in the measurement of innovation outputs. These result in a likely overestimation of innovation incidence, especially for measures of product or process innovation, and in difficulties when conducting benchmarking across countries.

ES versus UNESCO Data

Clear evidence of the problems with benchmarking and comparing different datasets is illustrated in figure 2B.1. The figure shows how the ES tends to find higher innovation rates than UNESCO data for the same country.

The Problem with Subjective Measurement

Subjective data have strong limitations as measures of actual outcomes. In an influential study, Bertrand and Mullainathan (2001) show the likely bias when analyzing subjective data given their likely correlation with context variables. The possible sources of bias when using subjective data are numerous, such as those that derive from cognitive problems, as shown in Bertrand and Mullainathan (2001). A large amount of experimental evidence shows that certain characteristics of the survey, such as how the questions are structured in the survey, the ordering and the wording used, the format of the interview, or the quality of the translation, all significantly influence the outcome of

FIGURE 2B.1 UNESCO and Enterprise Survey Data Differ Greatly

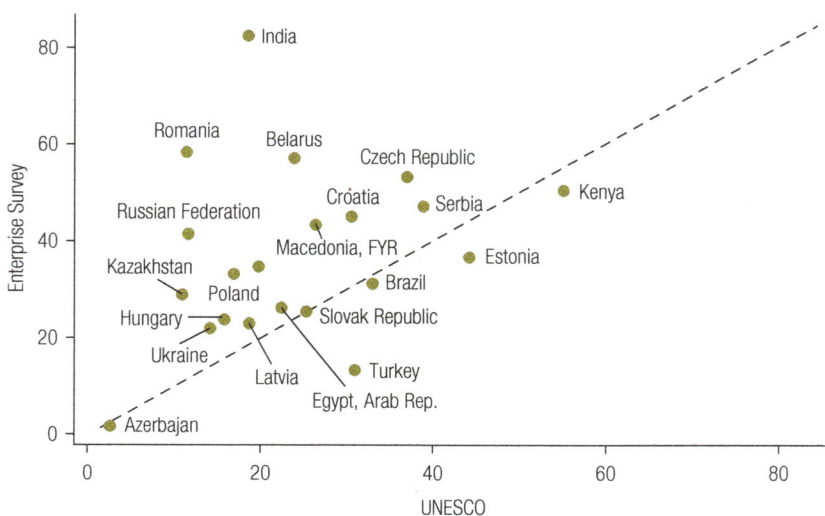

Sources: Enterprise Surveys (www.enterprisesurveys.org) and United Nations Educational, Scientific, and Cultural Organization (UNESCO) Statistics.

Note: The two axes show the percentage of innovative firms in manufacturing according to each data source.

survey responses. For example, whether the question is formulated in a positive way or in a negative way is more likely to translate into a positive or a negative answer. In addition, Schwarz (1999) describes how closed versus open response formats or the rating scale can also bias the response obtained.

The sources of bias identified in the literature on subjective measurement are particularly relevant for innovation surveys, given the subjective nature of many of the questions used in innovation surveys. For example, the *Oslo Manual* (OECD 2005) defines product innovation "as the introduction of new or significantly improved product (goods and/or services)." However, "significantly improved" is a relative and subjective term that may be understood differently by different people.

The use of standard survey instruments in most innovation surveys in OECD countries has mitigated the impact of cognitive issues, like ordering or wording, on the quality of the data collected. However, methodological issues related to the respondent's understanding of innovation or to the type of survey instrument used have yet to be solved. The correlation between innovation and core economic indicators for EU countries, for instance, has pointed out the existence of the "Norwegian puzzle," which shows relatively lower innovation rates for Norwegian firms than would be expected when comparing the Norwegian economy to that of other countries. The results of an experiment conducted by Statistics Norway suggest that this is partially explained by the survey instrument used. The experiment shows that innovation rates are significantly different when captured by a stand-alone innovation survey versus a combined R&D and innovation survey (Wilhelmsen 2014). Similarly, an experiment conducted in the Flanders region of Belgium shows that innovation rates are considerably and systematically higher when measured with a short questionnaire than when using a long questionnaire (Hoskens 2015). Although it is not clear which survey instrument is more accurate in measuring innovation rates, this difference shows that survey methodology can greatly impact innovation measurement.

Context, cultural differences, and social desirability are likely to affect how respondents understand and respond to innovation questions. Respondents are likely to have different views on what is considered innovation, depending on the context in which they live and operate. Whereas in the United States firms consider innovation as something new and unique, in Europe firms are more likely to include improvement as elements of innovation (Galindo-Rueda and Van Cruysen 2016). Furthermore, self-reported innovation may be biased by social desirability that, in turn, might have a differential effect on respondents from different cultural backgrounds (Johnson and Van de Vijver 2003). Because innovation is commonly associated with increased productivity and growth, it may be perceived as a desirable outcome. Therefore, respondents to innovation surveys may be inclined to over-report innovations in the absence of follow-up questions to ascertain the accuracy of the answer.

Is the U-shaped Relationship between Innovation and per Capita Income an Artifact of Such Measurement Issues?

Figure 2B.2 replots the ES-reported share of firms focusing on innovations that are new to the firm or the local market only as imitation (green line). Then it also plots the average labor productivity differential—for each country between firms that report innovating and those that do not (blue line). This differential diminishes with distance from the frontier. Although we cannot be certain of the direction of causality, this is consistent with the poorer countries having different subjective ideas of what defines an innovation: a lower quality of "innovation" implies less productivity impact in the firm. Alternatively, it is consistent with lower-productivity firms being less able to distinguish incidental from impactful innovation when surveyed.

Results from an Experiment

Cirera and Muzi (2016) show the results of an experiment conducted by the Enterprise Analysis Unit of the World Bank Group in 15 countries to test two different approaches to measuring innovation in developing countries. The first, more economical, approach uses a short questionnaire embedded in a general firm-level survey, namely the ES. The second, much more expensive, approach uses a stand-alone, longer questionnaire and provides more information. The same question about innovation is asked twice

FIGURE 2B.2 Returns to Innovation and Productivity

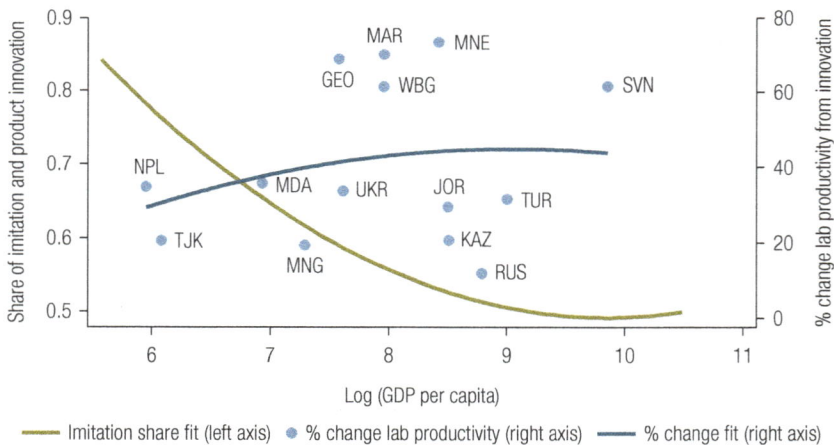

Source: Elaboration using Enterprise Survey data (www.enterprisesurveys.org).

Note: The productivity differential is calculated as the coefficient associated to the estimation of Cobb–Douglas productivity function augmented to include innovation as a knowledge input. The coefficient on the innovation dummy is then transformed to a percentage change. The x axis measures the logarithm of gross domestic product (GDP) per capita.

(often to the same person), once without many other questions on innovation and again after some weeks with an entire set of questions on innovation.

The results of the experiment show large variation in responses within the same firm, in some countries averaging more than 30 percent. As figure 2B.3 shows, differences in reported innovation are sizable across types of innovations and countries. However, the magnitude and direction of these differences vary widely, and no country shows consistently lower or higher differences across types of innovation. This is indicative of significant problems with subjectivity and survey design.

Cirera and Muzi (2016) find that cognitive issues do not seem to play a key role in explaining inaccuracies because neither the use of explanatory cards nor the experience of the respondent seems to matter. Also, a lower-quality interview is more likely to produce inaccurate responses, whereas whether the firm reports making informal payments and the size of the firm are likely to reduce inaccuracies. The time elapsed between interviews is a strong predictor of differences in reported innovation between surveys, likely the result of the recall effect. The results point toward issues of subjectivity, incentives, and framing as sources of bias.

FIGURE 2B.3 **Differences in Innovation Rates Reported between Short and Long Questionnaires Are Large**

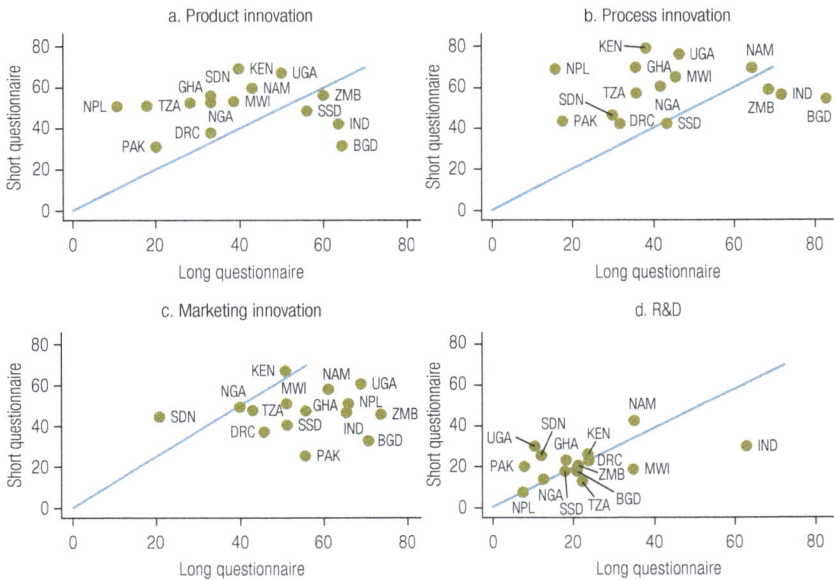

Source: Cirera and Muzi 2016.
Note: The two axes show the share of responses for each type of questionnaire.

Cirera, López-Bassols, and Muzi (2017) provide an analysis of different innovation measurement frameworks and suggest some key elements to better measure innovation outcomes. These are summarized here:

- **Describing the innovation introduced.** The experience of the World Bank innovation surveys suggests that a key variable to define innovation is the description of the innovation introduced and how this differs from existing products or process. This is instrumental to be able to determine the accuracy of the report of an innovation.
- **Avoiding framing the responses.** To avoid framing, some surveys in countries such as Canada and Australia do not use the term "innovation" throughout the survey. These questionnaires are labeled as business strategies or business processes questionnaires. Questions can be made about changes and about improvements that do not require a positive association with innovation.
- **Degree of novelty.** The notion of "new or significantly improved" is difficult to operationalize because it is attempting to assess changes to some characteristics (of a product or process) that should somehow be measurable, but are usually lacking a reference point (Smith 2005). Distinctions made between innovations that are new only to the firm (imitation or adoption) and those that are new to the local, national, or international market are not very informative regarding the degree of novelty of innovations. In many cases, firms are not aware of or do not have full information to assess whether such innovations are truly new to the local or national market. This is even more important in the case of process innovation, where there may be little information available about other firms' production processes.

This means that when possible one should ask about specific changes and provide some metric of novelty. A more relevant distinction should be made at two levels. First, at the level of the firm it is important to differentiate between a completely new product (diversification) from a simple product upgrade. Second, it is important to identify whether the new product or process embodies a new technological attribute or type of product that has not been in the market versus whether it is mainly imitation or technology adoption. More clarity in these definitions of novelty is of critical importance in comparing countries and reconciling these surveys with economic theories of diffusion and technology adoption. Surveys could thus consider testing alternative formulations that make a clearer distinction between invention and imitation/adoption (see also Nieminen and Lehtoranta 2015).

- **Intention and impacts.** Another problem related to the previous one concerns the intention of the changes introduced and to what extent they had a measurable impact on the firm's activities. For example, in difficult business environments—characterized by lack of reliable inputs, electricity shortages, customs delays, and so on—firms may have to constantly change some of their production processes to adapt and survive with little efficiency or improvement effects. Intention of improvement is therefore important to define innovation.

- **Implementation**. A further challenge for measurement is the requirement that an innovation needs to be *implemented* (that is, introduced to the market or within the firm), which is key to distinguishing innovation from other related activities such as invention. However, in some cases it may be difficult to identify when this happens because the innovation process often includes small incremental steps that are not in themselves innovative. In any case the survey needs to ask whether the innovation is implemented.

Increasing the Scope for Measuring Innovation Inputs

As has been shown in chapter 2, most innovation occurs without formal R&D activities. Chapter 4 describes some of these inputs in more detail. Below we suggest some of the key capabilities for innovation that need to be measured in surveys.

Technological Capabilities

The first category includes several knowledge-based activities and assets that firms develop or purchase to strengthen their technological potential. The two main suggestions for innovation surveys are to

1. Expand the list of innovation inputs currently included in the Oslo framework by identifying more precisely certain types of tangible and intangible assets that can be acquired or sourced externally (for example consultancy services and technology gained through firm acquisition); and
2. Consider key activities that may be related to R&D but are supporting the creation of new knowledge (for example, design and engineering).

Some of these activities are more prevalent in technologically mature economies and firms closer to the technological frontier that have the capability to create more radical innovations. However, firms in less developed countries can start accumulating some of these capabilities in line with the process of increasing the accumulation of R&D as they converge to the technological frontier. Moreover, design and engineering are critical capabilities in sectors such as knowledge-intensive business services (Pina and Tether 2016).

Production Capabilities

The second category involves a broad set of capabilities needed to improve production processes, through both internal factors and relations with external agents. Two key areas proposed for this category are

1. Collecting additional information regarding the firm's involvement and position within value chains (local or global); and

2. Considering the use of modern production techniques such as lean manufacturing methods.

These activities are important complementary capabilities for innovation and can vary considerably in terms of their sophistication as firms get closer to the technological frontier.

Organizational/Managerial Capabilities

The third category includes capabilities related to the effective deployment and use of internal resources, in particular the firm's human and organizational capital. As chapter 4 shows, managerial practices are part of core competences and critical inputs for innovation because they determine the way in which knowledge is accumulated and used, particularly for firms farther away from the technological frontier. This involves documenting how the firm is organized as well as the use of various processes and practices aimed at collecting and using strategic information and knowledge more efficiently, both internally and externally. Future surveys need to further develop several questions on the role of structured management practices and management quality (see, for example, Bloom and Van Reenen 2007, 2010) using data from the World Management Survey), including on

- The use of structured management and modern production techniques;
- Performance monitoring and target setting; and
- Talent management and incentives.

Notes

1. Sutton (2001) for example, treats the role of R&D broadly construed as "increasing the consumers' willingness-to pay" for a firm's product, complementary to its role in decreasing the cost of production. See also Hallak and Schott (2011) and Khandelwal (2010).
2. See also the World Bank Enterprise Survey, http://www.enterprisesurveys.org.
3. For more information about Orbis, see the BvD website, https://www.bvdinfo.com/en-gb /about-us/overview.
4. For more information, see the World Management Survey website, http://worldmanagementsur vey.org.
5. UNESCO data summarize data on innovation incidence on the basis of national surveys of selected middle- and high-income countries.
6. The World Bank Enterprise Survey and its linked innovation modules were implemented during the period 2013–2015 in 53 countries over four regions—Europe and Central Asia (ECA), the Middle East and North Africa, South Asia, and Sub-Saharan Africa. This is the most comprehensive set of cross-country surveys on innovation information carried out to date with the same questionnaire. Most firms in the sample are concentrated in the manufacturing sector (49 percent) and wholesale and retail (29 percent), although the sector composition varies by country. The countries with the largest representation in the sample are Russia (12 percent) and India (10 percent), and some countries in ECA have fewer than 250 firms in the innovation modules. The core innovation questionnaire is based on *Oslo Manual* guidelines, and the questions are similar to Community Innovation Survey (CIS) questionnaires. The mode of data collection in both surveys is face-to-face interviews.

7. Whereas the Enterprise Survey uses a comparable questionnaire for all countries, UNESCO collects information from national statistics offices. In some cases (for example, Azerbaijan or Kenya) both incidence rates are similar; in other cases (for example, India) there are significant differences across sources. Including one or the other data source does not change the main fitted line in figure 2.2.

8. For these reasons, we follow Jaffe and Trajtenberg (2002); Branstetter (2001); Furman, Porter, and Stern (2002); Furman and Hayes (2004) and Ulku (2007), among others, and use the number of utility patents granted by the USPTO. The USPTO demands that the invention be "novel and nontrivial, and has to have commercial application" (Jaffe and Trajtenberg 2002, 3–4). In the absence of a global patenting agency, the United States remains the principal locus of patenting activity, and the USPTO offers reliable panel data for the period 1963 to 2000 for a large number of countries. Granted patents are assigned by country of origin on the basis of the country of residence of the first inventor.

9. See Branstetter, Guangwei, and Veloso (2015) for a discussion of why this number is exaggerated. The bulk of patents are filed by multinationals from the United States or Taiwan, China, and hence we are not measuring the innovative activity of domestic firms.

10. Although concerns about remaining endogeneity suggest caution in putting too much weight on this estimate, it nonetheless contrasts importantly with firm-level estimates using the same techniques, which imply substantially lower elasticities. One interpretation is that the aggregate estimations capture spillover effects among firms and industries, although the lack of comparability of the aggregate and micro samples leaves this as a conjecture only.

11. By region, in Sub-Saharan Africa only 26 percent of innovators do any R&D, 56 percent in South Asia, 28 percent in Europe and Central Asia, and 18 percent in the Middle East and North Africa.

References

Alston, Julian M., T. J. Wyatt, Philip G. Pardey, Michele C. Marra, and Connie Chan-Kang. 2000. "A Meta-analysis of Rates of Return to Agricultural R&D." IFPRI Research Report 113, International Food Policy Research Institute, Washington, DC.

Aroca, Patricio, and Roger R. Stough. 2015. "Lessons from a Study of Innovation in a Chilean Mining Region." Unpublished paper, Universidad Adolfo Ibáñez, Chile.

Bell, Martin, and Keith Pavitt. 1993. "Technological Accumulation and Industrial Growth: Contrasts Between Developed and Developing Countries." *Industrial and Corporate Change* 2 (2): 157–210.

Bertrand, Marianne, and Sendhil Mullainathan. 2001. "Do People Mean What They Say? Implications for Subjective Survey Data." *American Economic Review* 91 (2): 67–72.

Bloom, Nicholas, Renata Lemos, Raffaella Sadun, Daniela Scur, and John Van Reenen. 2014. "JEEA-FBBVA Lecture 2013: The New Empirical Economics of Management." *Journal of the European Economic Association* 12: 835–76.

———. 2016. "International Data on Measuring Management Practices." *American Economic Review* 106 (5): 152–56.

Bloom, Nicholas, and John Van Reenen. 2007. "Measuring and Explaining Management Practices across Firms and Countries." *Quarterly Journal of Economics* 122 (4): 1351–1408.

———. 2010. "Why Do Management Practices Differ across Firms and Countries?" *Journal of Economic Perspectives* 24 (1): 203–24.

Blundell, Richard, Rachel Griffith, and John Van Reenen. 1995. "Dynamic Count Data Models of Technological Innovation." *Economic Journal* 105 (429): 333–44.

Blundell, Richard, Rachel Griffith, and Frank Windmeijer. 2002. "Individual Effects and Dynamics in Count Data Models." *Journal of Econometrics* 108 (1): 113–31.

Bosch, Mariano, Daniel Lederman, and William F. Maloney. 2005. *Patenting and Research and Development: A Global View.* Washington, DC: World Bank.

Branstetter, Lee G. 2001. "Are Knowledge Spillovers International or Intranational in Scope? Microeconometric Evidence from the US and Japan." *Journal of International Economics* 53 (1): 53–79.

Branstetter, Lee, Li Guangwei, and Francisco Veloso. 2015. "The Rise of International Coinvention." In *The Changing Frontier: Rethinking Science and Innovation Policy,* edited by Adam B. Jaffe and Benjamin F. Jones, 135–68. Chicago: University of Chicago Press.

Cirera, Xavier. 2017. "Management Practices as an Input for Innovation and Productivity in Developing Countries." Unpublished paper, World Bank, Washington, DC.

Cirera, Xavier, Vladimir López-Bassols, and Silvia Muzi. 2017. "Measuring Firm Innovation: A Review of Existing Approaches." Unpublished paper, World Bank, Washington, DC.

Cirera, Xavier, and Silvia Muzi. 2016. "Measuring Firm-Level Innovation Using Short Questionnaires: Evidence from an Experiment." Policy Research Working Paper 7696, World Bank, Washington, DC.

Cirera, Xavier, and Leonard Sabetti. 2016. "The Returns to Innovation and Imitation in Developing Countries." Unpublished paper, World Bank, Washington, DC.

Cohen, Wesley M., and Daniel A. Levinthal. 1990. "Absorptive Capacity: A New Perspective on Learning and Innovation." *Administrative Science Quarterly* 35 (1): 128–52.

Collard-Wexler, Allan, and Jan De Loecker. 2014. "Reallocation and Technology: Evidence from the US Steel Industry." *American Economic Review* 105 (1): 131–71.

Crépon, Bruno, Emmanuel Duguet, and Jacques Mairesse. 1998. "Research, Innovation and Productivity: An Econometric Analysis at the Firm Level." *Economics of Innovation and New Technology* 7 (2): 115–58.

Fagerberg, Jan, Martin Srholec, and Bart Verspagen. 2010. "The Role of Innovation in Development." *Review of Economics and Institutions* 1 (2): Article 2.

Furman, Jeffrey L., and Richard Hayes. 2004. "National Innovative Productivity among 'Follower' Countries, 1978–1999." *Research Policy* 33 (9): 1329–54.

Furman, Jeffrey L., Michael E. Porter, and Scott Stern. 2002. "The Determinants of National Innovative Capacity." *Research Policy* 31 (6): 899–933.

Galindo-Rueda, Fernando, and Adriana Van Cruysen. 2016. "Testing Innovation Survey Concepts, Definitions and Questions: Findings from Cognitive Interviews with Business Managers." OECD Science, Technology and Innovation Technical Paper, Organisation for Economic Co-operation and Development, Paris.

Hall, Bronwyn H. 2011. "Innovation and Productivity." NBER Working Paper 17178, National Bureau of Economic Research, Cambridge, MA.

Hall, Bronwyn H., Zvi Griliches, and Jerry Hausman. 1986. "Patents and R&D: Is There a Lag?" *International Economic Review* 27 (2): 265–83.

Hall, Bronwyn H., Jacques Mairesse, and Pierre Mohnen. 2010. "Measuring the Returns to R&D." In *Handbook of the Economics of Innovation,* edited by Bronyn H. Hall and Nathan Rosenberg, 1033–1082. Vol. 2. Amsterdam: Elsevier.

Hall, Robert E., and Charles I. Jones. 1999. "Why Do Some Countries Produce So Much More Output per Worker Than Others?" *Quarterly Journal of Economics* 114 (1): 83–116.

Hallak, Juan Carlos, and Peter K. Schott. 2011. "Estimating Cross-Country Differences in Product Quality." *Quarterly Journal of Economics* 126 (1): 417–74.

Hausman, Jerry, Bronwyn H. Hall, and Zvi Griliches. 1984. "Econometric Models for Count Data Models with an Application to the Patents—R&D Relationship." *Econometrica* 52 (4): 909–38.

Hoskens, Machteld. 2015. "Short vs. Long Form: Method Effects in Measuring Innovation." Paper presented at the OECD NESTI/EUROSTAT Scoping Workshop on the third revision of the Oslo Manual, Oslo, Norway.

Hsieh, Chang-Tai, and Peter J. Klenow. 2009. "Misallocation and Manufacturing TFP in China and India." *Quarterly Journal of Economics* 124 (4): 1403–48.

Jaffe, Adam B., and Manuel Trajtenberg. 2002. *Patents, Citations, and Innovations: A Window on the Knowledge Economy*. Cambridge, MA: MIT Press.

Johnson, Timothy P., and Fons Van de Vijver. 2003. "Social Desirability in Cross-Cultural Research." In *Cross-Cultural Survey Methods,* edited by Janet A. Harkness, Fons J. R. Van de Vijver, and Peter P. Mohler, 195–204. Hoboken, NJ: Wiley.

Jones, Charles I. 2016. "The Facts of Economic Growth." *Handbook of Macroeconomics* 2: 3–69.

Khandelwal, Amit. 2010. "The Long and Short (of) Quality Ladders." *Review of Economic Studies* 77 (4): 1450–76.

Klenow, Peter J., and Andres Rodriguez-Clare. 1997. "The Neoclassical Revival in Growth Economics: Has It Gone Too Far?" *NBER Macroeconomics Annual 12*: 73–103.

Kline, Stephen J., and Nathan Rosenberg. 1986. "An Overview of Innovation." In *The Positive Sum Strategy: Harnessing Technology for Economic Growth*, edited by R. Landau and N. Rosenberg, 275–304. Washington, DC: National Academy Press.

Klinger, Bailey, and Daniel Lederman. 2006. "Diversification, Innovation, and Imitation Inside the Global Technological Frontier." Policy Research Working Paper No. 3872, World Bank, Washington, DC.

Kortum, Samuel, and Josh Lerner. 2000. "Assessing the Contribution of Venture Capital to Innovation." *Rand Journal of Economics* 31(4, Winter): 674–92.

Maloney, William F., and Mauricio Sarrias. 2017. "Convergence to the Managerial Frontier." *Journal of Economic Behavior & Organization* 134 (C): 284–306.

Mohnen, Pierre, and Bronwyn H. Hall. 2013. "Innovation and Productivity: An Update." *Eurasian Business Review* 3 (1): 47–65.

Nieminen, Mika, and Olavi Lehtoranta, eds. 2015. "Measuring Broad-Based Innovation, VTT Technology 242." VTT Technical Research Centre of Finland, Espoo.

OECD (Organisation for Economic Co-operation and Development). 2005. *Oslo Manual: Guidelines for Collecting and Interpreting Innovation Data*, 3rd ed. Paris: OECD Publishing.

Pina, Katia, and Bruce S. Tether. 2016. "Towards Understanding Variety in Knowledge-Intensive Business Services by Distinguishing Their Knowledge Bases. *Research Policy* 45 (2): 401–13.

Restuccia, Diego. 2016. "Structural Change, Misallocation, and Aggregate Productivity." University of Toronto, NBER, and World Bank, Washington, DC.

Restuccia, Diego, and Richard Rogerson. 2008. "Policy Distortions and Aggregate Productivity with Heterogeneous Establishments." *Review of Economic Dynamics* 11 (4): 707–20.

Rozkrut, Dominik. 2015. "Are Micro Enterprises Different in Their Innovative Behavior?" Uniwersytet Szczeciński (US), al. Papieża Jana Pawła II 22a, Szczecin, Poland, 70–453.

Schwarz Norbert. 1999. "Self-Reports: How the Questions Shape the Answers." *American Psychologist* 54 (2): 93–105.

Smith, Keith. 2005. "Measuring Innovation." In *The Oxford Handbook of Innovation*, edited by Jan Fagerberg, David C. Mowery, and Richard R. Nelson, 148–77. Oxford, UK: Oxford University Press.

Sutton, John. 2001. *Technology and Market Structure: Theory and History*. Cambridge, MA: MIT Press.

Ulku, Hulya. 2007. "R&D, Innovation, and Growth: Evidence from Four Manufacturing Sectors in OECD Countries." *Oxford Economic Papers* 59 (3): 513–35.

Wilhelmsen, Lars. 2012. "A Question of Context: Assessing the Impact of a Separate Innovation Survey and of Response Rate on the Measurement of Innovation Activity in Norway." Document 51/2012, Statistics Norway, Oslo.

———. 2014. "Assessing a Combined Survey Strategy and the Impact of Response Rate on the Measurement of Innovation Activity in Norway." Statistics Newsletter for the Extended OECD Statistical Network.

World Bank. 2005. *Turkey Investment Climate Survey 2005*. Washington, DC: World Bank.

World Management Survey. 2012. http://worldmanagementsurvey.org/.

3. The Innovation Paradox and the National Innovation System

Introduction

The stylized facts presented in the previous chapter pose what we term the *innovation paradox*: Given how high the rates of returns to innovation are thought to be and, further, that they are thought to rise with distance from the technological frontier, why do poor countries not invest far more than they do? This chapter argues that the key to the paradox lies in the absence of critical complementary factors, which depresses the return to innovation and makes low rates of innovation investment rational. This insight has important implications for how we benchmark innovation performance and how we conceive of the National Innovation System (NIS).

The Innovation Paradox

As noted in the introduction, estimates of the returns to research and development (R&D) are generally extremely high, and the most recent and reliable estimates appear to confirm this. Bloom, Schankerman, and Van Reenen (2013) and Lucking, Bloom, and Van Reenen (2017) find social returns of 55.0–57.7 percent depending on the sample period, compared to a private return of 13.6–20.7 percent. Doraszelski and Jaumandreu (2013) find an average private return across sectors of 40 percent for Spain (1996–2000), roughly double that of, for instance, investments in infrastructure. As much of the literature argues, the advanced countries should be investing multiples of the amounts they presently do (Jones and Williams 1998 and Bloom, Schankerman, and Van Reenen 2013).

The potential gains from Schumpeterian catch up suggest that the case is even stronger for developing countries. Griffith, Redding, and Van Reenen (2004) argue using data from the Organisation for Economic Co-operation and Development (OECD) that returns rise much higher with increased distance from the technological frontier, reflecting the progressively greater gains from knowledge transfer afforded to follower countries. Simple extrapolations from their estimates suggest that returns could reach the triple digits, far higher than returns to physical or human capital. By this logic, innovation should be the central policy focus for growth-minded countries and investment in innovation a priority. In fact, to reframe Lucas's (1988) famous observation about growth: confronted with the rates of return found in the literature, it would be hard for governments to think of anything else.

Yet, chapter 2 shows that not only do developing countries not make heroic investments in innovation but they also invest far less in every type of innovation than rich countries do. As an example, figure 2.7 established that the poor countries invest far less as a share of their gross domestic product (GDP) than do rich countries in R&D: the Scandinavian countries, Japan, and the United States rank highest in investment, and Africa and parts of Asia rank lowest.[1] What can explain this seeming irrationality on the part of developing country firms and governments? We will argue below that distance from the frontier could indeed increase the gains from Schumpeterian catch-up, but the increased scarcity of complementary factors necessary for R&D to have an impact prevents these potential returns from being realized.

Innovation Complementarities

Adopting a new technology may involve not only R&D to identify and modify the technology to the local context but also investment in physical machinery (physical capital), very likely, training (human capital) to enable employees to run the machines, as well as upgrading management skills to plan and execute longer-term projects.[2] R&D spending will have little impact without well-trained engineers, and any new ideas will be useless without able private sector entrepreneurs to take them to market. The centrality of these complementarities would seem to be supported by the fact that the increased aggregate intensity in innovation effort as countries develop, tracks the long-documented increase also in capital intensity, educational attainment, and now managerial capability.

Conceptually, this is an often overlooked but absolutely critical point. Innovation is not a free-floating activity but can be considered the accumulation of "knowledge capital" that enters a firm or national production function along with physical and human capital (see Klenow and Rodriguez-Clare 2005 and box 3.1). Mainstream economic theory highlights how these factors interact with and often enhance each other. In the present context, this means we cannot consider innovation activity separate from the stock of these other factors of production, which are also scarcer in developing countries. In turn, behind the provision of each of these complementary factors lies a further set of institutions and markets, ranging from schools to financial markets to trade agreements, that are also likely to be weaker in developing countries.

This discussion clearly has important implications for how developing countries should benchmark their innovation performance and how they conceptualize their National Innovation Systems. The next two sections focus on these topics.

Complementarities: A Basic Neoclassical Intuition

Drawing on Klenow and Rodriguez-Clare (2005), we begin simply assuming that firms produce goods combining labor L, physical capital K, human capital h, and technological progress or knowledge capital A. Adopting a standard mathematical simplification, firm i's production function is given by

$$Y_i = k_i^{\alpha} (A_i h_i L_i)^{1-\alpha} \qquad \text{(B3.2.1)}$$

The terms α and $(1-\alpha)$ capture output elasticities of capital and labor, respectively, and dictate constant returns to scale.

Beginning with such a standard formulation highlights several key issues. First, as most of the NIS and neoclassical literature agrees, the central actor in innovation policy must be the generator of wealth, the firm, that appears on the right-hand side of figure 3.4. Second, it critically argues that, technological progress augments both capital K and labor L and allows us to produce more output for each. Third, in the same way that we think about K and h as accumulating physical or human capital, innovation can be thought of as accumulating knowledge capital A that includes all the learning and firm capabilities stressed by the NIS literature. Fourth, our production function also implies that production decisions are made jointly—that is, a decision to "innovate" is also likely to imply investments in machinery K and training h. Hence, innovation is not a free-floating factor outside of the production process but needs to be thought of it as part of it.

How is knowledge A accumulated? There is general agreement that, whereas rich countries need to invent new knowledge, firms in developing countries can benefit from accessing the existing stock of knowledge in the world A^* and applying it to the home stock of knowledge, A (that is, Schumpeterian catch-up). The degree of technological lag can be expressed as A/A^*, where 1 implies the country is at the frontier and less than 1 implies room for catch-up. The potential for knowledge accumulation through transfer is $(1-A/A^*)$.

However, as the NIS literature has stressed, this transfer does not occur automatically: the firm needs to identify and adapt this technology to its particular context. To formalize this intuition, the change (accumulation) of knowledge, $\dot{A}_i$, is given by

$$\dot{A}_i = \lambda R_i (1 - A_i / A^*) \qquad \text{(B3.2.2)}$$

where, R_i (R&D broadly considered) is the investment in knowledge capital made by the firm and the efficiency of that effort is denoted by λ, which we assume is the same for all firms. Therefore, λR term captures the productivity of firms in the country in producing innovation from innovation-related expenditures. We could think of both terms as partly reflecting the capabilities of firms listed as the second group of factors under "the firm" in figure 3.4. The firm's demand to accumulate any factor (in this case R) will depend on its capabilities ranging from its core competencies to its particular capability to identify and absorb new technologies. But then weak management or a lack of technological familiarity (a low λ) can result in misspent innovative effort.

Benchmarking Innovation Performance: How Do We Know Whether a Society Is Investing Enough in Innovation?

Ideally, societies should invest in innovation up to the point where marginal social returns are equated to the cost of borrowing. Jones and Williams (1998), for example, estimate a rate of return to R&D for the United States of 28 percent, which they argue implies that a quadrupling of investment was in order. Bloom, Schankerman, and Van Reenen's (2013) estimates dictate a doubling of R&D spending. Their estimates are broadly consistent with the OECD literature (for a review, see Hall, Mairesse, and Mohnen 2010), which suggests that these findings may be generalizable for the advanced countries.[3]

As discussed above, we would expect the returns to R&D to be much higher for developing countries. The imitation face of R&D facilitates the adoption of new technologies, and, as Schumpeter argues, countries further from the frontier have greater potential gains from catch-up and hence should have higher rates of return. Indeed, as noted in chapter 1, Griffith, Redding, and Van Reenen (2004) find that the return to R&D in the OECD increases as we move from frontier countries to those farther from the frontier.[4] Extrapolating their results to poor countries suggests the return to R&D could easily be 200 to 300 percent. This logic gives legitimacy to simple benchmarking techniques that assume that more is better: given Kenya's low gross domestic expenditure on R&D (GERD) compared with that of, for instance, the Republic of Korea, Kenya should invest more. This argument is often implicitly made in policy circles. For instance, the Lisbon declaration in Europe set a goal of raising the target for R&D expenditures from 1.9 to 3 percent of GDP by 2010 to close the gap with the United States (2.7 percent) and Japan (3.0 percent). Given Chile's comparatively low investment rate, former President Lagos proposed a goal of 1.5 percent by the same date for Chile.

But above we document that developing countries invest far less than rich countries in all types of innovation despite the expected high returns. This is precisely the innovation paradox. Should we not expect governments to divert a very large share of their resources toward supporting R&D?

The answer is probably no. Figure 3.1 presents estimates of the rate of return to innovation activities and to R&D intensity at the country level, using the enterprise surveys, for those countries for which the returns were statistically significant. What is clear is that when significant, the returns are positive and often very high for those few firms that perform R&D. However, they are not obviously higher than those reported for the advanced countries. In fact, for several countries, they are substantially lower. How do we square this with the Griffith, Redding, and Van Reenen (2004) findings of increased returns with distance from the frontier?

Using panel country-level data, Goñi and Maloney (2017) estimate the relationship between returns to R&D and country income. Consistent with Griffith, Redding, and

FIGURE 3.1 **The Returns to Innovation and R&D in Developing Countries Are Not Higher in the Poorest Countries**

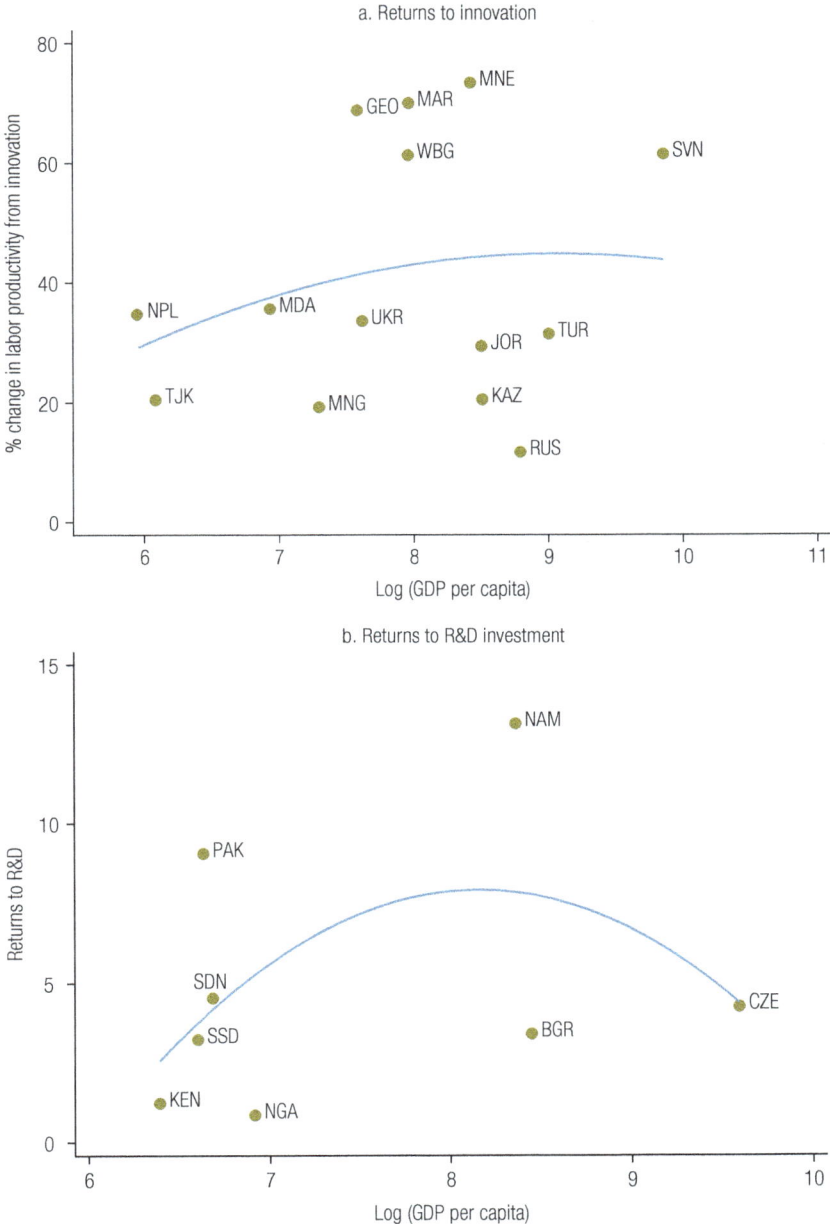

a. Returns to innovation

b. Returns to R&D investment

Source: Elaboration using Enterprise Survey data (http://www.enterprisesurveys.org/).

Note: Panel a shows the percentage share in labor productivity associated with the introduction of product or process innovation. This is calculated using the coefficient on the innovation dummy that enters an augmented production function with capital and labor scaled by labor. The coefficient is estimated by ordinary least squares. In the absence of a convincing instrument, or even a panel dimension, these estimates are simple ordinary least squares, which may suggest that they are, further, biased upward. Further, the figure does not include country estimates that are not statistically different from zero. Panel b shows the returns to R&D estimates using a similar approach but using R&D expenditure intensity as knowledge input. GDP = gross domestic product; R&D = research and development.

Van Reenen (2004), they find that the rate of return to R&D increases with distance from the frontier up to the income level of modern Argentina or Chile. However, moving still farther from the frontier, the rate of return begins to fall and may even be negative for quite poor countries (figure 3.2). This is consistent with figure 3.1, as well as the Bosch, Lederman, and Maloney (2005) estimates of the knowledge-generation function of patenting from R&D, which show that developing countries produce less additional knowledge per R&D expenditure than advanced countries, yielding implicit rates of return to R&D that are perhaps 50 percent (or less) of those found in the advanced countries.

A likely explanation is that, as countries are farther from the technological frontier, the potential gains from Schumpeterian catch-up in fact increase but the stock of the complementarity factors discussed above decreases. Below a certain level of development, the second effect begins to outweigh the first. That is, governments could try to invest directly in R&D; but if they lack the necessary complementary factors—a capital market that would enable firms to buy the necessary accompanying machinery, managers who know how to take new ideas to market, higher-order human capital necessary to translate greater spending into good quality innovation, and capacity to ensure the investments are allocated well—the returns will be low. Moreover, to the degree that

FIGURE 3.2   Returns to R&D Trace an Inverted U-Shape across the Development Process

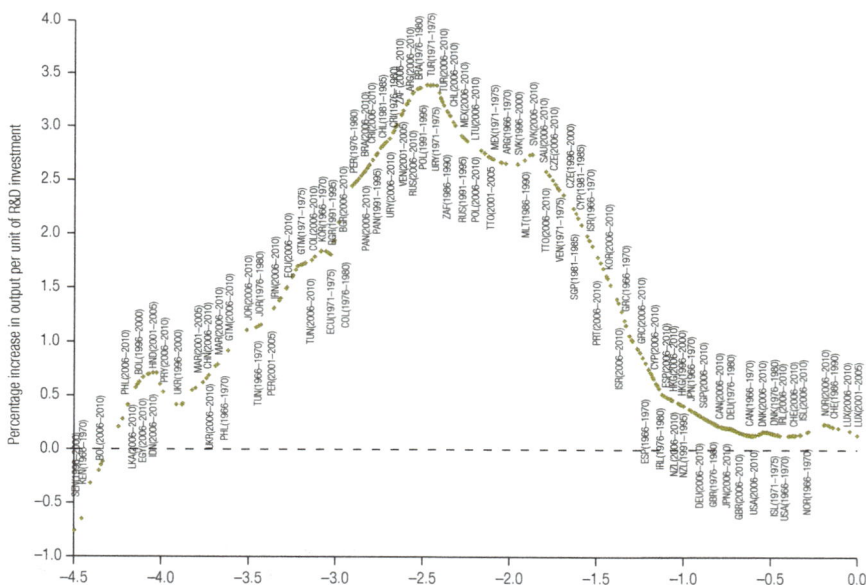

Source: Goñi and Maloney 2017.

Note: Graph uses quinquennials of cross-country data from 1960 to 2010 to estimate the rates of return to research and development (R&D) across the development process: 0 is the frontier, and moving left represents progressively less developed countries. See box 3.1 for details.

such spending crowds out investments in human capital or infrastructure, the returns could potentially be negative.

The discussion highlights how comparing raw innovation measures, such as GERD, across countries can be very misleading. The assumption that returns in poor countries would be at least as high as in the rich countries, so that low levels of R&D signal substantial underinvestment, is probably invalid. For Nepal to target Korea's level of R&D/GDP would almost certainly involve a vast waste of resources.[5] Given Nepal's lower level of physical and human capital, we would not expect Nepalese firms to be able to use the same amount of newly produced or adopted knowledge. Hence, finding that developing countries invest less in R&D than frontier countries does not necessarily imply that they should do more *relative to their investments in other complementary factors*.

Innovation Benchmarking in the Presence of Complementarities: Simulating Innovation Shortfalls

Some idea of the importance of this last point can be gleaned by calibrating the simple neoclassical model of innovation and growth developed by Klenow and Rodriguez-Clare (2005) (see box 3.2) with the stock of existing human and physical capital, and then asking whether the observed innovation (knowledge capital) is high or low given the existing levels of these types of capital. If lower than expected, we can think of there being innovation-related barriers, disincentives, or other failures that keep countries from reaching the optimal level of investment. As is clear from figure 3.3, there is essentially no relationship between the magnitude of this deviation from optimal and observed GERD.[6] Korea's high R&D appears, in fact, low relative to its human and physical capital,

FIGURE 3.3 **Simulated Deviations from Optimal Innovation Investment Are Not Correlated with R&D/GDP**

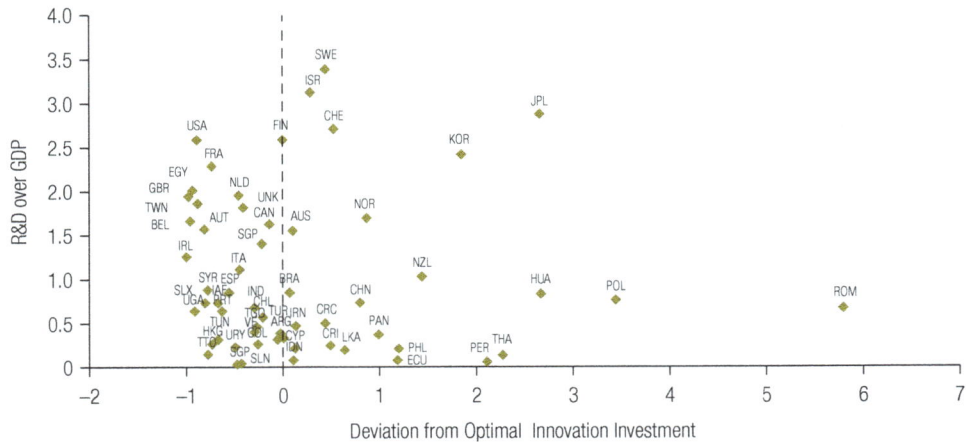

Source: Maloney 2017 based on Klenow and Rodriguez-Clare 2005; Maloney and Rodriguez-Clare 2007.
Note: Abbreviations are ISO country codes.

suggesting a "tax," whereas Colombia, Senegal, and Tunisia have higher investment than might be expected (or efficient) given their other factors of production.

Though the methodology necessarily makes some heroic assumptions, it makes the same fundamental point as made above with regard to the rates of return. Low R&D/GDP levels in Colombia, Senegal, and Tunisia are not necessarily due to problems particular to innovation, or even less to weak science, technology, and innovation institutions. The reason could lie, for instance, in a lack of complementary factors—such as bad schools limiting human capital accumulation or weak financial markets impeding physical capital accumulation.

Complementarities and the NIS

The previous discussion suggests that it is a mistake to narrowly focus innovation policies on promoting R&D or to relegate innovation policy solely to a science and technology ministry. A much broader view of the overall accumulation problem of the country and the constellation of markets, institutions, and individuals and the links among them that are often grouped under the term National Innovation System (NIS) is needed.[7]

There are many definitions of the NIS, and views differ on which policies and institutions should be included (see Freeman 1987; Lundvall 1992, 1997; Nelson 1993; and Soete, Verspagen, and Ter Weel 2010).[8] Figure 3.4 supports a broader interpretation than is often used, to take into account the complementarities discussed above. It also seeks to bring together many of the concerns of both the NIS and the neoclassical economics literature (see Maloney 2017). Broadly speaking, the left panel and lower central and right panels (blue triangles) depict elements that have priority in the NIS literature, including human capital, firm support mechanisms and STI institutions, innovation-specific credit and subsidy policies, and the capabilities of the entrepreneurs. The rest of the diagram attempts to capture some of the concerns raised by our focus on missing complementary factors. In particular, it highlights that firms make accumulation decisions of knowledge capital (innovation), human capital, and physical capital together (see box 3.2 for a formal exposition). Clearly, the division between the two sets of variables is not so sharp, but nevertheless the figure is useful in providing an integrated view.

We break figure 3.4 into demand and supply for knowledge capital (innovation broadly construed). The bidirectional arrows crudely capture the feedback relationship between firms and knowledge institutions and that much accumulation of knowledge in advanced economies occurs in what is called "Pasteur's quadrant" of the innovation space—where basic research and applied technology interact in a mutually reinforcing and nonlinear way (Stokes 1997; Edquist, 2004).

Figure 3.4 highlights two critical facts. First, innovation cannot be supply driven; there must be demand from firms that have the capabilities to innovate and the

FIGURE 3.4 **The Expanded National Innovation System (NIS)**

Government oversight, resolution of market and systemic failures, coordination

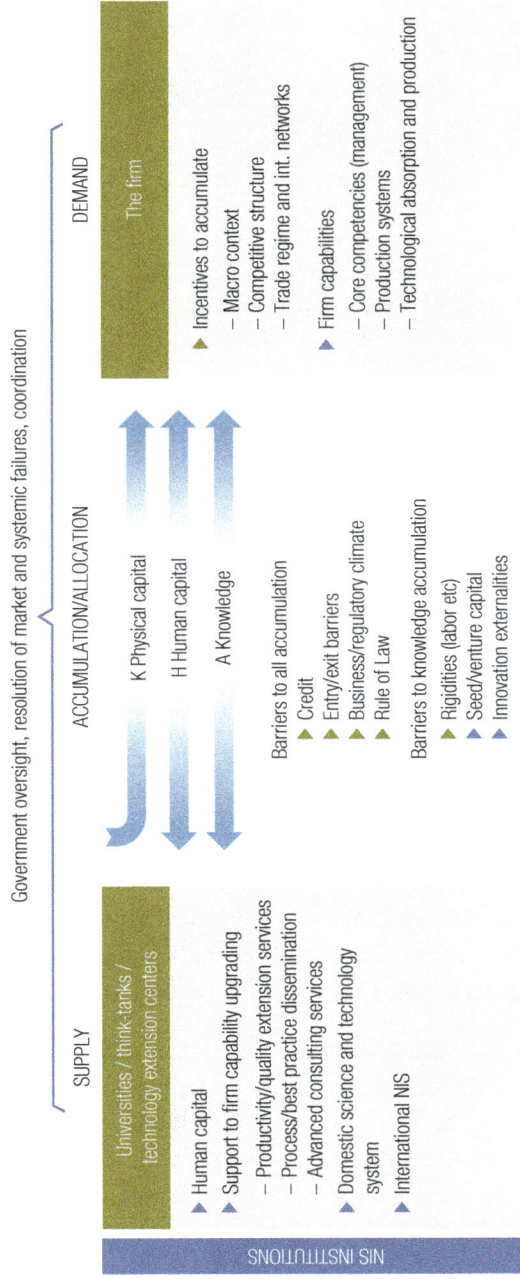

NIS INSTITUTIONS

SUPPLY

Universities / think-tanks / technology extension centers

▲ Human capital
▲ Support to firm capability upgrading
  – Productivity/quality extension services
  – Process/best practice dissemination
  – Advanced consulting services
▲ Domestic science and technology system
▲ International NIS

ACCUMULATION/ALLOCATION

K Physical capital

H Human capital

A Knowledge

Barriers to all accumulation
▲ Credit
▲ Entry/exit barriers
▲ Business/regulatory climate
▲ Rule of Law

Barriers to knowledge accumulation
▲ Rigidities (labor etc)
▲ Seed/venture capital
▲ Innovation externalities

DEMAND

The firm

▲ Incentives to accumulate
  – Macro context
  – Competitive structure
  – Trade regime and int. networks
▲ Firm capabilities
  – Core competencies (management)
  – Production systems
  – Technological absorption and production

Source: Maloney 2017.

57

One approach to estimating the returns to R&D (see Jones and Williams 1998 and Hall, Mairesse, and Mohnen 2010 for a review) begins from a simple production function where $Y = Q(A, K, L)$, where output Y is produced as a function of ideas or knowledge capital A and a collection of factors, in our case labor L and physical capital K.

As an approximation, Goñi and Maloney (2017) in figure 3.2 estimate $\Delta lnY = \alpha + \beta_A \, \Delta lnA + \beta_K \Delta lnK + \beta_L \Delta lnL + e$, where α captures period fixed effects. They employ the common transformation $\beta_f \Delta lnF = r_F \, F/Y$, where r_F is the rate of return on any factor F and F/Y is the share of investment F in output. They use this transformation for both physical (Investment/GDP) and knowledge capital (R&D/GDP), but leave labor in growth terms.

An extensive literature struggles with controlling for the potential endogeneity of R&D: it may be that R&D drives growth, but it may also be that expectations of future growth drive R&D, for example. Lagged values of R&D are often used (Hall and Mairesse 1995; Griffith et al. 2006), although this can be questioned because R&D investments tend to be persistent over time. Credible external instruments are sometimes available: Bloom et al. (2013) use changes in the firm-specific tax price of R&D (exploiting changes in federal and state-specific rules). Crepon–Duguet–Mairesse (CDM) models (Crépon, Duguet, and Mairesse 1998) explicitly measure the interactions in a structural model including an equation for innovation inputs, outputs, and the production function.

In the absence of good country-level instruments, Goñi and Maloney use lagged values and the national intellectual property rights regimes (Ginarte and Park 1997) as instruments—the latter, as Rodrik (2001) notes, largely being driven by considerations related to trade agreements with the advanced countries. The results are robust to instrumenting. Figure 3.2 is estimated using a varying parameter technique developed by Hastie and Tibshirani (1993) and Fan and Zhang (1999, 2000) that allows the full parameter vector to vary across the development process and Cai et al. (2006) who extend the methodology to accommodate endogeneity in the conditioning set. The data are cross-country quinquennial averages.

incentives to do so, including to accumulate capabilities. Second, as noted above, the accumulation decisions of the traditional (capital and labor) and innovation (knowledge) parts of the economy need to be jointly considered.

The first group of variables on the demand side comprises the overall set of incentives to invest and accumulate. This includes the macro context, competitive structure, trade regime, and international networks that determine whether firms seek to innovate. The second set of variables captures firm capabilities discussed in the next chapter: the core managerial competencies, production systems, and higher-end capabilities for technological absorption and innovation that enable a firm to recognize an opportunity and mobilize itself to take advantage of it. Of particular salience is the ability to quantify and manage the risk intrinsic to any project. Development is, by nature, a process of placing a series of bets on opportunities of uncertain returns, and entrepreneurs need to develop the capabilities to quantify and manage the associated risk (see, for example, Maloney and Zambrano 2016). These capabilities can be seen as increasingly demanding in sophistication as "innovation" moves from simple improvements to actual long-term R&D.

There are clear interactions between the two sets of variables. For instance, a larger international market increases the likely benefits of upgrading and innovating while better capabilities permit taking advantage of these markets.

On the supply side are all the sources of knowledge that support firm demand. This begins with the basic supply of human capital, from the worker level to the entrepreneur to engineers and scientists. The second set are institutions that support firms, including the kinds of productivity and quality extension services found around the world, services to disseminate new technologies or best practices, and higher-end consulting services in specialized topics. These are discussed in depth in chapter 7. The science and technology system adapts existing knowledge or generates new knowledge for the use of firms. Finally, the global innovation system generates most new knowledge; therefore, being firmly plugged in along manifold dimensions is key. Because many of these institutions are nonmarket (government research institutes, universities, and so on), the question about what mechanisms and incentives link them to one another is prominent in the NIS literature.

The center panel makes the point that NIS policy must concern itself with barriers to all types of accumulation, both because physical capital is a complement and because the accumulation of knowledge capital is subject to all the same accumulation barriers as physical capital—capital markets, business climate, or ability to diversify risk—which we normally abstract from in the advanced country literature because those markets function reasonably well. Hence, low investment in managerial capabilities or innovation may be due to a variety of accumulation investment barriers that are commonly discussed in the World Bank *Doing Business* analyses, rather than innovation-related market or systemic failures.

Clearly, innovation-specific issues are still important, and they are captured in the next group down. For instance, there may be an absence of seed/venture capital that would enable new innovative start-ups to emerge and existing firms to place new innovative bets. In addition, there may be specific restrictions on the workforce restructuring required for the adoption of new technologies. Finally, there are all the standard information-related market failures discussed above, those related to the appropriation of knowledge that have given rise to R&D subsidies and tax incentives, and to intellectual property rights systems.

There is evidence that the latter are important. The analysis of Bosch, Lederman, and Maloney (2005) suggests that the security of intellectual property rights, the quality of research institutions, and the degree of collaboration with the private sector plausibly explain half the difference in the elasticity of knowledge creation between advanced and follower countries. Nguyen and Jaramillo (2014) found that lower institutional quality in terms of rule of law, regulatory quality, or property and patent right protection lowers the return to innovation for a large sample of firms in developing countries. In Vietnam, the concern of many start-ups about having their ideas compromised during the process of filing for local patents impeded all subsequent mobilization of financing and scaling up.

But more general accumulation issues impinge as well. Aghion et al. (2012), Bond, Harhoff, and Van Reenen (2010), Hall and Lerner (2009), and Mulkay, Hall, and Mairesse (2000) stress credit constraints as a reason for underinvestment in innovation and Bloom (2007) the depressing impact of uncertainty. Allard, Martinez, and Williams (2012) show that political stability plays an important role in the development of the NIS, given the need for long-term accumulation of human capital. More generally, Baker, Bloom, and Davis (2016) show how policy uncertainty reduces investment, which is likely to have even more effect on innovation projects with long gestations. Other studies have documented the role of more democratic regimes (Srholec 2011), corruption (DeWaldemar 2012), or efficient institutions (Amendolagine et al. 2013). Various works have demonstrated a correlation between exporting firms and innovation, suggesting openness is also important (Almeida and Fernandes 2008).

Overall, the NIS concept provides a framework to understand the environment within which firm innovation occurs. It also highlights how demand for innovation, specifically the ability of the firm to recognize, articulate, and execute an innovation-related project, is at the center of the discussion. This dictates a deeper examination of firm capabilities and a recognition that innovation occurs along a continuum of sophistication ranging from basic business practices, to more advanced production systems (just-in-time, for example), to technical literacy to manage formal R&D. Evolving into more R&D–intensive products also requires a greater set of skills and contracting institutions for managing technological complexity (Krishna and Levchenko 2013), financial literacy and deeper capital markets for managing riskier products (Acemoglu and Zilibotti 1997; Krishna, Levchenko, and Maloney 2017), greater technological literacy, and high-quality science and technology institutions.

Overseeing this evolution and the overall functioning of the NIS is the government, which is also tasked with the resolution of market and systemic failures and coordination among various actors.

Concluding Remarks

The innovation "paradox" arises from the coexistence of great potential gains from Schumpeterian catch-up in developing countries with low innovation investment by firms, and the surprising lack of effectiveness by governments in increasing these investments by several orders of magnitude. Our proposed answer to this paradox stresses that innovation demands a broad set of complementarities in terms of physical and human capital. These, in turn, depend on all the underlying conditions that facilitate the accumulation of any type of capital, as well as those seen as particular to innovation, such as intellectual property rights, or resolution of market failures. Advanced countries have many of these worked out: financial markets function, business climates are friendly, and skilled human capital abounds. A marginal increase in R&D spending under these conditions may have a high rate of return. However, developing countries lack many or all of these; hence, the expected rate of return to knowledge capital investment is far below what Schumpeterian models would predict.

This implies that benchmarking innovation performance must go beyond comparing raw levels of GERD to incorporate the stock of these complementarities—countries with low levels of physical or human capital probably should not try to accumulate advanced country levels of knowledge capital. In turn, the conception of the NIS needs to have a broad scope to reflect the fact that innovation policy cannot consist of simply offsetting innovation-related market failures. It must also ensure that a broader set of complementary factors, necessary for firms to receive the potentially high rates of return from technological adoption, are present.

The next chapter takes up one complementary input—that related to firm capabilities and management skills—as a critical missing item on the developing country innovation agenda.

Notes

1. Roseboom (2003) argues that underinvestment is the rule in agricultural R&D as well.
2. Correa, Fernandes, and Uregian (2008) find that the technology choices of firms in Europe and Central Asia are related to access to appropriate complementary inputs such as skilled labor, managerial capacity, R&D, finance, and to a lesser extent good infrastructure.
3. However, these rates of return are substantially below those from other studies using cross-country data for the G-7 (Group of Seven countries: Canada, France, Germany, Italy, Japan, the United Kingdom, and the United States) (see, for example, Coe and Helpman 1995; van Pottelsberghe de la Potterie and Lichtenberg 2001; and Kao, Chiang, and Chen 1999). Again, returns to R&D have been most studied and, although we stress above the need to look beyond R&D, the lessons apply generally.
4. In their model Griffith, Redding, and Van Reenen (2004) find the returns to R&D have a dual source—the first one related to R&D itself and the second via the effect of R&D into technology transfer by allowing countries and firms to converge to the technological frontier. This model could be generalized to other innovation inputs, such as technology licensing, training, purchase of equipment, and so on, because they facilitate technology transfer in these countries and firms farther away from the frontier.
5. See Lee (2013, 45–50) for a recent discussion of several more sophisticated measures.
6. This was previously done in more detail for several Latin American countries in Maloney and Rodriguez-Clare (2007), but here we seek to make a general point focusing on a global sample of countries. There are numerous issues of calibration discussed by Maloney and Rodriguez-Clare, including the fundamental problem of exclusively treating total factor productivity (TFP) differences as reflecting innovation performance as opposed to, for instance, allocation inefficiencies.
7. See also Freeman (1995) and Lundvall et al. (2002) for a discussion of the origins of the term. Freeman traces the origin of the concept of a National Innovation System to Friedrich List's ([1841] 1909) discussion of the system of institutions and policies, most related to the learning

about new technology and applying it, during Germany's catch-up with England. See also Smits, Kuhlmann, and Shapira (2010) for a recent review as well as Lee (2013) in the context of leapfrogging in Asia and Latin America.

8. Nelson (1993) define the NIS somewhat narrowly as "a set of institutions whose interactions determine the innovative performance of national firms," especially those supporting R&D efforts. Lundvall (1992) suggests a broader view that includes national education systems, labor markets, financial markets, intellectual property rights, competition in product markets, and welfare regimes. Edquist's (1997) view includes "all important economic social, political organizational institutional and other factors that influence the development, diffusion and use of innovations" (Soete, Verspagen, and ter Weel 2010).

References

Acemoglu, Darren, Simon Johnson, and James Robinson. 2005. "The Rise of Europe: Atlantic Trade, Institutional Change, and Economic Growth." *American Economic Review* 95 (2): 546–79.

Acemoglu, Darren, and Fabrizio Zilibotti. 1997. "Was Prometheus Unbound by Chance? Risk, Diversification, and Growth." *Journal of Political Economy* 105 (4): 709–51.

Aghion, Philippe, Philippe Askenazy, Nicolas Berman, Gilbert Cette, and Laurent Eymard. 2012. "Credit Constraints and the Cyclicality of R&D Investment: Evidence from France." *Journal of the European Economic Association* 10 (5): 1001–24.

Allard, Gayle, Candace A. Martinez, and Christopher Williams. 2012. "Political Instability, Pro-Business Market Reforms, and Their Impacts on National Systems of Innovation." *Research Policy* 41 (3): 638–51.

Almeida, Rita, and Ana Margarida Fernandes. 2008. "Openness and Technological Innovations in Developing Countries: Evidence from Firm-Level Surveys." *Journal of Development Studies* 44 (5): 701–27.

Amendolagine, Vito, Amadou Boly, Nicola Daniele Coniglio, Francesco Prota, and Adnan Seric. 2013. "FDI and Local Linkages in Developing Countries: Evidence from Sub-Saharan Africa." *World Development* 50 (C): 41–56.

Baker, Scott R., Nicholas Bloom, and Steven J. Davis. 2016. "Measuring Economic Policy Uncertainty." *Quarterly Journal of Economics* 131 (4): 1593–1636.

Bloom, Nicholas. 2007. "Uncertainty and the Dynamics of R&D." *American Economic Review* 97 (2): 250–55.

Bloom, Nicholas, Benn Eifert, Aprajit Mahajan, David McKenzie, and John Roberts. 2013. "Does Management Matter? Evidence from India." *Quarterly Journal of Economics* 128 (1): 1–51.

Bloom, Nicholas, Mark Schankerman, and John Van Reenen. 2013. "Identifying Technology Spillovers and Product Market Rivalry." *Econometrica* 81 (4): 1347–93.

Bond, S., D. Harhoff, and J. Van Reenen. 2010. "Investment, R&D, and Financial Constraints in Britain and Germany." In *Contributions in Memory of Zvi Griliches*, edited by Jacques Mairesse and Manuel Trajtenberg, 433–60. Cambridge, MA: National Bureau of Economic Research.

Bosch, Mariano, Daniel Lederman, and William F. Maloney. 2005. *Patenting and Research and Development: A Global View*. Washington, DC: World Bank.

Cai, Zongwu, Mitali Das, Huaiyu Xiong, and Xizhi Wu 2006. "Functional Coefficient Instrumental Variables Models." *Journal of Econometrics* 133 (1): 207–41.

Coe, David T., and Elhanan Helpman. 1995. "International R&D Spillovers." *European Economic Review* 39 (5): 859–87.

Correa, Paulo G., Ana M. Fernandes, and Chris J. Uregian. 2008. "Technology Adoption and the Investment Climate: Firm-Level Evidence for Eastern Europe and Central Asia." *World Bank Economic Review* 24 (1): 121–47.

Crépon B., E. Duguet, and J. Mairesse. 1998. "Research, Innovation and Productivity: An Econometric Analysis at the Firm Level." *Economics of Innovation and New Technology* 7 (2): 115–58.

De Waldemar, Felipe Starosta. 2012. "New Products and Corruption: Evidence from Indian Firms." *Development Economies* 50 (3): 268–84.

Doraszelski, Ulrich, and Jordi Jaumandreu. 2013. "R&D and Productivity: Estimating Endogenous Productivity." *Review of Economic Studies* 80 (4): 1338–83.

Edquist, Charles, ed. 1997. "Systems of Innovation: Technologies, Institutions, and Organizations." London: Pinter.

———. 2004. "Systems of Innovation—Perspectives and Challenges." In *The Oxford Handbook of Innovation*, edited by Jan Fagerberg and David C. Mowery, 181–208. Oxford, UK: Oxford University Press.

Fan, Jianqing, and Wenyang Zhang. 1999. "Statistical Estimation in Varying Coefficient Models." *Annals of Statistics* 27 (5): 1491–1518.

———. 2000. "Simultaneous Confidence Bands and Hypothesis Testing in Varying-Coefficient Models." *Scandinavian Journal of Statistics* 27 (4): 715–31.

Freeman, Christopher. 1987. *Technology Policy and Economic Performance: Lessons from Japan*. London: Pinter.

———. 1995. "The 'National System of Innovation' in Historical Perspective." *Cambridge Journal of Economics* 19 (1): 5–24.

Ginarte, Juan C., and Walter G. Park. 1997. "Determinants of Patent Rights: A Cross-National Study." *Research Policy* 26 (3): 283–301.

Goñi, Edwin, and William F. Maloney. 2017. "Why Don't Poor Countries Do R&D? Varying Rates of Factor Returns across the Development Process." *European Economic Review* 94 (C): 126–47.

Griffith, Rachel, Elena Huergo, Jacques Mairesse, and Bettina Peters. 2006. "Innovation and Productivity across Four European Countries." *Oxford Review of Economic Policy* 22 (4): 483–98.

Griffith, Rachel, Stephen Redding, and John Van Reenen. 2004. "Mapping the Two Faces of R&D: Productivity Growth in a Panel of OECD Industries." *Review of Economics and Statistics* 86 (4): 883–95.

Hall, Bronwyn H., and Josh Lerner. 2009. "The Financing of R&D and Innovation." NBER Working Paper No. 15325, National Bureau of Economic Research, Cambridge, MA.

Hall, Bronwyn H., and Jacques Mairesse. 1995. "Exploring the Relationship between R&D and Productivity in French Manufacturing Firms." *Journal of Econometrics* 65 (1): 263–93.

Hall, Bronwyn H., Jacques Mairesse, and Pierre Mohnen. 2010. "Measuring the Returns to R&D." NBER Working Paper No. 15622, National Bureau of Economic Research, Cambridge, MA.

Hastie, Trevor, and Robert Tibshirani. 1993. "Varying-Coefficient Models." *Journal of the Royal Statistical Society: Series B (Methodological)* 55 (4): 757–96.

Jones, Charles I., and John C. Williams. 1998. "Measuring the Social Return to R&D." *Quarterly Journal of Economics* 113 (4): 1119–35.

Kao, Chihwa, Min-Hsien Chiang, and Bangtian Chen. 1999. "International R&D Spillovers: An Application of Estimation and Inference in Panel Cointegration." *Oxford Bulletin of Economics and Statistics* 61 (S1): 691–709.

Klenow, Peter J., and Andres Rodriguez-Clare. 2005. "Externalities and Growth." In *Handbook of Economic Growth*, Volume 1A, edited by Philippe Aghion and Steven N. Durlauf, 817–61. Amsterdam: Elsevier.

Krishna, Pravin, and Andrei A. Levchenko. 2013. "Comparative Advantage, Complexity, and Volatility." *Journal of Economic Behavior & Organization* 94: 314–29.

Krishna, Pravin, Andrei A. Levchenko, and William F. Maloney. 2017. "Growth and Risk: The View from International Trade." Unpublished report, World Bank, Washington, DC.

Lee, Keun. 2013. *Schumpeterian Analysis of Economic Catch-Up: Knowledge, Path-Creation, and the Middle-Income Trap.* Cambridge, UK: Cambridge University Press.

List, Friedrich. 1909. *The National System of Political Economy.* London: Longmans, Green and Co. (Original work published 1841).

Lucas, Robert E. 1988. "On the Mechanics of Economic Development." *Journal of Monetary Economics* 22 (1): 3–42.

———. 1990. "Why Doesn't Capital Flow from Rich to Poor Countries?" *American Economic Review* 80 (2): 92–96.

Lucking, Brian, Nicholas Bloom, and John Van Reenen. 2017. "Have R&D Spillovers Changed?" Stanford University, Stanford, CA. https://people.stanford.edu/nbloom/sites/default/files/lbv_ssrn.pdf.

Lundvall, Bengt-Åke, ed. 1992. *National Systems of Innovation: Towards a Theory of Innovation and Interactive Learning.* London: Pinter.

———. 1997. "Development Strategies in the Learning Economy." Paper submitted at STEPI's l0th Anniversary Conference, Seoul, May 26–29.

Lundvall, Bengt-Åke, Björn Johnson, Esben Sloth Andersen, and Bent Dalum. 2002. "National Systems of Production, Innovation and Competence Building." *Research Policy* 31 (2): 213–31.

Maloney, William F. 2017. "Revisiting the National Innovation System in Developing Countries." World Bank, Washington, DC.

Maloney, William F., and Andres Rodriguez-Clare. 2007. "Innovation Shortfalls." *Review of Development of Economics* 11 (4): 665–84.

Maloney, William F., and Andres Zambrano. 2016. "Entrepreneurship, Information, and Learning." World Bank, Washington, DC.

Mulkay Benoit, Bronwyn H. Hall, and Jacques Mairesse. 2000. "Firm-Level Investment and R&D in France and the United States: A Comparison." NBER Working Paper No. 8038, National Bureau of Economic Research, Cambridge, MA.

Nelson, Richard R, ed. 1993. *National Innovation Systems: A Comparative Analysis.* New York: Oxford University Press.

Nguyen, Ha, and Patricio A. Jaramillo. 2014. "Institutions and Firms' Return to Innovation: Evidence from the World Bank Enterprise Survey." Policy Research Working Paper 6918, World Bank, Washington, DC.

Rodrik, Dani. 2001. "The Global Governance of Trade as If Development Really Mattered." Unpublished report, Harvard University, Cambridge, MA.

Roseboom, Johannes. 2003. "Underinvestment in Agricultural Research and Development Revisited." ISNAR Briefing Paper 60, International Service for National Agricultural Research, The Hague, The Netherlands. http://ebrary.ifpri.org/cdm/ref/collection/p15738coll11/id/304.

Smits, Ruud, Stefan Kuhlmann, and Philip Shapira, eds. 2010. *The Theory and Practice of Innovation Policy: An International Research Handbook.* Cheltenham, UK: Edward Elgar.

Soete, Luc, Bart Verspagen, and Bas Ter Weel. 2010. "Systems of Innovation." In *Handbook of the Economics of Innovation*, edited by Bronwyn H. Hall and Nathan Rosenberg, 1159–80. Amsterdam: Elsevier.

Srholec, Martin. 2011. "A Multilevel Analysis of Innovation in Developing Countries." *Industrial and Corporate Change* 20 (6): 1539–69.

Stokes, Donald E. 1997. "Pasteur's Quadrant: Basic Science and Technological Innovation." Washington, DC: Brookings Institution Press.

van Pottelsberghe de la Potterie, Bruno, and Frank Lichtenberg. 2001. "Does Foreign Direct Investment Transfer Technology across Borders?" *Review of Economics and Statistics* 83 (3): 490–97.

4. Managerial Practices as Key Firm Capabilities for Innovation

Introduction

In the previous chapter, we described the variety of complementary factors required for innovation expenditures, narrowly considered, to be effective. This chapter focuses on a particular set of complementarities—the capabilities firms develop that enable them to identify new technological opportunities, develop a plan to exploit them, and then cultivate the human resources necessary to execute it. Without these complementarities, moving beyond the simplest types of innovation is not feasible. Hence, a central dynamic of the development process is a progressive increase in sophistication in both production and technological capabilities, and especially a subset of those—managerial capabilities—as firms approach the technological frontier.

This view differs from the simplification typically employed in mainstream economics that firms are fully rational, possess full information, and will simply follow with perfect foresight the path to the technological frontier. In this view, policy should focus first on eliminating the external barriers to firm growth—for example, distortions in the business climate or financial markets. Innovation policy should then primarily redress the market failures pertaining to innovation in all countries, such as imperfect appropriability of the rents from ideas.

By contrast, an ample literature in the National Innovation System tradition has long argued that firms need to learn how to approximate the neoclassic firm by acquiring a range of capabilities without which they cannot manage innovation projects effectively. Teece and Pisano (1994), and more in the mainstream Sutton (2012), Sutton and Trefler (2016), or Hallak (2006), among others, have also stressed the acquisition of these capabilities as fundamental to both productivity and quality upgrading. Of great importance has been the recent introduction of the World Management Survey (WMS) discussed in chapter 2, which has permitted a quantum leap in the comparative quantitative analysis of management practices and their implications for productivity and innovation. In particular, the WMS has documented that developing country firms are indeed lagging in a wide range of capabilities that are critical to the Schumpeterian catch-up process: few managers in developing countries can take a long-term view, have sophisticated project evaluation skills, or have a human resource policy that would staff research and development (R&D) projects. Hence, there may be no effective partner for matching grant schemes, or R&D subsidies and the variety of market failures in innovation may be compounded by others that drive weak management.

Redressing these capability deficiencies emerges as a critical element in most accounts of the "East Asian miracle," which stress the increasing capacity of entrepreneurs to engage in a continual process of adaptation and innovation across many sectors (see, for example, Teece, Pisano, and Shuen 1997). Matthews (1996) and Cho and Mathews (2000), for example, downplay R&D–focused paradigms and focus on how in Asia latecomer firms acquired capabilities through accelerated organizational learning and have proceeded through stages of technological capability enhancement.[1] In the Republic of Korea, Kim (1997) argues that the accumulation of technological capability—firm learning capacity—was more important than most sectoral interventions commonly cited[2] (see also Katz 1987; Lall 1987). The acquisition of these capabilities, as Hobday (2000) notes, is neither automatic nor painless but was in East Asia a difficult process with much trial and error, investments in training, and creativity. This economic learning process—acquiring the capacity to absorb, adapt, diffuse, disseminate, and improve ideas—is arguably one of the core dynamics of the development process, regardless of the underlying production structure of the economy.

This chapter first describes the capabilities firms require for successful innovation. It then discusses managerial and organizational practices at the core of the innovation and productivity process. The third section provides the first systematic evidence, drawing again on the same datasets used in chapter 2, about the relationship between managerial and organizational practices and innovation processes; and the final section concludes.

Firm Capabilities for Innovation

Defining Capabilities for Innovation

Sutton (2012) defines capabilities as those elements of the production process that cannot be bought "off the shelf" on the market like a normal input and hence must be learned and accumulated by the firm. This idea lies behind the ample literature on resource-based theories of the firm (see Penrose 1959; Rumelt 1984; Wernerfelt 1984; and Lockett, Thompson, and Morgenstern 2009). These capabilities range from basic organizational skills, to logistical abilities (see Syverson 2008), to planning routines and systems of human resource management.

In more complex settings, the "organizational capital" literature (Prescott and Visscher 1980; Atkeson and Kehoe 2005) studies the firm characteristics driving differential performance across firms. This literature views the organizational structure of the firm, rather than market position or propriety knowledge, as the main source of firm value. In the *dynamic capabilities* framework (Teece and Pisano 1994; Teece 2000;

Helfat et al. 2007), the organization's key competencies are those that enable it to integrate, build, and reconfigure resources in rapidly changing environments (Teece, Pisano, and Shuen 1997).[3] A review of the early literature in capabilities and some of the existing conceptualizations of this concept can be found in annex 4A. Here we focus on some of these key capabilities for innovation.

The Importance of Organization Competencies for Learning and Innovation

The central role that organizational practices play in firms' knowledge management has been emphasized by the literature. Some case studies focusing on the East Asian experience emphasize that the rapid learning process described above was facilitated by the introduction of managerial and organizational processes, establishment of dedicated design and engineering departments, or development of quality management processes (Bell and Figueiredo 2012). More recently, Garicano and Rossi-Hansberg (2015) emphasize that the capacity of a firm to exploit new technologies greatly depends on its organization. Individuals are time-bound in their ability to deploy knowledge to solve problems. Organizational hierarchies relax this constraint by creating layers of teams where "expert" workers manage less knowledgeable workers, thus increasing the experts' time availability and enabling them to specialize.

The process of organizational articulation and capabilities accumulation requires the articulation of internal incentives to ensure workers are allocated to tasks where they can be more productive, are incentivized (or not penalized) to propose improvements at early stages, and are later incentivized to propose and execute more sophisticated innovation. Although large-scale quantitative evidence is still sparse, some studies find that performance-based reward systems have a positive influence on the creativity and innovative behavior of individual employees (De Jong and Den Hartog 2007; Ederer and Manso 2013; Gibbs et al. 2015) and, in some cases, on the firm's overall innovation-related activities and outcomes (Leiblein and Madsen 2008). These activities include firms' patenting propensity (Chen, Chen, and Podolski 2014) and quality (Mao and Weathers 2015).

Though this report focuses primarily on innovation, it is important to highlight that we use the term capabilities amply. For example, much of the existing analysis in the strategic management literature on firm capabilities focuses on capabilities that are needed to build and maintain a firm's competitive advantage, including the knowledge and routines required to maintain existing production. One example is provided by the response of the Aquafresh company in Ghana when faced with intense competition from Asian producers. Sutton and Kpentey (2012) document how the firm began in clothing and textiles but, under competitive pressure, reinvented itself as a maker of soft drinks. It could achieve this not because of its expertise in clothing and textiles but rather because it was a well-functioning firm that could identify an alternative path and reorient itself to changing market conditions.[4]

A useful taxonomy to understand these capabilities is provided by ul Haque et al. (1995) and Bell (2009), who differentiate capabilities—including physical, knowledge, human, and organizational capital—that are needed for the use of existing technology from those needed for adapting or creating new technologies.[5] Specifically, the authors distinguish two useful subsets of capabilities:

1. Production capabilities: those that make use of existing technologies and organizational configurations to maintain production; and
2. Technology/innovation capabilities: those that enable firms to improve existing technologies or processes or to develop new ones.[6]

However, the distinction between production and innovation capabilities is often blurred. Some of the routines and organization structures that start as basic production capabilities evolve to become innovation capabilities. These can include design (Galindo-Rueda and Millot 2015), engineering, market intelligence, and other "change-generating knowledge and skill" (Bell 2009, p. 14). For example, firms need some technical or engineering capabilities for maintenance as production capabilities. These, however, may evolve over time in some firms to a dedicated engineering department to test new technologies, which will be key for innovation. Thus, the capabilities needed for innovation are multidimensional, depend on the type of innovation introduced, and evolve over time. Figure 1.2 in chapter 1 summarizes this general typology, differentiating within innovation capabilities needed for technology adoption and imitation from those needed for invention and technology generation.

The Capabilities Escalator

Case studies suggest that firms progressively build on their accumulated capabilities, facilitating more and more sophisticated investments and innovation. Bell and Figueiredo (2012), for example, characterize the manufacturing sector as proceeding in different stages corresponding to discrete levels of innovation complexity. From implementing minor adaptations and imitation of products and processes using a few qualified technicians, successful firms moved to more incremental innovation using engineers in organized units for product development and introducing better marketing and managerial practices. Subsequently, a second transition to more advanced innovation and catching up involved various types of engineers and designers, R&D departments, and collaboration with knowledge providers, with more centralized knowledge management and more sophisticated lean production processes. Firms that reach the technological frontier tend to have internationally recognized R&D departments, sophisticated organizational practices and incentives, and strong collaboration with knowledge providers.

Figure 4.1 attempts to capture this accumulation of capabilities across several dimensions as firms gain in sophistication. Moving from left to right, the figure represents the process of catching up, where innovation shifts from simple technology adaptations and improvements in products and processes to more R&D–intensive technology and product generation. Moving toward the frontier requires increased sophistication in some of these capabilities, in some cases with more intensive resources and routines that are more organized, as well as more specialized human capital such as engineers and designers.

Figure 4.1 highlights three key insights. First, production capabilities, some of which are managerial and organizational, are important for incremental innovation. Target setting or quality management and monitoring are key elements of innovation projects (see box 4.1 for an example in Vietnam). These capabilities evolve and become more sophisticated as firms converge to the frontier. For example, basic capabilities, such as simple task assignment or maintenance work, become more sophisticated in training or technology management. Second, a core set of managerial and organizational capabilities are important for both production and innovation along the entire catch-up path. These managerial and organizational capabilities are still critical for adopting frontier technologies. Finally, related to the previous insight, many of these capabilities are complementary, as suggested in box 4.1. Their absence significantly constrains the ability to accumulate other technological capabilities and learning.

BOX 4.1

Managerial Practices and Innovation in Vietnam

The WMS data indicate that Vietnamese firms are strong on monitoring but weak on setting long-run targets, on introducing new technologies and best practice in operations, and on developing human resource policies. Interviews with firms suggest that "many managers have mentioned that they meet their targets all the time, and anything less than 100 percent target achievement is considered unacceptable by senior management." A target of 100 percent is probably too high given that it suggests targets are too easy, and that the firm is not experimenting or taking the risks necessary to be innovative in the long run. However, "Regardless of any forward-thinking and strategic policies, Vietnamese managers emphasize that their principal objective is profit and *the focus is always on the short term*" (Bloom et al. 2015; italics added).

This is consistent with Newman et al. (2015), who report that 84 percent of firms surveyed had no program of either technology adaptation or R&D. A longer time horizon articulating a vision of long-run firm and product upgrading as well as the human resources necessary for innovation is largely absent. For example, "Developing talent is considered expensive and often unnecessary, as it is perceived to be easy to replace workers and even managers" (p. 180). This is a critical lacuna because active innovation requires a dominance of best practice and a multiyear strategy for the firm.

Source: Newman et al. 2015.

FIGURE 4.1 **Firm Capabilities for Innovation**

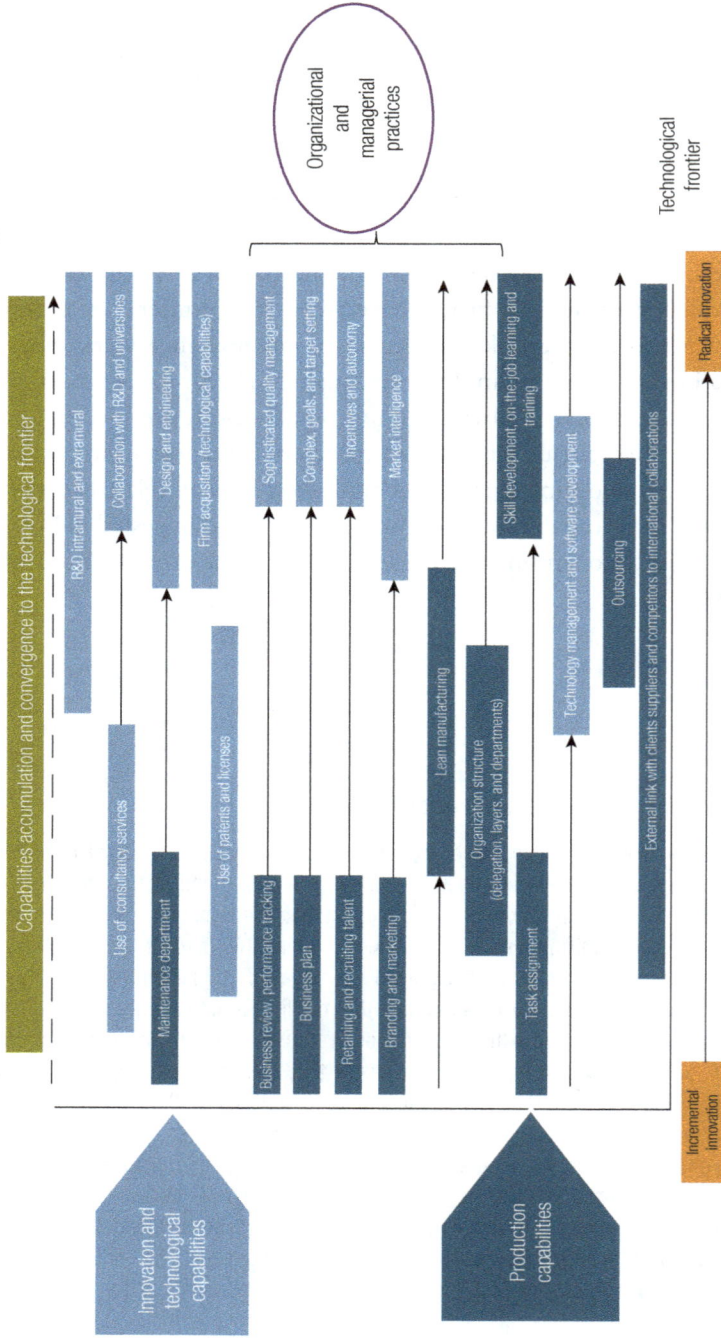

Source: Cirera, López-Bassols, and Maloney 2017.

Note: Those capabilities in blue are the ones that are often used intensively for innovation. However, in practice, some can also be used in normal production processes; and, vice versa, production capabilities are also key complementarities in the innovation process. R&D = research and development.

Measuring Capabilities

As noted, the schematic in figure 4.1 is derived primarily from detailed case studies. To date, there has been very little attempt to systematically explore the role of capabilities broadly construed in innovation empirically; in fact, the issue is frequently absent in policy discussions. This may be partly due to the limited availability of information about these capabilities in traditional innovation and enterprise surveys. The *Oslo Manual*, the internationally recognized reference book on the measurement of innovation, which provides guidelines for the innovation surveys described in box 2.1, identifies activities that are necessary for producing innovation outputs (OECD 2005). This list, which includes R&D, the acquisition of machinery and equipment, training, and so on, has evolved over time but is still limited to a range of activities heavily focused on R&D–based innovation (see annex 2B). Even here, detailed measurement of necessary human capital–related capabilities, such as engineers or scientists, remains thin. In the broader growth literature, Murphy, Shleifer, and Vishny (1991) document at the country level that the density of engineering graduates affects growth more, for instance, than that of lawyers. However, firm-level data on such technical human capital, not to mention how it is deployed and organized within the firm, remain unavailable. The lack of information on these other firm capabilities has impeded efforts to measure their importance and thus shape the innovation policy debate. This is perhaps less problematic in the case of technological capabilities because many policy makers believe engineering or scientific capability to be important for innovation.

However, the absence of data on the basic organization of firms and how they are managed has led to this key complementary capability being largely overlooked in innovation policy. Two examples are the use of matching grants to promote R&D and public research institutes to provide knowledge to firms. In both cases, there may not be a partner to employ financing or knowledge effectively. The rest of the chapter is devoted to this point, which is critical to reorienting the developing country innovation agenda.

The Data Revolution in Managerial Capabilities Measurement

Progress on the managerial data gap has been rapid in recent years. A data revolution in measuring firm management and organizational practices, which as figure 4.1 discusses relates to both productive and technological capabilities, has occurred in developed countries and is increasingly expanding to developing countries (see box 4.2). This wave of firm-level surveys, largely promoted by Bloom and Van Reenen (2007), focuses on a set of structured management practices such as monitoring and use of information for improving production; design, integration, and realism of production targets; and human resource policies and incentives, including bonuses, promotions, and dismissals. Initial surveys of this type include the 2010 Management and Organizational Practices Survey (MOPS) in the United States and the WMS,

The New Data on Management Quality

Three new sources of data permit benchmarking countries by management quality and studying consequent firm performance.

The **World Management Survey (WMS)** is conducted through phone interviews with representative samples of firms across the world along four principal dimensions (see Bloom and Van Reenen 2007):

1. *Operations*. The degree to which the firm acted upon encountering a problem in the production process
2. *Monitoring*. Whether the firm monitored production performance indicators and how many indicators
3. *Targets*. Time horizon of production targets, if any, short versus long term
4. *Incentives*. Whether managers were offered performance bonuses

The survey has been carried out in 34 countries, including both advanced and developing countries.

The **Managerial and Organizational Practices Survey** (MOPS) is a written-response questionnaire used in the United States that broadly follows these categories as well and a similar survey has been recently implemented in Mexico (ENAPROCE 2015) in a large representative sample of small, medium, and large firms (25,456 firms).

The innovation module of the World Bank Enterprise Survey includes a section on managerial practices based on a reduced set of questions of the MOPS (see annex 2A). The section is implemented on medium and large firms (above 50 workers).

For comparability across surveys, we focus on creating an index like the one proposed in Bloom and Van Reenen (2007) based on four major management dimensions: (1) operations, (2) monitoring, (3) targets, and (4) incentives.

As in Bloom and Van Reenen (2010), the scores of each management practice are standardized to have a mean of zero and standard deviation of one:

$$Z_{m_{ji}} = \frac{m_{ji} - \overline{m}_j}{\sigma_{mj}}$$

(B4.2.1)

where $z_{m_{ji}}$ is the standardized score for management practice j in firm i.

Then, for each firm, the unweighted average of each management practice is standardized to obtain a final measure of overall firm managerial quality, the management score:

$$m_i = (m_{operations} + m_{monitoring} + m_{targets} + m_{incentives}) / 4$$

(B4.2.2)

$$Z_i(m) = \frac{m_i - \overline{m}_m}{\sigma_m}$$

(B4.2.3)

implemented primarily in large firms in 35 countries, including Organisation for Economic Co-operation and Development (OECD) countries, some emerging economies, and an increasing number of low-income countries. Some more general business and innovation surveys, such as the Survey of Innovation and Business Strategy (SIBS) in Canada, the innovation survey of the Enterprise Survey Unit of the World Bank implemented in 48 countries, and the National Survey on Productivity and Competitiveness on small and medium enterprises (SMEs) and micro firms in Mexico, are adopting some of the questions used in the MOPS and the WMS.

These new data, either by themselves or matched with, for instance the Bureau van Dijk (BvD) Orbis firm data, provide a richer characterization of innovation activities and enable researchers to explore the importance of management practices in the innovation process. This work indicates that many developing country firms lack the management practices required to support robust innovation systems.

For example, developing country firms in the WMS sample frequently have very short time horizons and little in the way of long-run productivity plans, and, correspondingly, have very weak human resource policies. China, for instance, is world class at short-term targets, however it is among the worst in long-term planning and staffing for such plans. Vietnamese entrepreneurs focus exclusively on the short term and consider cultivation of human capital to be largely a waste of time (see box 4.1). Experience with undertaking randomized control trials (RCTs) in even reasonably sophisticated countries like Colombia suggests that many firms lack basic accounting and tracking routines. It is highly unlikely that such firms are capable of undertaking complex activities such as R&D, which have long gestation periods and are subject to substantial uncertainty.

New Empirical Evidence on Managerial Practices and Innovation

The Evidence Linking Managerial and Organizational Practices with Innovation

Despite the extensive qualitative evidence linking managerial and organizational practices to innovation, quantitative evidence establishing this link is extremely limited. In one of the few empirical studies on this issue, Peeters and Van Pottelsberghe (2005) use data from large firms in Belgium to identify seven capabilities, including technological, production, and managerial processes, that matter for innovation. These include corporate culture (for example, values, employee recognition and rewards, mainstreaming the firm's innovation strategy, and communication); work organization (for example, brainstorming, multidisciplinary teams, employee rotation, and information exchange across departments); generation of new ideas (for example, market surveys, competitive intelligence, recruitment, and patent searches); and project selection (for example, knowledge management).[7]

With the data described in box 4.2 above, we are able to offer a more comprehensive view of the link between managerial and organizational practices and innovation. The objective is to build a bridge between the innovation literature and the new management literature, and to provide evidence on the importance of these capabilities for innovation in both emerging markets and low-income countries.

All the three datasets employed here—the WMS, the Enterprise Survey (ES), and ENAPROCE for Mexico—use the same approach to measuring managerial practices pioneered by Bloom and Van Reenen (2007). The authors focus on a set of structured management practices that were identified by industry experts as key in explaining firms' performance. These include four different dimensions: (1) *operations* in terms of introduction of lean manufacturing and improvements, (2) *monitoring* for constant improvements, (3) use of appropriate *targets* and acting when problems arise, and (4) use of *incentives* to attract and retain talent. Although other managerial practices could also be identified and measured, this set has been shown to be a robust predictor of performance across countries and highly correlated with other practices (Bloom and Van Reenen 2012).

Managerial Practices Are Correlated with R&D Intensity and Other Innovation Inputs
Bloom et al. (2013), using U.S. data from the 2012 MOPS, show that there is a very high correlation between structured management and R&D expenditures and patents, after instrumenting for potential endogeneity. Figure 4.2 suggests that the correlation between management practices and R&D is robust, using two different global samples and controlling for the impact of income per capita in both. Panel a plots the average management index from the WMS data for large firms against the average R&D quality index, a component of the Global Innovation Index that measures business R&D intensity, the ability of countries to generate researchers, and the quality of their universities. In both cases, we plot the residuals of regressing these indices on GDP per capita to ensure that income per capita is not driving this relationship. The two indexes are highly correlated.

Panel b is based on data from the ES that include information on management and innovation in medium and large companies from a larger sample of countries. Again, there is a high correlation between the average management index and the average country R&D intensity (measured as dollars per worker), conditional on investing in this type of activity and controlling for the level of income per capita. Although clearly causality is difficult to establish, both are consistent with the idea that better management practices are necessary to increase R&D intensity and manage it efficiently.

Managerial Practices Are Also Correlated with Innovation Outputs
This positive correlation between the quality of managerial practices and innovation inputs is unsurprisingly found with outputs as well. Countries with better managerial practices on average also have higher overall innovation capacity, broadly construed.

FIGURE 4.2 The Quality of R&D and of Management Practices Are Highly Correlated

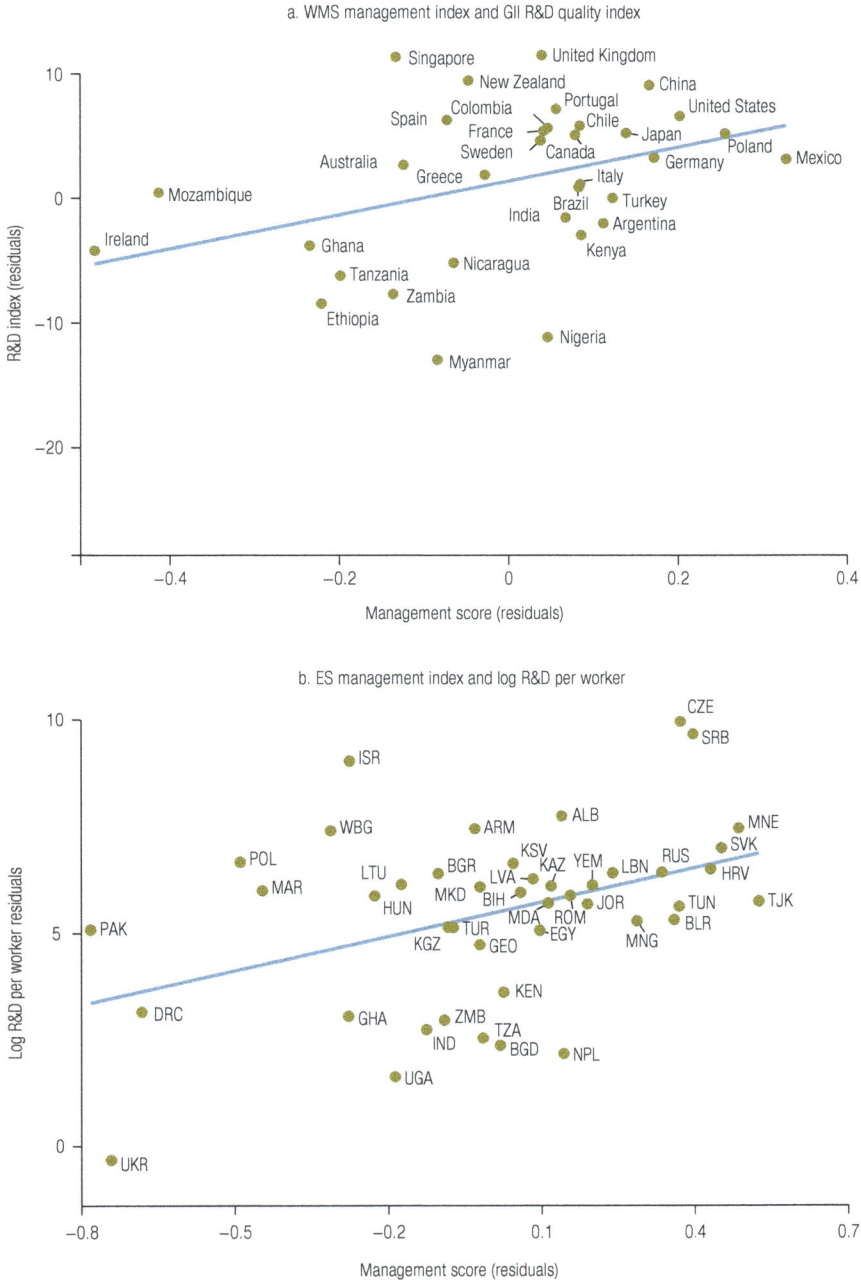

a. WMS management index and GII R&D quality index

b. ES management index and log R&D per worker

Source: Elaboration from Global Innovation Index 2015 and World Management Survey 2015 (panel a), and from Enterprise Survey data (www.enterprisesurveys.org) (panel b).

Note: In both graphs the residuals of regressing R&D and management on gross domestic product per capita are plotted to control for the impact of income per capita on the correlation. ES = Enterprise Survey; GII = Global Innovation Index; R&D = research and development; WMS = World Management Survey. The R&D quality index is comprised of business R&D intensity, the ability of countries to generate researchers, and the quality of their universities.

FIGURE 4.3 **Innovation Outputs Are Associated with Better Management Practices**

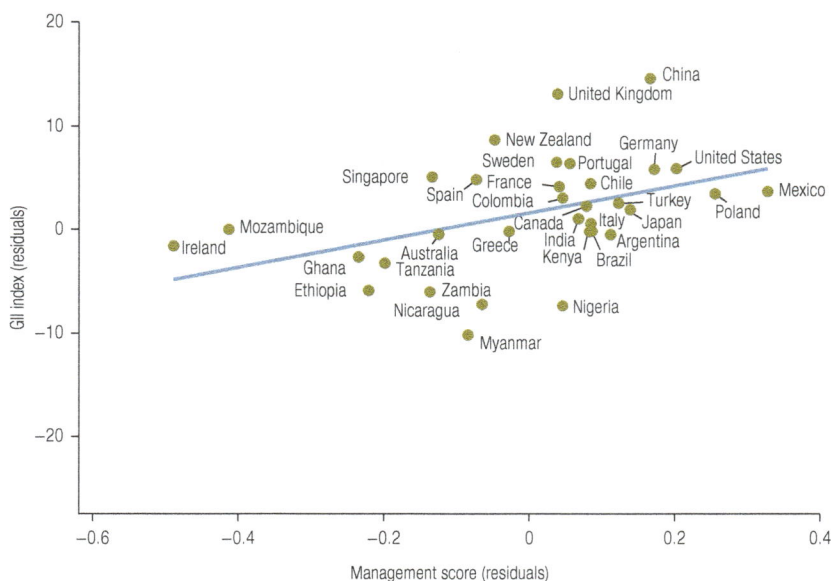

Source: Elaboration from Global Innovation Index 2015 and World Management Survey 2015.

Note: The residuals of regressing the Global Innovation Index and management on gross domestic product per capita are plotted to control for the impact of income per capita in driving the correlation.

Figure 4.3 shows that the average WMS management score is highly correlated with the Global Innovation Index (GII 2015), which captures overall innovation capacity, including the quality of framework conditions and other infrastructure. Those countries with better management practices also have more innovative capacity.

This correlation is also seen using firm-level data on innovation expenditures. Figure 4.4 shows the percentage of firms introducing innovations, decomposed by region and type of innovation (from the ES data). Better-managed firms in each region are more likely to introduce any innovation (product or process) and are more likely to introduce a product new to the firm, the national market, or the international market.[8]

More recently, Bloom et al. (2017) also show this correlation between innovation inputs and outputs and management, using data from MOPS in the United States. Specifically, the authors show that those firms that are at the highest managerial quality quintiles are the ones that also have higher R&D intensity and file more patents per worker (figure 4.5).

Estimates of the Role of Managerial Practices in Knowledge Creation Functions

Identifying the separate effects of managerial capabilities versus technological capabilities requires more structured empirical exercises that control for a greater range of variables.

FIGURE 4.4 Better Management Quality Is Associated with Higher Innovation Outputs

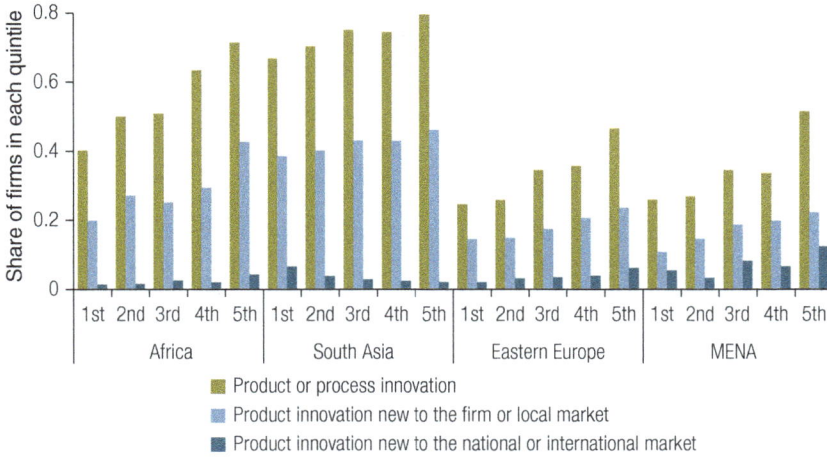

Source: Elaboration using Enterprise Survey data (www.enterprisesurveys.org).

Note: X axis shows quality of management practices by quartile in each region. MENA = Middle East and North Africa.

FIGURE 4.5 U.S. Firms with Higher Management Quality Undertake More R&D and Patent More

Source: Bloom et al. 2017.

Note: R&D = research and development. Based on MOPS survey for the United States and ordered by quintile of calculated management quality.

Drawing on both the ES and the WMS/Orbis datasets, we estimate the standard knowledge creation function described in chapter 2, which relates innovation outcomes to R&D, and add management quality and other covariates (see box 4.3). In a sense, we can think of management quality as capturing a broader set of management capabilities and R&D as capturing revealed capabilities that are more technological.

Estimating the Augmented Knowledge Creation Function

As discussed in chapter 2, a substantial literature estimates a knowledge creation function, where knowledge is generally represented by patenting. We do something similar. Depending on the exercise, I represents process or product innovation, or patenting. In each case, we add management as an additional capability, along with a set of firm-level controls:

$$I = \beta_R R\&D + \beta_M M + Controls + e \qquad \text{(B4.3.1)}$$

As the dependent variables are frequently discrete—0 or 1, or count variables, such as number of patents filed in the firm— we use appropriate estimation techniques. For instance, Maloney and Sarrias (2017) use a negative binomial estimator to deal with count data (patents).

Because we are generally working with cross-sections of data—which do not permit using lagged variables—and lack other credible instruments, the coefficients are almost certainly biased and must be taken as suggestive. In several exercises, Cirera (2017) employs the Crépon–Douguet–Mairesse (CDM) model (Crépon, Douguet, and Mairesse 1998) to address endogeneity concerns using a system of equations. Specifically, the CDM model is a recursive system of equations that characterize the evolution of the innovative process in three stages. Equations in the first stage explain the firm's decision to invest in R&D on the basis of firm-specific, sectoral, and other factors. The second stage characterizes innovation outcomes, or the likelihood that the firm's investment in knowledge capital translates to successful innovations (a knowledge production function). In the third stage, an equation links innovation outputs to firm productivity.

Capabilities and Process and Product Innovation

Cirera (2017), using the ES data, confirms the relationship shown in figure 4.4, controlling for size, age, sector, and country effects. The latter ensures that management and R&D activity are not simply picking up the level of development per se. Figure 4.6 plots the coefficients from that exercise and shows that both R&D and management quality increase the probability of introducing product innovation, process innovation, and process innovations that involve automation.[9] Bartz, Mohnen, and Schweiger (2016) find consistent results with a similar model for ES data for Europe and Central Asia.

Capabilities and Patenting

Management quality also is significantly related to patenting and R&D. Figure 4.5 from Bloom et al. (2017) shows that, for the United States, patenting is associated with higher management skills. For a broader range of advanced and developing countries, Maloney and Sarrias (2017), using the WMS/BvD Orbis database, find broadly similar patterns (figure 4.7). Formal econometric estimation shows that management quality has a strong independent effect on patenting, quite apart from whatever support it gives to undertaking R&D—on average a one standard deviation increase in managerial quality leads to roughly five additional patents per firm.

FIGURE 4.6 **R&D and Management Quality Affect the Probability of Introducing a Process or Product Innovation**

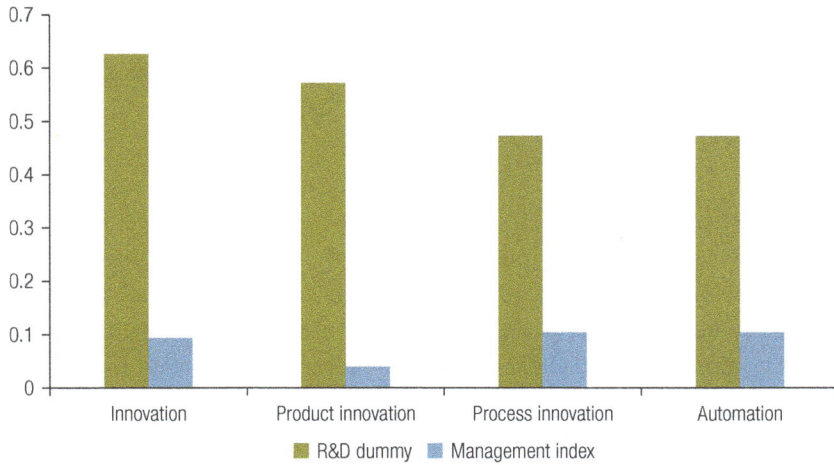

Source: Elaboration using Enterprise Survey data (www.enterprisesurveys.org).

Note: Marginal effects of a probit model estimating the probability of each type of innovation on whether firm does R&D, the management index, age, and country and sector dummies. R&D = research and development. All coefficients are statistically significant at the 99 percent confidence level.

FIGURE 4.7 **Globally, Firms with Higher Management Quality Undertake More R&D and Patent More**

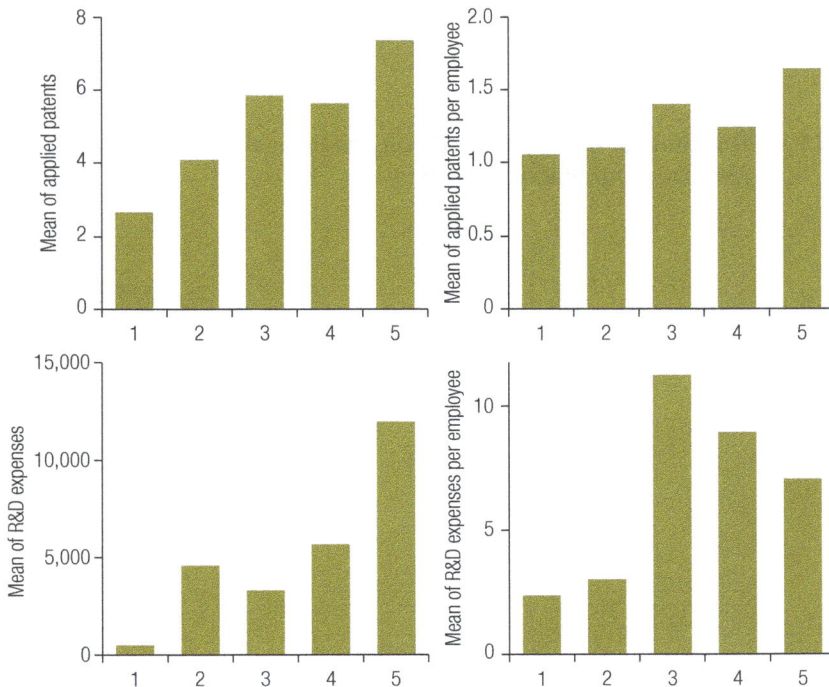

Source: Maloney and Sarrias 2017.

Interactions between Managerial Quality and Innovation

Finally, more detailed firm-level data from Mexico allow us to establish that the effect of management on innovation grows stronger with better management. Figure 4.8 shows the coefficients of the unconditional quantile regression of an index of innovation inputs and outputs[10]—and the quality of management increases and shows that the relationship becomes stronger for those firms that are at the top of each management quintile.

The Dual Impact on Productivity

In chapter 2, we discussed the positive impact that firm-level innovation has on productivity. In this chapter, we summarized some of the evidence suggesting that management quality has a substantial, positive impact on productivity and showed evidence that managerial and organizational practices are important inputs for innovation. This supports the view that good management practices have a dual positive effect on productivity: a direct effect through enabling a more efficient use of factors and an indirect effect through increasing the probability of innovating.

Cirera (2017), using ES data in a CDM framework (see box 4.3), finds evidence for this hypothesis. Better management practices drive innovation and subsequently productivity in developing countries in all regions analyzed. However, the indirect effect via innovation disappears for incremental innovation in lower-income countries and persists in middle- and high-income countries. As discussed in chapter 2, this suggests that some of the innovations introduced in the lower-income countries reflect small changes rather than substantial upgrading.

FIGURE 4.8 **The Effect of Management Quality on Innovation Index Increases with Management Quality in Mexico**

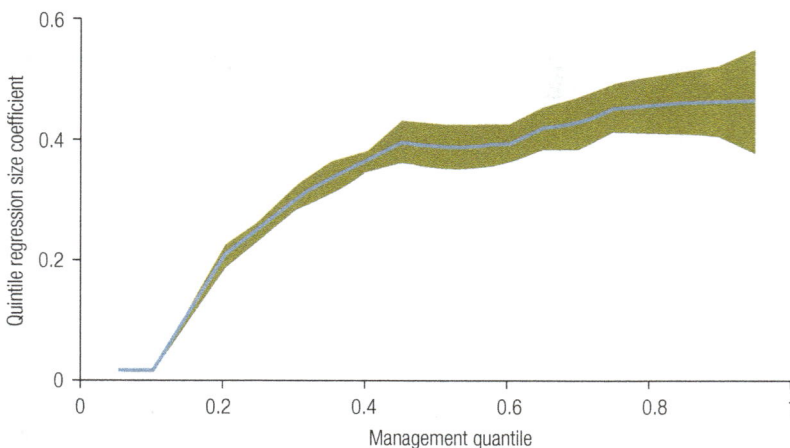

Source: Iacovone and Pereira-López 2017.
Note: Quantile Regression of management quality on innovation index using ENAPROCE.

The Innovation Paradox

Complementarities between Managerial Practices and R&D

Not only does management quality enter independently from R&D in knowledge generation but it also increases the efficacy of R&D in generating innovation outputs.[11] In figure 4.9 the efficiency of R&D (the y axis) is measured by the residuals generated by regressing the GII (2015) on the measure of R&D quality—an index that includes the quality of R&D institutions as well as the level of gross domestic expenditure on R&D (GERD). A negative value indicates that the country obtains lower-than-average innovation quality for a given R&D quality. Distance to the managerial frontier (the x axis) is measured by the difference between the country's management score and the maximum score (the U.S. score). As countries move farther from the managerial frontier, there is lower R&D efficiency in achieving innovation.

This positive complementarity between management and R&D is also evident using firm-level data. Iacovone and Pereira-López (2017) find that better managerial practices increase the efficiency in which R&D efforts translate into innovation activities in Mexico. In other words, an additional investment in R&D expenditure has a larger impact on innovation in a better-managed firm than the same investment in a poorly managed firm. Taken together, these findings suggest that lack of managerial and organizational complementary factors may be an important explanation for the low rates of return to R&D in poor countries documented in chapter 3.

FIGURE 4.9 Better Management Increases the Impact of R&D on Innovation

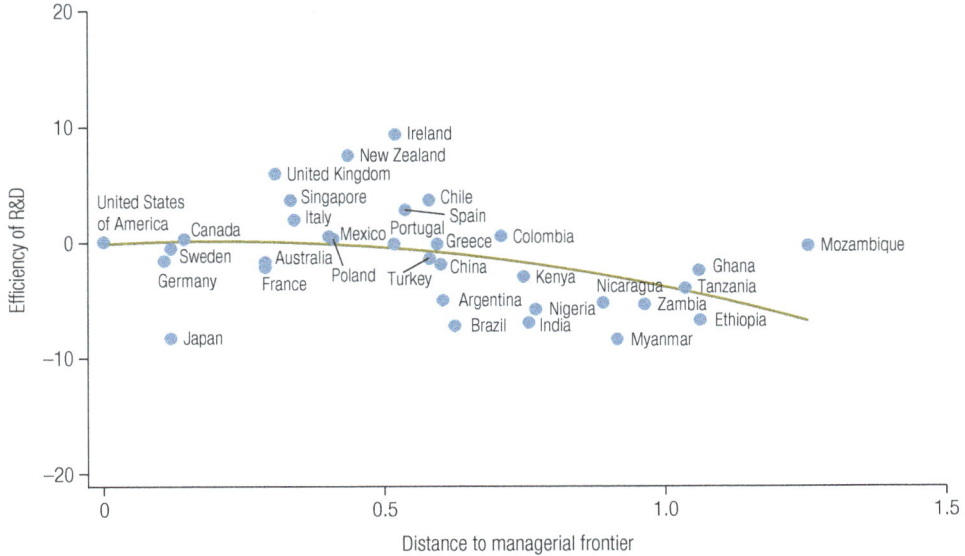

Source: Elaboration from Global Innovation Index 2015 and World Management Survey 2015.

Note: The figure shows the residuals of regressing the GII index on the R&D index vs distance to the managerial frontier defined as the absolute value of the country managerial index ratio with the US average managerial index 0 minus 1. 0 indicates the frontier, and positive values distance from average managerial quality in the United States.

FIGURE 4.10 Performance Monitoring and Incentives Are Associated with Greater Innovation Index

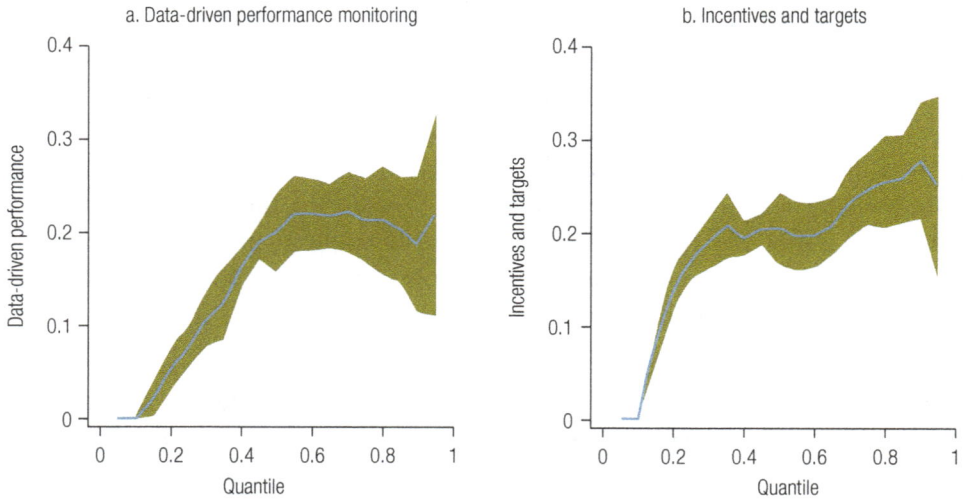

a. Data-driven performance monitoring

b. Incentives and targets

Source: Iacovone and Pereira-López 2017.

What Managerial Practices Matter for Innovation

Does the impact of management quality differ by type of practice? For example, as noted earlier, Chinese and Vietnamese firms are strong on monitoring but weak on setting long-run targets, on introducing new technologies and best practice in operations, and on developing human resource policies. The latter practices are likely to severely constrain innovation projects because setting targets and having a well-trained and incentivized labor force is critical to transform an idea to prototyping and commercialization. Iacovone and Pereira-López (2017) replicate the same exercise as in figure 4.9 using individual practices (figure 4.10). They find a similar correlation between both the innovation index and the use of data-driven performance monitoring and incentives and targets. This reinforces the view of some studies in the innovation management literature that emphasize continual improvement and risk management, where both types of practices play a very important role.

Concluding Remarks

This chapter has emphasized the importance of managerial and organizational practices as firm capabilities necessary for innovation and described their process of accumulation. The key messages can be summarized as follows:

- Managerial and organizational practices have a direct impact on innovation, even after controlling for the usual innovation inputs such as R&D.
- Managerial practices are important predictors of innovation and productivity across countries, across firm size, and across country income levels.

- Strong managerial and organizational practices enhance the impact of R&D on innovation and productivity and a lack of them may partly explain the lower returns to R&D found in poorer countries.
- Developing these capabilities is an important policy objective, especially in countries and firms that are more distant from the technological frontier.

Policy makers need to identify the barriers to accumulating these capabilities, as well as the set of complementary factors needed to maximize their impact. This requires that agencies and policies support the innovative efforts of enterprises in ways that are appropriate to the local National Innovation System (NIS) and business climate. We focus on these elements in part II of this report.

Annex 4A A Review of Firm Capabilities for Innovation

This annex summarizes the key capabilities highlighted by different literature over the last three decades as important for innovation (See Cirera, López-Bassols, and Maloney 2017). Despite the strong R&D myopia that has biased innovation policy and practice, the innovation literature has traditionally emphasized the importance of a broader set of capabilities for successful innovation, especially in developing countries. Recent advances in the measurement of managerial and organizational practices have opened the "black box" of these capabilities, and provided a more nuanced view of the different routines that are necessary to converge to the technological frontier.

Accumulating Capabilities Are the Key for Growth and Economic Catch-Up

During the 1980s, several authors studying the experiences of Latin American countries and the Newly Industrialized Countries (NICs) in East Asia emphasized the importance of acquiring technological capabilities during their process of growth convergence. A World Bank project, "The Acquisition of Technological Capability" led by Carl Dahlman and Larry Westphal, emphasizes that the acquisition and development of technological capabilities were at the center of the innovation process in the NICs. Rather than invention or the generation of indigenous technologies, acquiring the capabilities for efficient production requires the combination of foreign technologies with efforts to develop the skills and know-how required to effectively use this technology (Dahlman, Ross-Larson, and Westphal 1987). Although most of the debate around the East Asian "miracle" centered on the role of openness, which has an important impact on incentives to engage in innovation, a critical element explaining the growth success of these countries was the ability of firms to learn and accumulate capabilities over time, and thus catch up technologically.

Firm Capabilities: An Old Subject of Study with Different Conceptualizations

The longstanding interest in understanding the concept of firm capabilities is rooted in Penrose's (1959) seminal work on the nature (and growth) of the firm. In this framework, firms own a number of *resources* that support (and constrain) their growth (Cantwell 2000; Jacobides and Winter 2005). However, views on the nature of these capabilities differ. On the one hand, neoclassical theories of the firm have traditionally conceptualized these capabilities and the process of technology adoption as a *black box* (Rosenberg 1982). Under this paradigm, firms were seen as organizations with the main objective of reducing transaction costs (Coase 1937). Important efforts were made in the late 1970s and 1980s to explain differences in firm growth, for example emphasizing managerial talent (Lucas 1978) or learning (Jovanovic 1982). These models, while explaining critical features of firms' dynamics, fail to offer a clear conceptualization of the processes that enable firms to learn and acquire tacit knowledge.

Instead, they focus primarily on how differences in capabilities were revealed in performance—that is, firm growth or market share changes—or, as in Sutton (2005), in attributes such as quality and cost.

On the other hand, organizational theory, management-related fields, and most of the innovation literature have examined the concept of firm capabilities in more detail, using primarily case studies and qualitative information. These studies focus on identifying the precise set of capabilities (and combinations of capabilities) that firms must acquire, develop, and accumulate to introduce innovations or maintain competitive advantages. Although these strands overlap to some extent, they provide different conceptualizations of firm capabilities, which has resulted in a lack of a unifying framework to understand capabilities. This contributed to the widely accepted view in policy and media circles that innovation is generated primarily by accumulating a limited subset of these capabilities—research and development—for technology generation and radical new products. As we discussed earlier, this model is at odds with the innovation processes typical of firms farther away from the technological frontier.

To build a bridge between this literature and the industrial organization tradition, Sutton (2000, 2005, 2012) distinguishes between two conceptualizations. First, there is a firm's *underlying* capability ("the set of elements of 'know-how' or 'working practices' held collectively by the group of individuals comprising the firm"; Sutton 2005, p. 3). Second, there is a firm's *revealed* capability, which is the observable (and performance-relevant) outcome reflecting the firm's productive capacities in terms of both quality and productivity.

Different conceptual models emphasize various aspects of firm capabilities, but some key characteristics are consistently highlighted throughout these studies. Specifically, capabilities are (1) primarily internal to the firm, (2) firm-specific, (3) knowledge-based, and (4) not easily replicable.[12] More important, these knowledge capabilities manifest in routines, management practices, specialized departments, or assets that are acquired by firms internally or externally, that can be measured, and that are the result of specific investments in learning and know-how accumulation over time. A key element in these frameworks is that innovation is seen as a product of the firm's "combinative capabilities to generate new applications from existing knowledge" (Kogut and Zander 1992), or as a change in established routines (Nelson and Winter 1982). Even for more basic technologies, this requires investments in capability building that increase firms "absorptive capacity" (Cohen and Levinthal 1990) to facilitate the process of technology transfer.

Notes

1. This strategy is based on the creation in these countries of an institutional framework, involving both public and private sectors, that provides a capacity not just to receive the imported technologies, but to *absorb, adapt, diffuse,* or *disseminate* them and ultimately improve them through the efforts of indigenous technologists and engineers. Technological capability is acquired and enhanced through a process of organizational learning at the level of the firm and at the level

of the industry. The whole process can be described as one of "economic learning" (Cho and Mathews, 2000, p. 4).

2. This is consistent with findings that developing countries lag across all sectors and the recent literature that casts doubt on the policy maker's capacity to identify sectors with desirable externalities (Lederman and Maloney 2012, Maloney and Nayyar 2017) or whether the efforts to choose sectors were an important part of the Asia growth miracle (Noland and Pack 2003). Dodgson (2000, p. 261) states, "An important policy question for less technologically developed nations, such as Malaysia and Indonesia, is whether the present emphasis on electronics is likely to produce any longer-term sustainable comparative advantages. One might justifiably ask whether emphasis could be better placed on more traditional and historical, but still potentially high technology, high value-added industries, such as tropical cash crops in Malaysia and textiles in Indonesia."

3. Dynamic capabilities are closely linked to organizational processes (Eisenhardt and Martin 2000), particularly organizational learning, which can lead to the alteration of capabilities through external sourcing as well as through internal knowledge creation. Innovation depends on the leveraging of organizational capabilities, processes, and resources. Organizational capabilities are often explicitly linked to different innovation activities (Grant 1996), including the commercialization of new products or the implementation of new (or improved) processes (Chandler 1992). Organizational capabilities in a broad sense include the human capital of the firm's employees (management and others) as well as the structure of organizational incentives that enable evaluation and transmission of skills and knowledge within the organization (Ulrich and Lake 1990). Among organizational capabilities, the use of knowledge management policies and practices within firms has become increasingly widespread. This includes various management techniques and tools that are being deployed by firms to optimize their use of knowledge in support of their innovation activities (OECD 2003; Kremp and Mairesse 2004).

4. Visits to firms in the auto parts sector in Colombia revealed the wide variance in such capabilities across firms. Faced, again, with increased competition from Asia, some firms simply lowered their prices, which over the long term is not a viable strategy. Others sought to retail the low end of the Asian products but maintain market share at the higher end, hoping that competition would not extend there soon. The most adept organizations were able to seek out new sectors that could repackage or reapply their existing technological abilities to markets with more slope in the demand curve. One, for instance, moved into the metal skeletons of the vertical gardens that are ubiquitous in Bogotá but that require tailoring to local context and hence are not susceptible to being mass-produced abroad.

5. Bell (2009, p. 11) highlights the dynamic nature of these technological and innovation capabilities that reflect the "capacity [of firms] to create new configurations of product and process technology and to implement changes and improvements to technologies already in use."

6. Lall (1992) distinguishes three uses of technological capabilities: (1) investment: relating to the initial phases of technology acquisition and deployment; (2) production: quality control, maintenance, research, design, innovation; and (3) linkage capabilities: enabling effective inward and outward knowledge flows.

7. Other studies include Bartz, Mohnen, and Schweiger (2016), who show for a sample of countries in Europe and Central Asia that better managerial practices increase innovation incidence and productivity. Cosh, Fu, and Hughes (2012) study the relationship between organization structure and innovation in the United Kingdom's small and medium enterprises. The authors find that having a formal organizational structure of decentralized decision making and written business plans is an important predictor of the ability to innovate.

8. Firms in South Asia in the radical innovation group are an exception. However, there are very few radical innovators in the sample and average differences across groups are not significant.

9. Because the R&D and management variables are in different units—management is a standardized score and R&D is a dummy whether the firm invests in R&D—we cannot compare their relative effects.

10. This continuous index is calculated by Iacovone and Pereira-Lopez (2017) based on data from ENAPROCE (2015) on different innovation inputs and outputs, such as the use of intellectual property and investments in technology. The index measures whether a firm: purchases licenses over products, processes, or machinery and equipment aimed at updating, upgrading, and improving its production processes and uses them as they are; assimilates and documents the technologies comprised by the licenses; adapts and modifies technologies purchased to increase efficiency; generates its own technology; files for patents over technologies developed; and sells the technology it generates to other companies.

11. See, for example, the discussion of the role of organizational practices in the development of capabilities in the experience of firms catching up in East Asia and Latin America (Bell and Figueiredo 2012).

12. While our focus is on firm-level capabilities, capabilities have also been considered at the level of countries. See for example Hidalgo and Hausmann (2009) and Hausmann and Hidalgo (2011) who model the link between *country capability endowments* and *product capability requirements*, or Daude, Nagengast, and Perea (2016) who examine the determinants of national *export capabilities*.

References

Atkeson, Andrew, and Patrick J. Kehoe. 2005. "Modeling and Measuring Organization Capital." *Journal of Political Economy* 113 (5): 1026–53.

Bartz, Wiebke, Pierre Mohnen, and Helena Schweiger. 2016. "The Role of Innovation and Management Practices in Determining Firm Productivity in Developing Economies." MERIT Working Papers 034, United Nations University—Maastricht Economic and Social Research Institute on Innovation and Technology.

Bell, Martin. 2009. "Innovation Capabilities and Directions of Development." STEPS Working Paper 33, STEPS CEntre, Brighton, UK.

Bell, Martin, and Paulo N. Figueiredo. 2012. "Innovation Capability Building and Learning Mechanisms in Latecomer Firms: Recent Empirical Contributions and Implications for Research." *Revue Canadienne d'Études du Développement* 33 (1): 14–40.

Bloom, Nicholas, Erik Brynjolfsson, Lucia Foster, Ron S. Jarmin, Megha Patnaik, Itay Saporta-Eksten, and John Van Reenen. 2017. "What Drives Differences in Management?" NBER Working Paper No. W23300, National Bureau of Economic Research, Cambridge, MA.

Bloom, Nicholas, Raissa Ebner, Kerenssa Kay, Renata Lemos, Raffaella Sadun, Daniela Scur, and John Van Reenen. 2015. "Management Practices in Vietnam." Background paper for *Vietnam 2035: Toward Prosperity, Creativity, Equity, and Democracy*. World Bank, Washington, DC.

Bloom, Nicholas, Benn Eifert, Aprajit Mahajan, David McKenzie, and John Roberts. 2013. "Does Management Matter?: Evidence from India." *Quarterly Journal of Economics* 128 (1): 1–51.

Bloom, Nicholas, and John Van Reenen. 2007. "Measuring and Explaining Management Practices across Firms and Countries." *Quarterly Journal of Economics* 122 (4): 1351–1408.

———. 2010. "Why Do Management Practices Differ across Firms and Countries?" *Journal of Economic Perspectives* 24 (1): 203–24.

Cantwell, John A. 2000. "A Survey of Theories of International Production." In *The Nature of the Transnational Firm*, edited by C. N. Pitelis and R. Sugden, 10–56. London: Routledge.

Chandler, Alfred D. 1992. "Organizational Capabilities and the Economic History of the Industrial Enterprise." *Journal of Economic Perspectives* 6 (3): 79–100.

Chen, Chen, Yangyang Chen, and Edward J. Podolski. 2014. "Employee Treatment and Corporate Innovative Success: Evidence from Patent Data." *Journal of Corporate Finance*. http://ssrn.com/abstract=2461021.

Cho, Dong-Sung, and John Mathews. 2007. *Tiger Technology: The Creation of a Semiconductor Industry in East Asia*. Cambridge, UK: Cambridge University Press.

Cirera, Xavier. 2017. "Management Practices as an Input for Innovation and Productivity in Developing Countries." Unpublished report, World Bank, Washington, DC.

Cirera, Xavier, Vladimir López-Bassols, and William F. Maloney. 2017. "Firm Capabilities for Innovation: A Conceptual Framework"Unpublished report, World Bank, Washington, DC.

Coase, Ronald. 1937. "The Nature of the Firm." *Economica* 4 (16): 386–405.

Cosh, Andy, Xiaolan Fu, and Alan Hughes. 2012. "Organisation, Structure and Innovation Performance in Different Environments." *Small Business Economics* 39 (2): 301–17.

Cohen, Wesley, and Daniel A. Levinthal. 1990. "Absorptive Capacity: A New Perspective on Learning and Innovation". *Administrative Science Quarterly* 35 (1): 128–52. Special Issue: Technology, Organizations, and Innovation.

Crépon B., E. Duguet, and J. Mairesse. 1998. "Research, Innovation and Productivity: An Econometric Analysis at the Firm Level." *Economics of Innovation and New Technology* 7 (2): 115–58.

Dahlman, Carl J., Bruce Ross-Larson, Larry E. Westphal. 1987. "Managing Technological Development: Lessons from the Newly Industrializing Countries." *World Development* 15 (6): 759–75.

Daude, Christian, Arne Nagengast, and Jose Ramon Perea. 2016. "Productive Capabilities: An Empirical Analysis of Their Drivers." *Journal of International Trade & Economic Development* (Taylor & Francis Journals) 25 (4): 504–35.

De Jong, Jeroen P. J., and Deanne N. Den Hartog. 2007. "How Leaders Influence Employees' Innovative Behaviour." *European Journal of Innovation Management* 10 (1): 41–64.

Dodgson, Mark. 2000. "Strategic Research Partnerships: Their Role, and Some Issues of Measuring Their Extent and Outcomes—Experiences from Europe and Asia." Paper presented to the Workshop on Strategic Research Partnerships, National Science Foundation, SRI International, Washington, DC, October 13.

Ederer, Florian, and Gustavo Manso. 2013. "Is Pay-for-Performance Detrimental to Innovation?" *Management Science* 59 (7): 1496–1513.

Eisenhardt, Kathleen M., and Jeffrey A. Martin. 2000. "Dynamic Capabilities: What Are They?" *Strategic Management Journal* 21 (10–11): 1105–21.

ENAPROCE. 2015. http://www.inegi.org.mx/est/contenidos/proyectos/encuestas/establecimientos /otras/enaproce/default_t.aspx.

Galindo-Rueda, Fernando, and Valentine Millot. 2015. "Measuring Design and Its Role in Innovation." OECD Science, Technology and Industry Working Papers 2015/1, Organisation for Economic Co-operation and Development, Paris.

Garicano, L., and E. Rossi-Hansberg. 2015. "Knowledge-Based Hierarchies: Using Organizations to Understand the Economy." NBER Working Paper No. 20607, National Bureau of Economic Research, Cambridge, MA.

GII (Global Innovation Index). 2015. https://www.globalinnovationindex.org/.

Gibbs, M., S. Neckermann, and C. Siemroth. 2015. "A Field Experiment in Motivating Employee Ideas." *Tinbergen Institute Discussion Papers* 14–045/VII, Tinbergen Institute.

Grant, Robert M. 1996. "Toward a Knowledge-Based Theory of the Firm." *Strategic Management Journal* 17: 109–22.

Hallak, J. 2006. "Product Quality and the Direction of Trade." *Journal of International Economics* 68 (1): 238–65.

Hausmann, R., and C. Hidalgo. 2011. "The Network Structure of Economic Output." *Journal of Economic Growth* (16): 309–42.

Helfat, Constance E., Sydney Finkelstein, Will Mitchell, Margaret Peteraf, Harbir Singh, David Teece, and Sidney G. Winter. 2007. *Dynamic Capabilities: Understanding Strategic Change in Organizations*. Malden, MA: Wiley-Blackwell.

Hidalgo, C., and R. Hausmann. 2009. "The building blocks of economic complexity." *Proceedings of the National Academy of Sciences* 106 (26): 10570–575.

Hobday, Michael. 2000. "East versus Southeast Asian Innovation Systems: Comparing OEM- and TNC-Led Growth in Electronics." In *Technology, Learning, and Economic Development: Experiences of Newly Industrializing Economies*, edited by Linsu Kim and Richard R. Nelson, 129–60. Cambridge, UK: Cambridge University Press.

Iacovone, Leonardo, and Mariana Pereira-López. 2017. "Management Practices as Drivers of Innovation: New Evidence from Mexico." Unpublished report, World Bank, Washington, DC.

Jacobides, Michael G., and Sidney G. Winter. 2005. "The Co-evolution of Capabilities and Transaction Costs: Explaining the Institutional Structure of Production." *Strategic Management Journal* 26 (5): 395–413.

Jovanovic, Boyan. 1982. "Selection and the Evolution of Industry." *Econometrica* 50 (3): 649–70.

Katz, Jorge M., ed. 1987. *Technology Generation in Latin American Manufacturing Industries*. Basingstoke, UK: Palgrave Macmillan.

Kim, Linsu. 1997. *Imitation to Innovation: The Dynamics of Korea's Technological Learning*. Boston: Harvard Business School Press.

Kogut, Bruce, and Udo Zander. 1992. "Knowledge of the Firm, Combinative Capabilities, and the Replication of Technology." *Organization Science* 3 (3): 383–97.

Kremp, Elizabeth, and Jacques Mairesse. 2004. "Knowledge Management, Innovation and Productivity: A Firm-Level Exploration Based on French Manufacturing CIS3 Data." NBER Working Paper 10237, National Bureau of Economic Research, Cambridge, MA.

Lall, Sanjaya. 1987. *Learning to Industrialize: The Acquisition of Technological Capability by India*. Basingstoke, UK: Macmillan.

———.1992. "Technological Capabilities and Industrialization." World Development 20 (2): 165–86.

Lederman, Daniel, and William F. Maloney. 2012. *Does What You Export Matter? In Search of Empirical Guidance for Industrial Policies*. Washington, DC: World Bank.

Leiblein, Michael J., and Tammy L. Madsen. 2008. "Unbundling Competitive Heterogeneity: Incentive Structures and Capability Influences on Technological Innovation." *Strategic Management Journal* 30 (7): 711–35.

Lockett, Andy, Steve Thompson, and Uta Morgenstern. 2009. "The Development of the Resource-Based View of the Firm: A Critical Appraisal." *International Journal of Management Reviews* 11: 9–28.

Lucas, Robert E. 1978. "On the Size Distribution of Business Firms." *Bell Journal* 9: 509–23.

Maloney, William F., and Gaurav Nayyar. 2017. "Industrial Policy, Information, and Government Capacity." Working Paper, World Bank, Washington, DC.

Maloney, William F., and Mauricio Sarrias. 2017. "Management Quality and Innovation." Working Paper, World Bank, Washington, DC.

Mao, Connie X., and Jamie Weathers. 2015. "Employee Treatment and Firm Innovation." Working Paper, Temple University, Philadelphia.

Matthews, J. 1996. "Organizational Foundations of the Knowledge-Based Economy." In *Employment and Growth in the Knowledge-Based Economy*, edited by D. Foray and Bengt-Åke Lundvall, 157–80. Paris: OECD Publishing.

Murphy, Kevin M., Andrei Schleifer, and Robert W. Vishny. 1991. "The Allocation of Talent: Implications for Growth." *Quarterly Journal of Economics* 106 (2): 503–30.

Nelson, Richard R., and Sidney G. Winter. 1982. *An Evolutionary Theory of Economic Change*. Cambridge, MA: Belknap Press/Harvard University Press.

Newman, Carol, John Rand, Theodore Talbot, and Finn Tarp. 2015. "Technology Transfers, Foreign Investment and Productivity Spillovers." *European Economic Review* 76 (May): 168–87.

Noland, Marcus, and Howard. Pack. 2003. *Industrial Policies in an Era of Globalization*. Washington, DC: Peterson Institute for International Economics.

OECD (Organisation for Economic Co-operation and Development). 2003. *Measuring Knowledge Management in the Business Sector—First Steps*. OECD/Statistics Canada.

———. 2005. *Oslo Manual: Guidelines for Collecting and Interpreting Innovation Data*. 3rd edition. Paris: OECD Publishing.

Peeters, Carine, and Bruno Van Pottelsberghe. 2005. "Innovation Capabilities and Returns to Scale." CEB Working Paper 05-002, Université Libre de Bruxelles, Brussels.

Penrose, Edith. 1959. *The Theory of the Growth of the Firm*. New York: Oxford University Press.

Prescott, Edward C., and Michael Visscher. 1980. "Organizational Capital." *Journal of Political Economy* 88 (3): 446–61.

Rosenberg, Nathan. 1982. *Inside the Black Box: Technology and Economics*. Cambridge, UK: Cambridge University Press.

Rumelt, D. 1984. "Towards a Strategic Theory of the Firm." *Alternative Theories of the Firm* 2002 (2): 286–300.

Sutton, John. 2000. "Rich Trades, Scarce Capabilities: Industrial Development Revisited." Keynes Lecture in Economics, British Academy, London.

———. 2005. *Competing in Capabilities: An Informal Overview*. Washington, DC: World Bank.

———. 2012. *Competing in Capabilities: The Globalization Process*. Oxford, UK: Oxford University Press.

Sutton, John, and Bennet Kpentey. 2012. *An Enterprise Map of Ghana*. International Growth Centre, London.

Sutton, John, and Daniel Trefler. 2016. "Capabilities, Wealth, and Trade." *Journal of Political Economy* 124 (3): 826–78.

Syverson, Chad. 2008. "Markets: Ready-Mixed Concrete." *Journal of Economic Perspectives* 22.1 (Winter): 217–34.

Teece, David J. 2000. "Firm Capabilities and Economic Development: Implications for the Newly Industrializing Economies." In *Technology, Learning and Innovation, Experiences of Newly Industrializing Economies*, edited by L. Kim and R. Nelson, 105–128. Cambridge, UK: Cambridge University Press.

Teece, David J., and Gary Pisano. 1994. "The Dynamic Capabilities of Firms: An Introduction." *Industrial and Corporate Change* 3 (3): 537–56.

Teece, David J., Gary Pisano, and Amy Shuen. 1997. "Dynamic Capabilities and Strategic Management." *Strategic Management Journal* 18 (7): 509–33.

ul Haque, Martin Bell, Carl Dahlman, Sanjaya Lall, and Keith Pavitt. 1995. "The Development of Technological Capabilities, Trade, Technology, and International Competitiveness." World Bank, Washington, DC.

Ulrich, David, and Dale Lake. 1990. *Organizational Capability: Competing from the Inside Out*. New York: Wiley & Sons.

Wernerfelt, Birger. 1984. "The Resource-Based View of the Firm." *Strategic Management Journal* 5 (2): 171–80.

World Management Survey. 2015. http://worldmanagementsurvey.org/.

5. Building and Accumulating Managerial Capabilities

Introduction

In the previous chapter, we argued that management and organization capabilities are critical to innovation. We offered evidence that management practices are essential complements to other inputs, such as research and development (R&D), and have an independent effect on product and process innovation, and patenting. For developing countries, capabilities in this area are not only critical to production efficiency but also constitute the building blocks of innovative capabilities. Thus, innovation policy in developing countries should prioritize the accumulation of managerial capabilities for countries at the bottom of the capabilities escalator.

In this chapter the report focuses on how firms can build and acquire these capabilities. The recent availability of data on management quality enables the identification of factors that determine managerial capability: in particular, human capital, competition, and ownership structure, which are discussed in the first part of this chapter. Also, outward orientation or links to multinational enterprises (MNEs) can contribute to build these managerial capabilities. In the second part of the chapter, we discuss how integration with global value chains (GVCs) offers a valuable source of learning for building these capabilities.

What Determines Managerial Practices

In chapter 3, we discussed how firms' ability to innovate depends on the overall incentives framework. Innovation could be constrained by innovation-related market failures, such as a weak intellectual property regime, or by basic problems in the business environment, such as barriers to investment or high costs of doing business. In this section, we describe the process of accumulation of managerial capabilities and the role of external and internal factors in explaining differences in the quality of management across firms.

What Underlies the Differences in Average National Management Scores?

Managerial capabilities in the frontier countries, such as Germany, Japan, Sweden, and the United States, greatly exceed those in Africa and parts of Asia (see figure 2.12 in chapter 2).

FIGURE 5.1 **U.S. Firms' Management Scores Exceed Those in Poor Countries across the Distribution**

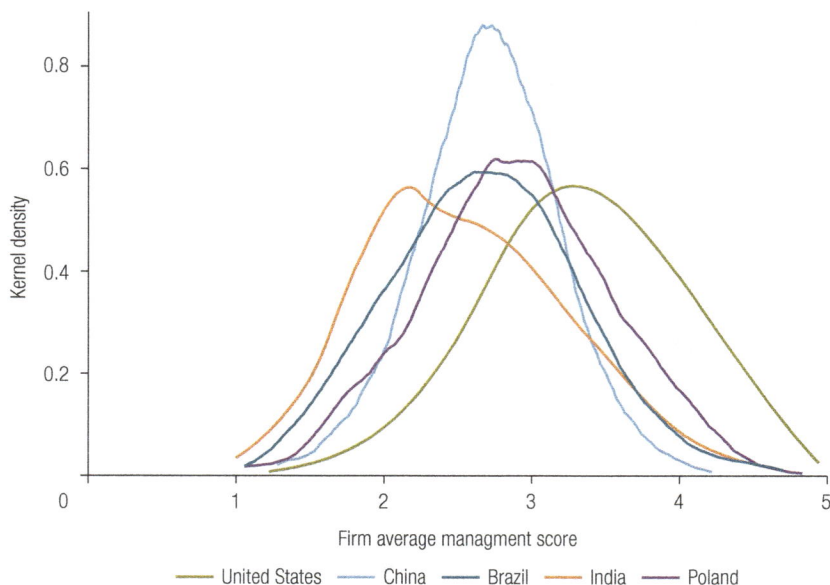

Source: World Management Survey 2012.

Average scores in monitoring, employment of just-in-time processes, internal feedback mechanisms, long-run planning and goal stretching, and human resource policies in poor countries are well below those in frontier countries.

Moreover, these lower average scores reflect poorer management across the entire distribution of firms, not a plethora of poorly managed firms coexisting with an efficient modern sector with firms performing close to the frontier (Maloney and Sarrias 2017). The distribution of management scores in the United States is farthest to the right in figure 5.1, suggesting that management quality of the better-managed firms in the United States substantially exceeds that of the better-managed firms in developing countries. In fact, the vast majority of firms in all of the region-representative countries shown fall below the average firm in the United States. As Maloney and Sarrias (2017) show, the difference between the median standardized management (z) score (see box 4.2) in a country and that in the United States moves uniformly with the average country z-score (panel a of figure 5.2). This suggests that convergence to the frontier is a question of moving not just the worst firms but the whole distribution.

Another way of demonstrating that lower average management quality in poor countries reflects problems across firms is to compare the average z-score in each country to the ratio of the difference in management quality with U.S. firms at the

FIGURE 5.2 **Improving Management Quality Implies Moving the Entire Distribution of Firms, Not Just the Laggards**

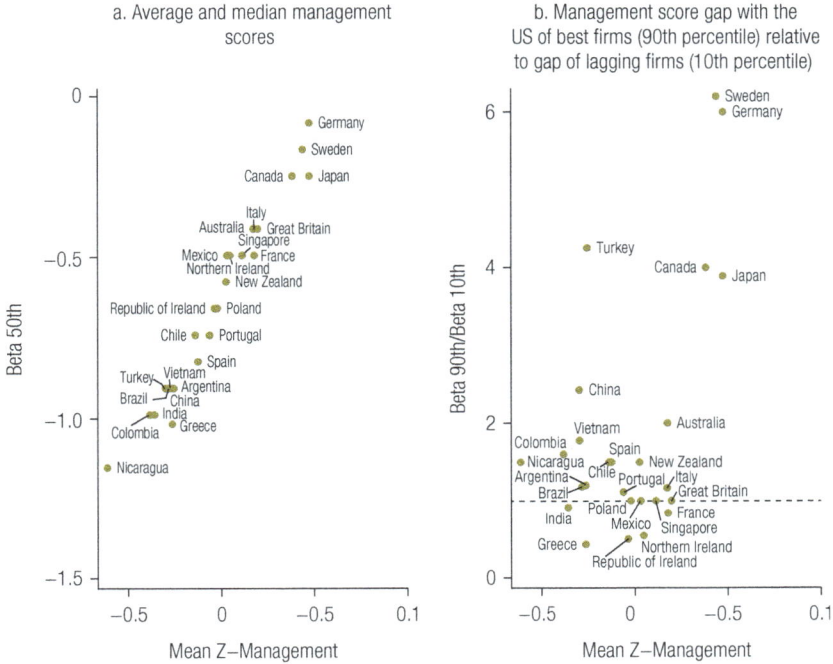

a. Average and median management scores

b. Management score gap with the US of best firms (90th percentile) relative to gap of lagging firms (10th percentile)

Source: Maloney and Sarrias 2017.

Note: The statistic in panel b is calculated by taking the difference of the management score of the 90th quantile in country X for the 90th quantile firm in the United States divided by the analogous difference for firms at the 10th quantile.

90th percentile (best-managed firms) over the 10th percentile (worst-managed firms) (panel b of figure 5.2). In theory, if the low average management quality in poor countries reflects many badly managed firms but the good firms are at the frontier, then this ratio should be below 1, as it is for Greece and Ireland. However, the ratio is close to or above 1 for many countries, suggesting that the best firms lag as much as or more than the worst firms. The ratio tends to be higher for richer countries, suggesting that this lag of the best becomes more pronounced with development. Thus, the United States marks the frontier not because its median firm is better managed— these firms are in fact very similar to those in Germany, Japan, and Sweden—but because its best firms are better by far. In some countries, like China and Turkey, the management quality of the best firms is well below that of U.S. firms, compared to countries with similar levels of average management quality (see also box 5.1). In sum, management quality upgrading requires lifting performance across the entire distribution.

Why Do China's Best Firms Lag in Management Quality?

China's rapid growth has been driven more by reasonable management skills across the bottom and center of the distribution combined with scale and low costs, rather than by stellar managerial performance at the top. Management quality at the 10th percentile (worst-managed firms) is only 0.58 points below the worst of U.S. firms, roughly the same as in Great Britain. However, managerial quality in China's top firms is 1.4 points below that of the top U.S. firms, among the worst ratios in the sample. Chinese managers are very good at some key capabilities for production, such as clarity of goals and measurement scores. However, in some key practices for innovation, such as just-in-time management and long-run strategic thinking, the scores are farther from the managerial frontier.

Similarly, a review of five prominent Chinese industries finds that, although aggregate production growth has been impressive, management quality at the individual firm level is well below the frontier (Cooke 2008, p. 25). In general, firms "rely on their low-cost advantage and mass production mode as their main competitive advantage instead of product innovation and quality of products and services." Arguably, Chinese managers are astute in terms of short-run assembly line management but often lack vision or plans for long-term technological advancement. Further, performance management often is based more on morality, political attitudes, seniority, and maintenance of harmonious relations with colleagues than on productivity-related indicators.

What Factors Affect Management Quality?

Bloom and Van Reenen (2007, 2010) exploring the World Management Survey (WMS), identify competition, human capital, ownership structure, the business environment, and learning spillovers as drivers of firm management scores. and Bloom et al. (2017) argue that these account for about a third of the dispersion of structured management practices across U.S. plants. We take several of these in turn.

Competition

Competition plays an important role in explaining differences in managerial practices for four frontier countries, either by forcing the worst firms to exit or by stimulating firms across the distribution to work harder (Bloom and Van Reenen 2007, 2010). Maloney and Sarrias (2017) confirm this effect for the frontier countries but find it less significant for developing countries. This may be because the proxy used to represent competition is less well measured in developing countries. However, like any type of innovation activity, the impact of competition on managerial practices is theoretically ambiguous. Competition can stimulate efforts at upgrading, particularly for firms close to the frontier (Aghion et al. 2005). For example, a significantly greater number of firms in European Union (EU) manufacturing sectors that were more affected by Chinese competition upgraded their technology, did more R&D, and increased patenting (Bloom, Draca, and Van Reenen 2016). On the other hand, competition reduces the rents resulting from innovation and hence reduces the incentive to improve practices.

Competition may even force firms furthest from the frontier to exit.[1] To some degree, this weeding-out effect is a normal process of improving quality. However, firms "close" to this threshold are unlikely to have the resources to invest in upgrading.

Case studies offer support for the view that the impact of competition on upgrading differs according to distance from the frontier. More competition likely would force improvements in operations in state-owned enterprises in China (see box 5.1) or large protected companies in many countries (see Rijkers, Freund, and Nucifora 2015 on Tunisia, for example). However, many Colombian small and medium enterprises (SMEs) faced with increased competition from Asian imports found it difficult to develop a counter strategy, including the necessary upgrading, until supported by outside consulting firms with more experience.

Human Capital

Human capital is an important determinant of management practices (see Bloom and Van Reenen 2007, 2010; Maloney and Sarrias, 2017). For instance, firms with managers who have attended college tend to show higher management scores. However, there is also evidence that firms invest in on-the-job managerial upgrading in the stylized fact that longer-lived firms tend to have better management.[2] As figure 5.3 shows, the median managerial practice from the Enterprise Survey (ES) data is higher

FIGURE 5.3 Managerial Practices Are Better in Older Firms

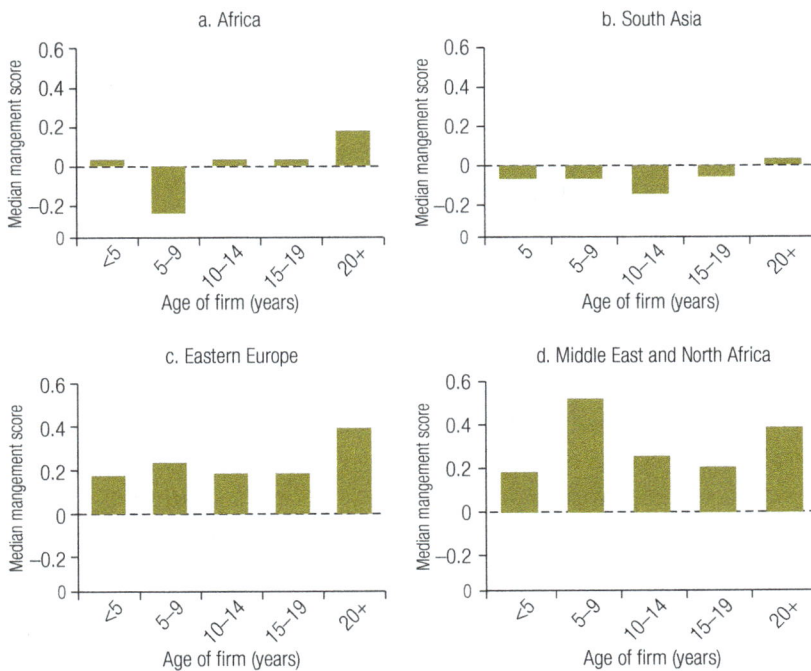

Source: Elaboration using Enterprise Survey data (www.enterprisesurveys.org).

for firms that have been in business more than 20 years than in younger firms, for all regions except the Middle East and North Africa. It is difficult to reach robust conclusions about the accumulation of managerial capabilities without longitudinal data, but this can be suggestive that management quality changes over the life cycle of the firm, and external factors and own upgrading efforts could play a role in improving management practices over the life cycle.

Foreign experience can also improve human capital by exposing managers to frontier practices, and managers who studied abroad score much better in management quality. This exposition to best practices by the top managers who set the vision and standards of the firm can have an appreciable impact on firms; performance.[3]

In sum, learning through education and experience can drive improvements in managerial quality. In part, this may reflect better-educated entrepreneurs displacing existing firms. However, firms appear to improve over the life cycle, and, as is discussed in chapter 7, business advisory interventions can have important effects on management quality and productivity. Convergence to the managerial frontier requires not only competition to remove badly managed firms but also, and potentially more important, programs to support the diffusion and adoption of good managerial practices.

Ownership Structure

Ownership structure is consistently found to be significantly associated with management quality (see, for example, Bloom and Van Reenen 2010; Maloney and Sarrias 2017). Government-owned companies tend to be managed badly. Firms with diffuse ownership (many shareholders) tend to be among the best. Family-owned firms, which are prevalent in developing countries, tend to have substantially worse managerial performance. Family owners may not contract professional managers, in part because they wish to pass management to elder sons, who may be less talented (Lemos and Scur 2016). Alternatively, family owners may be unwilling to hire professional management because weak contracting environments make it difficult for owners to maintain control (Bloom and Van Reenen 2007; McKenzie and Woodruff, 2012).

Iacovone, Maloney, and Tsivanidas (2017), employing the Bureau van Dijk Orbis and the World Value Survey (WVS) data for Europe, show a strong relationship between family ownership and the contracting environment measured either as the rule of law index by the Worldwide Governance Indicators (figure 5.4) or as reported levels of trust in individuals from the World Values Survey. They find that weak trust is associated with more family management and having 25 percent lower productivity levels. Reluctance to bring in the necessary professional skills limits learning, the scale of operations, and the upgrading and innovating that can be undertaken.

FIGURE 5.4 **Weaker Contracting Environments Lead to a Higher Incidence of Family Management and Weaker Capabilities**

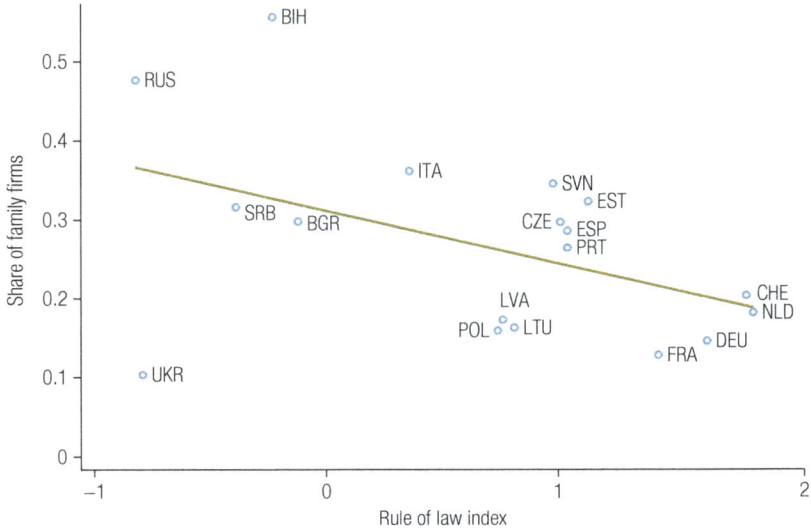

Source: Iacovone, Maloney, and Tsivanidas 2017.

External Sources of Learning

The value of external sources of learning has been long stressed by the innovation literature. This has been emphasized by the open innovation paradigm (Chesbrough 2003), establishing the importance of external collaboration and using external ideas in the process of technology adoption and technology generation. In this section, we focus on a specific set of channels that can facilitate learning and the accumulation of managerial and technical capabilities through participation in international markets and links to MNEs and GVCs.

Learning through Participation in International Markets

Firms that trade or operate across borders have better management practices (Bloom and Van Reenen 2010; Maloney and Sarrias 2017). Determining to what extent firms are learning from their international contacts or whether only better firms can operate successfully abroad is challenging. However, a sizeable literature explores this relationship.

Trade and Capabilities Building

As stressed in Chapter 3, firms can learn and accumulate capabilities for innovation by participating in international markets. First, openness to trade increases competition and increases the incentives for knowledge accumulation and innovation discussed earlier. Second, openness increases access to technology via imported inputs.[4]

In addition, access to export markets enables firms to upgrade their capabilities by learning about more sophisticated and contested markets, and enabling increases in scale.[5] Using firm-level data across 43 developing countries, Almeida and Fernandes (2008) find that exporters and importers are more likely to introduce technological innovations than nontrading firms are.

Firms that neither export nor import are less likely to introduce product innovations, appear to be worse managed, and are less likely to do R&D than firms that export, import, or do both (ES data for 44 countries in four regions—figure 5.5). Innovation and R&D incidence are higher in firms that both export and import, while managerial practices are also generally good for this group and for firms that import but do not export. Firms that export but do not import also show higher innovation activities incidence and are better managed than firms not exposed to trade—although less so than the other trade groups, perhaps because of being concentrated in low-value-added sectors.

The direction of causation between trade exposure, better quality management, and innovation may differ depending on the form of exposure to international markets. Importing firms learn through access to foreign inputs and technologies, whereas exporting firms can learn from competing in more demanding markets. At the same time, better-quality firms tend to have greater success in meeting the more stringent standards faced in international markets. Having these capabilities is key for competing in quality in world markets.[6]

There is some microevidence for the view that the direction of causality runs from upgrading capabilities to trade. Iacovone and Javorcick (2012), using detailed information on a sample of Mexican firms over the period 1994–2004, find evidence of quality

FIGURE 5.5 Firms Exposed to International Markets Have Better Managerial Practices and Are More Innovative

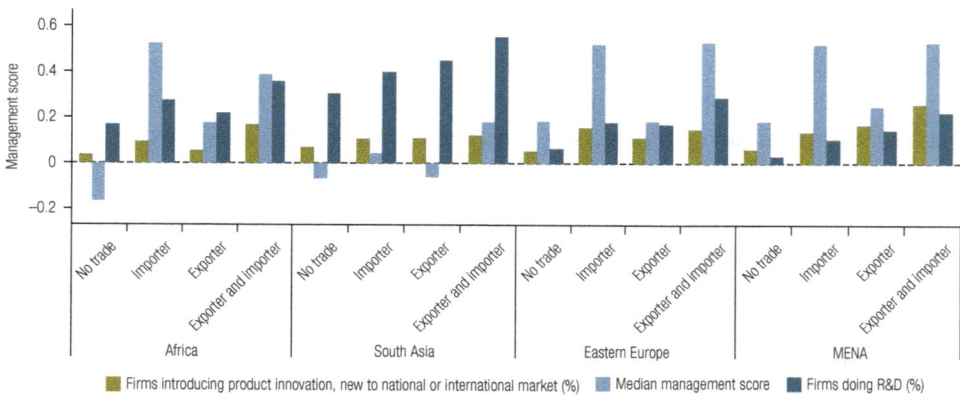

Source: Elaboration using Enterprise Survey data (www.enterprisesurveys.org).
Note: MENA = Middle East and North Africa; R&D = research and development.

The Innovation Paradox

upgrading (indicated by an increase in unit values) prior to entry into export markets. Also, Cirera, Marin, and Markwald (2015), using a unique dataset of Brazilian firms, show how innovative efforts and the strategic positioning of firms in the domestic market are key elements in explaining firms' export diversification (innovation). Thus, although there is evidence of learning through participating in international markets, improving firm capabilities also improves innovation via upgrading and export diversification.

Learning through Links to Foreign Direct Investment

Foreign Direct Investment and Spillovers

Links to foreign direct investment (FDI) can also provide important learning opportunities to firms. Firms with at least 25 percent foreign ownership[7] tend to be better managed, and are more likely to perform R&D and introduce product innovations (figure 5.6). Foreign firms may be a source of capabilities for domestic firms, but this cannot be measured on the basis of the ES dataset.

FDI can bring new technologies to a country through direct investments in subsidiaries. In some cases, this can trigger spillovers to local firms via supply links or by training staff that then create spin-offs or work for local companies. In a set of case studies, Chandra (2006) shows that FDI played a critical role in diversification and creation of new sectors in various developing countries (examples include electronics in Malaysia and Taiwan, China; salmon in Chile; fisheries in Uganda; and, to a lesser extent, horticulture in Kenya). FDI designed to serve local markets can also have positive effects on innovation via supplier linkages[8] and by offering products at lower prices, which increases competition facing some firms and lowers the cost of inputs for others.

FIGURE 5.6   Foreign-Owned Firms Are More Innovative

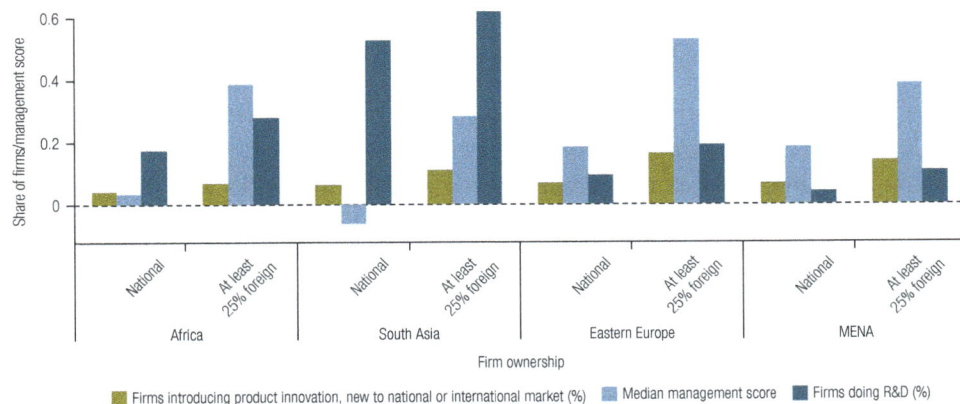

Source: Elaboration using Enterprise Survey data (www.enterprisesurveys.org).
Note: MENA = Middle East and North Africa. R&D = research and development.

However, in many cases large MNE presence has not induced any domestic capabilities spillovers. For example, there was little knowledge transfer to domestic SMEs from large electronics MNEs in Mexico. In addition, part of the justification of Singapore's aggressive policies to develop skills and firm capabilities was the lack of spillovers from existing MNEs.

Technology transfer from exposure to international markets and foreign-owned firms requires complementary capabilities on the part of domestic firms. Lall (1992) stresses the importance of linkage capabilities to effectively use and internalize knowledge flows. The ability to learn and adopt new capabilities and technologies requires the appropriate skills and managerial processes. Fu (2008) provides evidence that the spillovers from FDI in China are larger in regions with more educated workers. In most of the case studies of new sectors reviewed in Chandra (2006), local industrial development, training, and R&D activities play an important role in absorbing know-how through FDI. In this regard, capacity-building programs for local firms are critical to gaining benefits from FDI.

Capabilities transfer, however, has some differences from technology transfer. Technology transfer tends to be more sector specific, whereas capabilities, especially managerial practices, can be transferred from other sectors. In one of the few papers analyzing directly the transfer of managerial practices from MNEs to domestic firms, Fu (2012) finds evidence of the transfer of managerial practices from MNEs to U.K. firms. Domestic firms appear to adopt some managerial practices, and the transfer is not only intrasector but also occurs thorough upstream and downstream links to MNEs in other sectors. There is, however, some heterogeneity in adopting these managerial practices, and absorptive capacity and commitment from managers are critical to effectively adopt these practices and facilitate learning. In addition, these positive spillovers generally occur in capabilities that are more likely to be codified and that require less tacit knowledge (Fu, Helmers, and Zhang 2012).

Learning and Upgrading through Participation in GVCs

Perhaps one of the most valuable external sources of capabilities is participation in GVCs. GVCs are complex production systems made of multiple firms located in different countries linked together by multilayered sourcing networks and fast-evolving, technology-enabled business models (Gereffi, Humphrey, and Sturgeon 2005). Firms in such production networks, whether linked through "arm's-length transactions" where the buyer and seller act independently or through intragroup investment and trade, enjoy significant opportunities for transferring capabilities and absorbing foreign technology and innovation. Firms embedded in multinational production earn higher returns on innovation, face lower costs for R&D, and exploit scale better than firms selling to domestic markets (Guadalupe, Kuzmina, and Thomas 2012). As GVC participation becomes more stable, opportunities expand for supplier firms to become acquainted with newer, more advanced technologies, skills, and processes (Kugler and Verhoogen 2012), thereby boosting process innovation and even product innovation.

At the same time, relationships within GVCs differ, which affects the form and extent of technology transfer. For example, "captive" GVC relationships, where low-competence suppliers are heavily dependent on lead firms for highly codified, complex technical specifications, may offer little transfer of capabilities. By contrast, GVC relationships may be characterized by high interdependence between competent suppliers and lead firms, where upgrading opportunities are substantial and occur in both directions. Mariscal and Taglioni (2017) describe the degree of technological upgrading that is likely to occur in GVCs, depending on the level of technical dependence, forms of competition, costs of switching to alternate producers, codification and complexity of technical instructions, and competence of suppliers (table 5.1).

TABLE 5.1 Parameters Determining Firms' Governance Structures

	Governance Structure:					
		Market	**Captive**	**Hierarchical**	**Modular**	**Relational**
Factors influencing the governance structures	Nature of relational dependence between firms	Independent	High dependence	High dependence	Medium-high dependence	High dependence
	Technical dependence	Independent	High dependence	High dependence	Low dependence	High interdependence
	Price vs. nonprice competition	Price	Price (buyer-driven GVCs), nonprice (producer-driven GVCs)	Price or nonprice	Price or nonprice	Nonprice
	Switching costs to alternative producers	Low	Low	Medium, existence of sunk costs	Medium-high, existence of sunk costs	High
	Codification transactions	High	High	Low	Both minimally and highly codified transactions	Both lowly and highly codified transactions
	Complexity transactions	Low	High	High	High	High
	Competence suppliers	High	Low	Low	High	High
	Upgrading opportunity	High	Low	Depends on absorptive capacity of supplier	Low within relationship upgrading, high outside relationship	High, bidirectional

Source: Mariscal and Taglioni 2017.

Note: GVC = global value chain.

Mariscal and Taglioni (2017) describe how the different stages of GVC engagement have different implications for the capabilities requirements and learning opportunities (a more detailed description of the different stages of GVCs and how these affect capabilities can be found in annex 5A). These stages can be divided into: (1) the *protoconnecting stage*, where the ability to reach a minimum scale of transactions is key; (2) the *connected stage*, which requires a few basic capabilities (for example, production or managerial abilities, cheap access to key inputs of the production process) and the ability to correctly evaluate and leverage the firm core competences; (3) the *upgrading stage*, which requires high standards of quality and delivery and accordingly deep relationships with other participants in the chain; and (4) the *mature stage*, where the firm is in direct relationship with, or becomes, a lead firm, turnkey supplier, trading platform, or global buyer, requiring sufficient organizational capital and the ability to align own and buyer product market development and procurement strategies. Figure 5.7 summarizes the different types of innovation required at each stage, which can be used to guide innovation policy efforts.

At the initial stages of GVC engagement, firms need to have a correct understanding of their own capabilities and the basic skills they can provide. As connections to GVCs are established, more emphasis should be placed on fostering adaptive change and innovation through imitation of a narrow set of activities. Training by the lead firm or turnkey suppliers in a GVC and fostering turnover of managers from the foreign-owned firms to domestic firms may accelerate the process of learning.

As GVC engagement deepens, the institutional set-up to foster learning and upgrading should focus on policies that enable firms to acquire high-quality inputs at international prices to boost the quality of production, and that support the learning of

FIGURE 5.7   **Types of Innovation Differ at Different Stages of GVC Engagement**

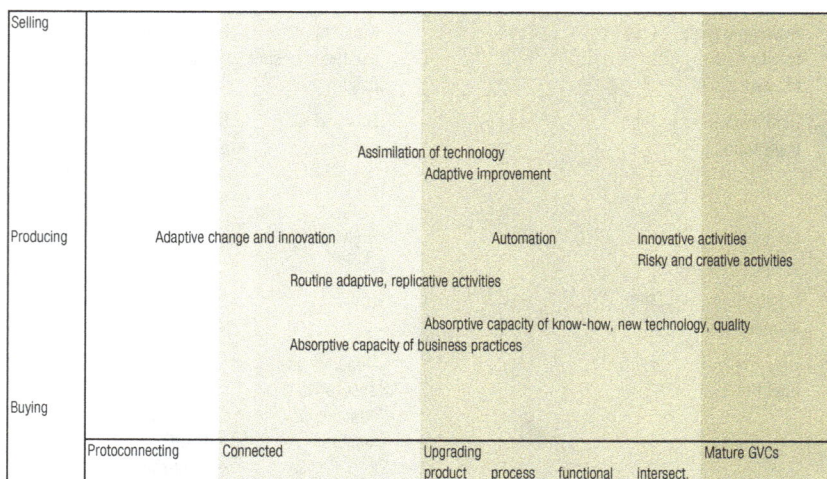

Source: Mariscal and Taglioni 2017.
Note: GVC = global value chain.

frontier business practices. Some of these instruments are discussed in chapter 7. Public support may be beneficial for firms' efforts to meet international standards, to automate production, and to achieve other adaptive improvements. Upgrading at the higher stages also requires the sort of complementary factors that were discussed in chapter 3—educational systems that focus on teaching advanced skills, improving the quality of vocational training, and promoting a general culture of meritocracy at all skill levels. Frederick's (2016) work on the apparel GVC in China provides a sector-level illustration of some of these dynamics (see box 5.2).

BOX 5.2

Lessons from China for Apparel Sector Innovation and Upgrading

China has been remarkably successful in the apparel industry, improving in all key areas and growing rapidly. China has performed well on numerous measures of upgrading (process, product, end-market, function, and intersectoral) by having a broad range of product categories, full-package offerings, "good-enough" compliance, and a distinct value proposition that entailed affordability, reliability, and the development of a good reputation (Frederick 2016).

Frederick (2016) attributes this to the following innovation policies and complementary factors:

- Industrial polices geared toward upgrading and assessing global dynamics, including grants and loans for technological upgrading; incentives for machinery to make more advanced products while removing incentives for lower-value products; targeting markets other than the EU and the United States, as well as the domestic market; investments in textile capabilities and technology and growth in key material segments; a "go-out" policy to encourage investment in low-value-added segments in neighboring countries; and support for domestic brand development
- A functional division of labor between sales and production, making use of agents and intermediaries to promote manufacturers and link up with global buyers
- Investments in connectivity through sourcing offices in Hong Kong SAR, China and near airports in mainland China that enable buyers to be both close and comfortable
- Continuous innovation and modifications in production processes to keep costs low and keep up with emerging competitors
- Developing long-term relationships that build on improvements in quality, speed, and price competition
- Correctly assessing the tipping point for buyers (where they may be inclined to change suppliers) and not exceeding those

Although China's success cannot directly be replicated, it does offer lessons for other countries, including the importance of developing long-term relationships and ties with foreign firms, targeting emerging markets without highly developed buyer–supplier relationships, and targeting niches within a highly diversified industry. China's success also offers opportunities for other countries through partnering with Chinese firms, both to transfer skills and knowledge and to access the Chinese market, and taking advantage of rising labor costs in China to undercut these suppliers.

Source: Engel and Taglioni 2017.

Concluding Remarks

In this chapter, we have examined factors that drive the accumulation of managerial capabilities. This is a learning process affected by, among other factors, capital, competition, and ownership structure as well as learning opportunities outside the firm: international trade, links to MNEs, and participation in GVCs. Getting the most of these interactions requires complementary investments from the recipient firms to improve absorptive capacity, especially in the case of links to MNEs.

One external factor missing in this chapter is the critical role of government policies to support capability upgrading. Convergence to the managerial frontier cannot be achieved only by getting rid of badly managed firms; it also requires firms across the distribution to innovate in their organization and management practices. The instruments to support this upgrading in the context of the overall policy mix supporting innovation are discussed in the next part of the report.

Annex 5A Capabilities at Different Stages of Connection in GVCs

In the framework proposed by Mariscal and Taglioni (2017), engagement starts with the *protoconnecting stage*, in which reaching a minimum scale of transactions is key. This is the case both in the sourcing and in the selling functions. The existence of intermediaries that play a matching role can help firms move the first steps toward international engagement (Ahn, Amiti, and Weinstein 2011). After having achieved significant size, the large intermediaries may become themselves companies engaging in GVCs, as traders or by gradually adding value through expanding into processing for some of the immediate upstream or downstream functions (Blum, Claro, and Horstmann 2010).

The actual initial stage of GVC engagement is the pure *connection stage*. At this stage, engagement in GVCs is not a robust situation but a rather unstable one and subject to market forces that may exclude the firm from continuing the connection (Blum, Claro, and Horstmann 2013). In this initial stage of engagement there will be important sunk costs of entry, which are partially determined by the organizational and managerial ability of firms (Arkolakis 2010). The relatively basic degree of capabilities needed to enter GVCs makes entry and exit from engagement pervasive, likely, but also flickering and unstable. At such a stage, it is mostly about meeting several minimum requirements, that is, a few basic capabilities that allow the firm to connect to either a foreign market or a lead firm. Basic capabilities (for example, production or managerial abilities, cheap access to key inputs of the production process) and the ability to correctly evaluate and leverage the firm core competences are the crucial elements to connecting to GVCs. From a sourcing perspective, this means that the firm is able to streamline its processes and product scope while also complementing well its production with a proper and effective access to the market of inputs (Csillag and Koren 2011; Goldberg et al. 2010). From a selling perspective, the key capability is about learning to align its goals to those of its actual and potential buyers and modulate its processes to fit seamlessly in their production processes (Kasahara and Rodriguez 2008; Van Biesebroeck 2005; De Loecker 2006).

As firms slowly move toward better connectivity, their learning processes as well as capabilities to target demand (Dhingra 2013) and absorptive capacities (De Loecker 2007, 2013; Iacovone and Crespi 2010) become key in shaping decisions. Examples of firms moving toward better connectivity include firms that evolve from occasionally supplying materials, components, or services to a global buyer (lead firm, trader, or turnkey supplier) to becoming registered suppliers of the same buyer. Alternatively, firms may go from being engaged marginally and intermittently in export/import activity to sourcing foreign goods and services and exporting to the global markets as part of the core business.

Upgrading (stage 3, figure 4.7) will rely on capabilities of handling greater firm size and complexity, increasingly effective sourcing strategies, and more sophisticated learning. An increase in firms' average size and productivity through more abundant capital and skills use is important for upgrading (Bustos 2011). Greater product complexity can be achieved by reinforcing intermediate management layers relative to plant workers (Caliendo et al. 2015). Sourcing is also key for upgrading. As part of this process, the organization of procurement practices and sourcing becomes an integral part of a firm's strategy and an increasingly important part of its competitive advantage (Antràs and Yeaple 2014). It matters not only which country you source from but also which domestic supplier links you create (Fieler, Eslava, and Xu 2014). On both the buying and the selling sides, feedback loops are strong for firms that manage to upgrade. On the selling side, connection to demanding and refined customers supports such learning (Fieler, Eslava, and Xu 2014). These have high standards of quality and delivery, and accordingly engage in deep relationship development with their suppliers. Selling to such customers already leads to upgrading inputs and skills, but the firm's ability to absorb quickly new technology and know-how, and to improve quality, determines the difference in performance relative to competitors (Costinot, Vogel, and Wang 2011).

The more firms upgrade toward the most *mature stages of GVC production* (stage 4, figure 4.7), the more they are in direct relation with, or become themselves, lead firms, turnkey suppliers, trading platforms, or global buyers. The two core capabilities of firms in the mature stage of GVCs are organizational capital and the ability to align own and buyer product market development and procurement strategies (or strategies of vertical and horizontal integration, within and across the boundaries of the firm). A most defining element for MNEs is the type of ownership (Yeaple 2013). Here core competences acquire a bias toward organizational capital because MNEs are defined by their broad spectrum of goods in manufacturing and services. Firms at this stage of engagement narrowly focus on core competences, which characteristically involves a strong focus on R&D, quality, brand, and strategies of vertical and horizontal integration (Di Comite, Thisse, and Vandenbussche 2014); and their comparative advantage will be based on offering highly specialized products (goods, services, and business models) at the technology frontier (Schott 2004). Of course, productive knowledge also matters, but this is applied so broadly across industries and products that product-specific expertise is not the defining capability of these firms anymore.

Such strong interdependence between buyers and suppliers comes with large benefits for all parties concerned. Suppliers connect to the most technologically relevant buyers with a large learning potential and virtuous feedback loops through direct and indirect exposure to new ways of managing and organizing production (Kee 2015). Product complexity also increases, with products themselves being both more elaborate and containing more value added, often in the form of embedded services and sophisticated technology (Kee and Tang 2016). From the skills perspective, companies increasingly specialize in nonroutine tasks (while outsourcing routine ones), and such nonroutine tasks become the key comparative advantage of the firm and increasingly central in the firm's organization. In fact, they are the worker-level reflection of a more complex organizational culture and structure, with multiple layers of high and middle management, where very specialized skills are transmitted through on-the-job learning and formal and informal training (Caliendo, Monte, and Rossi-Hansberg 2015). This is accompanied by functional upgrading, which is the process of altering the set of functions in which the firm is engaged. It involves increasing the set of functions the firm is doing and/or abandoning others, and it notably includes moving beyond purely production activities to more service-intensive and organizational tasks, like marketing, finance, innovation, product development, and so on.

Notes

1. Because of these two competing effects, Aghion et al. (2005) suggest that the relationship between innovation and competition follows an inverted U shape. See also Hashmi (2011) for the U-shape relationship revisited.

2. Data that track managerial performance over time for a consistent set of firms are generally unavailable, but an approximation for the degree of managerial quality over the life cycle can be based on the age of firms in each survey cross-section.

3. To name just two titans in late industrializing management history: Godai Tomoatsu, the father of Japanese industry, was one of a handful of Satsuma students who, against imperial law, studied in the United Kingdom to learn Western techniques. Dorabji Tata, a major founder of the Tata group in India, studied at Cambridge.

4. An empirical literature deals with the impact of increased openness on technology adoption indirectly by analyzing the impact of trade reform and increased imports on productivity. The main finding is that trade reform increases productivity by enabling firms to adopt better technologies thanks to cheaper imports, or by increasing competition. See Amiti and Konings (2007) for Indonesia, Kasahara and Rodriguez (2008) and Kasahara and Lapham (2013) for Chile, Luong (2011) for Mexico, and Muendler (2004), Schor (2004), and Cirera et al. (2015) for Brazil.

5. See Clerides, Lach, and Tybout (1998) for a definition of learning by exporting. Silva, Africano, and Afonso (2010) provide a detailed survey of the literature on learning by exporting. Further, Martins and Yang (2009) provide a meta-analysis for 33 empirical studies testing the hypothesis that firms become more productive after entering export markets.

6. Sutton (2007) develops a general equilibrium model where country capabilities are the core element of competition, and different costs and quality advantages determine market structure and incomes. In this model, the ability of countries to develop or accumulate these capabilities to compete in quality is a key determinant of their income per capita.

7. The ES data do not have information on the type of foreign investment.

8. Iacovone et al. (2015) show how the establishment of Walmart in Mexico induced and increased innovation efforts and raised productivity of local suppliers.

References

Aghion, Philippe, Nick Bloom, Richard Blundell, Rachel Griffith, and Peter Howitt. 2005. "Competition and Innovation: An Inverted-U Relationship." *Quarterly Journal of Economics* 120 (2): 701–28.

Ahn, JaeBin, Mary Amiti, and David E. Weinstein. 2011. "Trade Finance and the Great Trade Collapse." *American Economic Review* 101 (3): 298–302.

Almeida, Rita, and Ana Margarida Fernandes. 2008. "Openness and Technological Innovations in Developing Countries: Evidence from Firm-Level Surveys." *Journal of Development Studies* 44 (5): 701–27.

Amiti, Mary, and Jozef G. Konings. 2007. "Trade Liberalization, Intermediate Inputs, and Productivity: Evidence from Indonesia." *American Economic Review* 97 (5): 1611–38.

Antràs, Pol, and Stephen R. Yeaple. 2014. "Multinational Firms and the Structure of International Trade." In *Handbook of International Economics*, edited by Gita Gopinath, Elhanan Helpman, and Kenneth Rogoff, 55–130. New York: Elsevier.

Arkolakis, Costas. 2010. "Market Penetration Costs and the New Consumers Margin in International Trade." *Journal of Political Economy* 118 (6): 1151–99.

Bloom, Nicholas, Erik Brynjolfsson, Lucia Foster, Ron S. Jarmin, Megha Patnaik, Itay Saporta-Eksten, and John Van Reenen. 2017. "What Drives Differences in Management?" NBER Working Paper No. W23300, National Bureau of Economic Research, Cambridge, MA.

Bloom, Nicholas, Mirko Draca, and John Van Reenen. 2016. "Trade Induced Technical Change? The Impact of Chinese Imports on Innovation, IT, and Productivity." *Review of Economic Studies* 83 (1): 87–117.

Bloom, Nicholas, and John Van Reenen. 2007. "Measuring and Explaining Management Practices across Firms and Countries." *Quarterly Journal of Economics* 122 (4): 1351–1408.

———. 2010. "Why Do Management Practices Differ across Firms and Countries?" *Journal of Economic Perspectives* 24 (1): 203–24.

Blum, Bernardo S., Sebastian Claro, and Ignatius Horstmann. 2010. "Facts and Figures on Intermediated Trade." *American Economic Review* 100: 419–23.

Blum, Bernardo S., Claro Sebastian, Ignatius J. Horstmann. 2013. "Occasional and Perennial Exporters." *Journal of International Economics* 90 (1): 65–74.

Bustos, Paula. 2011. "The Impact of Trade Liberalization on Skill Upgrading Evidence from Argentina." Working Paper No. 1189, Department of Economics and Business, Universitat Pompeu Fabra, Barcelona, Spain.

Caliendo, Lorenzo, Giordano Mion, Luca David Opromolla, and Esteban Rossi-Hansberg. 2015. "Productivity and Organization in Portuguese Firms." CESifo Working Paper Series 5678, CESifo Group, Munich, Germany.

Caliendo, Lorenzo, Ferdinando Monte, and Esteban Rossi-Hansberg. 2015. "The Anatomy of French Production Hierarchies." *Journal of Political Economy* 123 (4): 809–52.

Chandra, Vandana. 2006. *Technology, Adaptation, and Exports: How Some Developing Countries Got It Right.* Washington, DC: World Bank.

Chesbrough, Henry William. 2003. *Open Innovation: The New Imperative for Creating and Profiting from Technology.* Boston: Harvard Business School Press.

Cirera, Xavier, Daniel Lederman, Juan A. Máñez, María E. Rochina, and Juan A. Sanchis. 2015. "The Export-Productivity Link for Brazilian Manufacturing Firms." *Economics* 9: 1–31.

Cirera, Xavier, Anabel Marin, and Ricardo Markwald. 2015. "Explaining Export Diversification through Firm Innovation Decisions: The Case of Brazil." *Research Policy* 44 (10): 1962–73.

Clerides, Sofronis, Saul Lach, and James Tybout. 1998. "Is Learning by Exporting Important? Micro-Dynamic Evidence from Colombia, Mexico and Morocco." *Quarterly Journal of Economics* 113 (3): 903–48.

Cooke, Fang Lee. 2008. *Competition, Strategy and Management in China.* Basingstoke, UK: Palgrave Macmillan.

Costinot, Arnaud, Jonathan Vogel, and Su Wang. 2011. "An Elementary Theory of Global Supply Chains." NBER Working Paper 16936, National Bureau of Economic Research, Cambridge, MA.

Csillag, Márton, and Miklós Koren. 2011. "Machines and Machinists: Capital-Skill Complementarity from an International Trade Perspective." CEPR Discussion Paper No. 8317, Centre for Economic Policy Research, London.

De Loecker, Jan. 2006. "Industry Dynamics and Productivity." PhD dissertation, Catholic University of Leuven.

———. 2007. "Do Exports Generate Higher Productivity? Evidence from Slovenia. *Journal of International Economics* 73 (1): 69–98.

Dhingra, Swati. 2013. "Trading Away Wide Brands for Cheap Brands." *American Economic Review* 103 (6): 2554–84.

Di Comite, Francesco, Jacques-François Thisse, and Hylke Vandenbussche. 2014. "Verti-zontal Differentiation in Export Markets." ECB Working Paper Series No. 1680, European Central Bank, Frankfurt-am-Main.

Engel, Jakob, and Daria Taglioni. 2017. "Global Value Chain Development Report 2017: Measuring and Analyzing the Impact of GVCs on Economic Development." World Bank, Washington, DC.

Fieler, Ana Cecilia, Marcela Eslava, and Daniel Yi Xu. 2014. "Trade, Technology and Input Linkages: A Theory with Evidence from Colombia." NBER Working Paper No. 19992, National Bureau of Economic Research, Cambridge, MA.

Frederick, Stacey. 2016. "Upgrading in the Apparel and Electronics Global Value Chains (GVCs): A Multi-layered Approach: China Country Case." Background Paper, United Nations Industrial Development Organization, Vienna.

Fu, Xiaolan. 2008. "Managerial Knowledge Spillovers from FDI: Evidence from UK Survey Data." Paper presented at the Academy of International Business Annual Conference, Milan, Italy.

———. 2012. "Foreign Direct Investment and Managerial Knowledge Spillovers through the Diffusion on Management Practices." *Journal of Management Studies* 49 (5): 970–99.

Fu, Xiaolan, Christian Helmers, and Jing Zhang. 2012. "The Two Faces of Foreign Management Capabilities: Spillovers and Competition from FDI in UK Retail Sector." *International Business Review* 21 (1): 71–88.

Gereffi, Gary, John Humphrey, and Timothy Sturgeon. 2005. "The Governance of Global Value Chains." *Review of International Political Economy* 12 (1): 78–104.

Goldberg, Pinelopi K., Amit Khandelwal, Nina Pavcnik, and Petia Topalova. 2010. "Imported Intermediate Inputs and Domestic Product Growth: Evidence from India." *Quarterly Journal of Economics* 125 (4): 1727–67.

Guadalupe, Maria, Olga Kuzmina, and Catherine Thomas. 2012. "Innovation and Foreign Ownership." *American Economic Review* 102 (7): 3594–627.

Hashmi, Aamir Rafique. 2011. "Competition and Innovation: The Inverted-U Relationship Revisited." Working Paper No. 1101, Department of Economics, National University of Singapore.

Iacovone, Leonardo, and Gustavo A. Crespi. 2010. "Catching Up with the Technological Frontier: Micro-Level Evidence on Growth and Convergence." *Industrial and Corporate Change* 19 (6): 2073–96.

Iacovone, Leonardo, and Beata Javorcik. 2012. "Getting Ready: Preparation for Exporting." CEPR Discussion Papers 8926, Centre for Economic Policy Research, Oxford, UK.

Iacovone, Leonardo, Beata Javorcik, Wolfgang Keller, and James Tybout. 2015. "Supplier Responses to Walmart's Invasion in Mexico." *Journal of International Economics* 95 (1): 1–15.

Iacovone, Leonardo, William F. Maloney, and Nick Tsivanidis. 2017. "Family Firms and Contractual Institutions." World Bank, Washington, DC.

Kasahara, Hiroyuki, and Beverly Lapham. 2013. "Productivity and the Decision to Import and Export: Theory and Evidence." *Journal of International Economics* 89 (2): 297–316.

Kasahara, Hiroyuki, and Joel Rodriguez. 2008. "Does the Use of Imported Intermediates Increase Productivity? Plant-Level Evidence." *Journal of Development Economics* 87 (1): 106–18.

Kee, Hiau Looi. 2015. "Local Intermediate Inputs and the Shared Supplier Spillovers of Foreign Direct Investment." *Journal of Development Economics* 87 (January): 106–18.

Kee, Hiau Looi, and Heiwai Tang. 2016. "Domestic Value Added in Exports: Theory and Firm Evidence from China." *American Economic Review* 106 (6): 1402–36.

Kugler, Maurice, and Eric Verhoogen. 2012. "Prices, Plant Size, and Product Quality." *Review of Economic Studies* 79 (1): 307–39.

Lall, Sanjaya. 1992. "Technological Capabilities and Industrialization." *World Development* 20 (2): 165–86.

Lemos, Renata, and Daniela Scur. 2016. "All in the Family? CEO Succession and Firm Organization." CSAE Working Paper WPS/2016-29, Centre for the Study of African Economies, Oxford, UK. https://www.csae.ox.ac.uk/workingpapers/pdfs/csae-wps-2016-29.pdf.

Luong, Tuan Anh. 2011. "The Impact of Input and Output Tariffs on Firms' Productivity: Theory and Evidence." *Review of International Economics* 19 (5): 821–35.

Maloney, William F. 2017. "Policies to Increase Firm Capabilities: Lessons from Japan and Singapore." Working Paper, World Bank, Washington, DC.

Maloney, William F., and Mauricio Sarrias. 2017. "Convergence to the Managerial Frontier." *Journal of Economic Behavior & Organization* 134 (C): 284–306.

Mariscal, Asier, and Daria Taglioni. 2017. "GVCs as Source of Firm Capabilities." Unpublished report, World Bank, Washington, DC.

Martins, Pedro S., and Yong Yang. 2009. "The Impact of Exporting on Firm Productivity: A Meta Analysis of the Learning-by-Exporting Hypothesis." *Review of World Economics* 145 (3): 431–45.

McKenzie, David, and Christopher Woodruff. 2012. "What Are We Learning from Business Training and Entrepreneurship Evaluations around the Developing World?" IZA Discussion Paper No. 6895, Institute for the Study of Labor, Bonn.

Muendler, Marc-Andreas. 2004. "Trade, Technology, and Productivity: A Study of Brazilian Manufacturers 1986–1998." CESifo Working Paper No. 1148, CESifo Group, Munich.

Rijkers, Bob, Caroline Freund, and Antonio Nucifora. 2015. "All in the Family State Capture in Tunisia." Policy Research Working Paper 6801, World Bank, Washington, DC.

Schor, Adriana. 2004. "Heterogeneous Productivity Response to Tariff Reduction: Evidence from Brazilian Manufacturing Firms." *Journal of Development Economics* 75 (2): 373–96.

Schott, Peter K. 2004. "Across-Product versus Within-Product Specialization in International Trade." *Quarterly Journal of Economics* 119 (2): 646–77.

Silva, Armando, Ana Africano, and Óscar Afonso. 2010. "Learning-by-Exporting: What We Know and What We Would Like to Know." University of Porto FEP Working Papers No. 364, University of Porto, Porto, Portugal.

Sutton, John. 2007. "Quality, Trade and the Moving Window: The Globalisation Process." *Economic Journal* 117 (524): F469–98.

Van Biesebroeck, Johannes. 2005. "Exporting Raises Productivity in Sub-Saharan African Manufacturing Firms." *Journal of International Economics* 67 (2): 373–91.

World Management Survey. 2012. http://worldmanagementsurvey.org/.

World Value Survey, wave 7, http://www.worldvaluessurvey.org/wvs.jsp/.

Yeaple, Stephen Ross. 2013. "The Multinational Firm." *Annual Review of Economics* 5: 193–217.

PART II

Government Capabilities and Policy

The evidence presented in part I of this report describes the nature of innovation in developing countries, the elements that explain the innovation paradox, and the critical role of managerial and organizational practices as a key innovation capability. In this second part, the report focuses on how governments can better support the accumulation and development of innovation capabilities. This requires confronting what we label the *innovation policy dilemma*: for developing countries, the greater magnitude of the market failures to be resolved and the multiplicity of missing complementary factors and institutions increase the complexity of innovation policy, at the same time that governments' capabilities to design, implement, and coordinate an effective *policy mix* to manage these failures and gaps are weaker.

Part II proposes a set of principles for agencies and the design of instruments to overcome this innovation policy dilemma. Chapter 6 describes a set of key principles for innovation policy making, and discusses how to strengthen policy capacity and agencies to effectively implement policies that enable firms to climb the capabilities escalator. Chapter 7 discusses the set of instruments that can facilitate the accumulation of innovation capabilities at different stages of technological development and, more important, the process through which the policy mix should be developed.

6. Supporting Innovation: Agencies and Government Capability

Introduction: The Innovation Policy Dilemma in Developing Countries

The previous chapters have established that countries farther from the frontier are more likely to lack critical innovation complementary factors across many markets and, in particular, firm capabilities. The logical extension of the innovation paradox is then why, given the potentially high returns, governments do not more actively engage in redressing these shortfalls.

Arguably, the answer is found in the fact that, while this increasing number of market and institutional failures in poorer countries augments the complexity of innovation policy, government ability to manage it decreases. As with firm capabilities, government capabilities are weaker farther from the frontier. This has often led to the absence of innovation on the policy agenda, ill-considered mimicking of advanced country institutional setups that may not respond to local issues, and, more generally, poor execution.

The chapter discusses some key principles, processes, and lessons to strengthen the capabilities needed in innovation agencies to develop an effective policy mix that supports innovation. It draws substantially on specific examples from recent evaluations using the Public Expenditure Reviews (PERs) in Science, Technology, and Innovation (STI) that have been implemented by the World Bank in a few Latin American countries (see box 6.1).

Core Elements of Good Innovation Policy Making

Governments require capabilities for policy making across four key dimensions:

1. Rationale and design of policy
2. Efficacy of implementation
3. Coherence of policies across the National Innovation System (NIS)
4. Policy consistency and predictability over time

The chapter takes up each of these in turn. Each dimension requires a set of government competencies in terms of human capital and policy processes that need to be built over time. The first refers to the ability to identify market failures and design

The Public Expenditure Review of Innovation Policy

The Public Expenditure Review (PER) on Science, Technology, and Innovation (STI) is an integrated and holistic evaluation of STI policies by the World Bank to help countries improve the quality of their policy making in innovation and allocate public resources to innovation more efficiently and effectively (see Correa, 2014, for an overview). By supporting the adoption of good practices in design, implementation, and coordination of innovation policy instruments, the PER facilitates strengthening the innovation policy mix, eliminating redundancies, and leveraging complementarities across the portfolio of instruments.

Specifically, the PER evaluates four stages of innovation policy interventions:

1. *General evaluation of the quality and coherence of the policy mix* based on the conditions of the country and its innovation system, including the portfolio mapping of STI programs and their assessment based on the coherence with existing innovation policy objectives
2. *Evaluation of the quality of design, implementation, and governance (functional analysis)* of existing instruments based on good practices
3. *Evaluation of the efficiency of existing instruments*, meaning their ability to produce the expected outputs with reasonable levels of resources
4. *Evaluation of the effectiveness of existing instruments and the system*, by analyzing their ability to generate the desired impact

Unlike traditional PERs, in the PER STI the unit of analysis is the individual innovation policy instrument, which allows evaluators to identify what is spent and with what objectives, as well as efficiency and effectiveness at a more detailed level.

appropriate policies. The second requires policy makers to be able to implement policies effectively, including evaluating, adapting, and modifying or terminating policies when needed. The third demands the ability to take an overview of the overall system and coordinate across ministries. The fourth needs policies that can maintain focus on the innovation agenda over time, overcoming fluctuations in political economy. None of these capabilities is easy to generate or maintain.

Rationale and Design of Innovation Policy

Designing policies appropriate to the local context requires a solid diagnostic of a problem to be redressed. Treating innovation policy in a systemic context does not imply that policy should be made by "organogram"—importing the same institutional boxes found in advanced country organizational maps (see Rodrik 2008; Andrews 2015; Andrews, Pritchett, and Woolcock 2013, 2017). Rather, as chapter 3 highlights, innovation can be low because of failures in many markets, some unrelated to the problems commonly facing advanced countries. Hence, a substantial effort is necessary to guarantee that policy solutions are aimed at the correct problem.

Market Failures

In the neoclassical tradition, policy is directed to resolving identified market failures. This both disciplines policy and informs its design. The traditional justification of innovation policy is based on some key market failures in knowledge markets (Arrow 1962; Nelson 1959):

1. ***Knowledge as a public good, spillovers, appropriability, and indivisibility.*** Knowledge shares some characteristics of *public goods*, such as nonexclusivity in consumption or nonexcludability in its use, which prevents agents that develop it from fully appropriating all the benefits generated. In other cases, innovation activities can *generate positive technological or knowledge externalities or spillovers* in other firms in the same cluster or location, such as the diffusion of a new technology, which also cannot be fully appropriated by the innovator. In addition, some of the knowledge investments needed for innovation are indivisible and may require large up-front investments that firms may not be able to do or afford by themselves.

2. ***Imperfect and asymmetric information.*** High uncertainty around the development, implementation, and commercialization of knowledge can generate significant *information asymmetries*[1] that result in lack of adequate financing of these activities or lack of ability to develop innovation projects.

3. ***Coordination failures.*** More generally, there can be significant coordination failures among actors in a system. As discussed in chapter 3, firms do not innovate alone and require the availability of complementary factors. In some cases, firms could coordinate their efforts in the provision of specific services such as certification or technology extension, but large information asymmetries prevent them from coordinating their efforts.

4. ***Missing or underdeveloped markets.*** In many developing countries, some of the important inputs needed to build firm capabilities, such as technical skills or business development services (BDS), are likely to be missing in the market.

Most innovation policies in advanced countries are driven by the need to resolve one or more of these failures. The first set of failures related to the characteristics of knowledge as a public good were developed in the context of a linear view of innovation that puts science and research and development (R&D) at the center stage, and that looks at innovation as primarily invention and technology generation. Although these are still important justifications for innovation policy, as introduced in part I, the first stage of the capabilities escalator is about developing the capabilities to be able to adopt existing technologies and knowledge and imitate existing product characteristics and attributes. In this context, some of these market failures, especially regarding imperfect and asymmetric information, can be more accentuated in countries farther away from the technological frontier.

False Failures: Lessons from the Expanded NIS

Figure 3.4 in chapter 3 suggests that low rates of innovation may be driven by failures in any number of markets working directly or through complementary factors. Firms may not innovate, not because of appropriation externalities, but because of weak firm capabilities, capital markets that do not permit longer-term borrowing, labor market barriers to reorganizing the workplace when new techniques are introduced, product market regulations or unfair playing fields that stifle demand. Alternatively, trade barriers may prohibit the import of necessary complementary machinery, or training programs may not be available to provide complementary labor. Hence, developing countries need to be especially careful in ensuring that they are solving the true problem and not simply assume a diagnosis common in advanced countries.

Systemic Failures

The NIS literature has expressed skepticism about the market failure approach and sees the innovation system as an array of interactions between firms and entrepreneurs—with bounded rationality—and institutions that are in constant evolution.[2] This approach is extremely useful in encouraging governments to think *systematically* about how a variety of necessary elements interact and need to be considered when designing innovation policies, much as chapter 3 encourages us to do.[3]

This report does not attempt to conclusively resolve the differences in these two approaches. Rather, it stresses that they cover a lot of common ground. Both accept the centrality of the firm and the importance of complementarities with factors of production and institutions to foster innovation activities (Maloney 2017). Many systemic issues can be recast through the lens of information asymmetries and coordination failures. For example, weak firm capabilities are seen in the NIS literature as reflecting systemic failures. These, in turn, may be manifestations of classic market failures: if financial markets are not lending for upgrading activities in SMEs, or if firms lack credible benchmarking of their managerial capabilities, an information asymmetry needs to be resolved. Infrastructure failures, such as missing research centers or quality certification (see chapter 7 for a more detailed description of these instruments)[4] can also be recast as problems of appropriability or coordination. Network failures again may be a problem of coordination among multiple actors, or information issues.[5]

These market failures, however, may in fact be much larger than those customarily assumed in the mainstream approach and hence justify the special emphases received in the systems literature. We can argue, as in the next chapter, that weak firm capabilities may be the result of asymmetric information (not knowing how to accumulate capabilities) or poorly functioning financial markets, but this does not in any way minimize the divergence from the standard view—that these are rational actors with full information—that such failures imply. Resolving them may be a very large task indeed.[6]

Working around Weak State Capability

A second reason for focusing on understanding the problem rather than on importing an institution from an advanced country organogram is that the agencies and ministries executing innovation policy are limited in their capabilities and this constrains the feasible set of policy measures to be taken. Hence, the public policy problem is how to resolve a documented failure subject to government capability constraints.

Clearly, improving the diagnostic, design, and execution capabilities of the government increases the set of possible policies. Unfortunately, the record on doing this is not encouraging. Some have even seen adverse outcomes from top-down initiatives where "a government succeeds in passing laws or creating new boxes in organization charts or declaring new administrative processes, but these 'reforms' are frequently not implemented or used" (Andrews and Pritchett, 2013, p. 1; see also Andrews 2013; Andrews, Pritchett, and Woolcock 2013). Furthermore, adding a steady supply of development aid or other finance triggered by nominal advances toward best practices can lead to "capability traps" where reforms are permanently ongoing but advances in functionality are small. Andrews, Pritchett, and Woolcock (2013) stress the perils of "isomorphic mimicry," where the outward forms of functional states and organizations are adopted to camouflage a persistent lack of function.

The critics of such top-down approaches stress that efforts to build capabilities should aim to solve problems in the local context as nominated and prioritized by local actors. These proponents of Problem Driven Iterative Adaptation (PDIA) prescribe experimentation with solutions to problems with iterative feedback, while engaging a broad set of actors in the first instance to ensure a given reform's viability and relevance, but in the second instance as a key part of a scaling strategy (Andrews, Pritchett, and Woolcock 2017). Here again, identifying the particular failure that needs to be remedied is the starting point of this iterative process.

The limitations of transplanting foreign good practices do not mean that those good practices are uninformative and should be rejected. First, good practices contain much insight into the kinds of incentives and design features that in other contexts have generated successful interventions. The diagnostics may often be similar, and the mechanisms proposed to remedy are potential building blocks for local policies. Second, it is not always so easy to identify what the relevant problems are. As Rodrik (2004) notes, the information flow from the private sector to policy makers is often poor. Where they exist, large business associations may represent only a small part of the private sector (not SMEs, for example). Careful surveys and focus groups can help, but, more fundamentally, firms often do not know what they do not know (see figure 7.5 in the next chapter). For example, the ubiquitous response that "taxes are too high" as the greatest obstacle to growth by firms with truly rudimentary management practices suggests a limited understanding of what is needed to improve firms' performance.

Finally, there may be several ways of resolving identified failures, and the best solution may depend on the context. For example, Camagni and Capello (2013) find that standard European innovation policies, such as R&D funding, facilitating foreign direct investment, or encouraging private-public R&D collaboration, among others, produce differing results across countries. Letting policy makers experiment and adapt on the basis of ongoing evaluation is most likely to allow for the evolution of appropriate solutions.

Managing High Levels of Complexity When Governments Lack the Capability to Do So

Although this governance dilemma has no simple resolution, there are several design lessons (see also box 6.2) that can be drawn to minimize policy failure.

Reducing failure dimensionality. The more complex the innovation project the more likely it is to fail. Although the NIS sketched in figure 3.4 suggests the large number of markets that need to function to maximize the returns from technological catch-up, minimizing to the degree possible the number of components of a particular initiative offers a higher probability of policy success. In early phases, a policy package focusing on raising firm capabilities while improving access to longer-term capital may be sufficient to generate substantial productivity gains (see chapter 7).

BOX 6.2

Good Innovation Policy Design Checklist

The project management and innovation literatures identifies the following key dimensions of good innovation policy design (RIME). These are evaluated in the PER review process.

1. Rationale:
   - Is there a documented market or system failure to be addressed?
   - Is there a clear statement of goals, beneficiaries, and measurable outcomes?
   - How will the proposed solution interact with the rest of the policy mix?
   - Does the proposed solution take into account how local context may make an alternative policy more efficient?
   - Does the measure consider the relative strengths of the public and private sectors?
   - Has the proposed solution anticipated potential capture in its design?
2. Intervention model:
   - Is there a logical model integrating theory, assumptions, and how inputs lead to outcomes and impacts?

3. Monitoring and evaluation methods:
   - Are there monitoring and evaluation (M&E) approaches and systems set up at the design stage?
   - Are there clear procedures for M&E feedback to inform the evolution of policy?

Source: Based on Rogers 2017; Wu and Ramesh 2014.

Weigh the relative strengths of markets and government (see, for example, Wu and Ramesh 2014). Choosing policies that minimize the need for high bureaucratic capabilities may lead to second-best design but better outcomes. In this regard, relying on private sector provision of services where possible or public-private partnerships and employing the capabilities of the latter can reduce the demands on the government.

Experiment with external services if domestic capabilities do not yet exist. Often the supply of services will be limited until a market is established. For instance, Italy drew on U.S. providers of extension services after World War II, and Singapore hired the Japanese Productivity Center to set up its firm upgrading program (See chapter 7). Another country recognized that it lacked the managerial capability to successfully staff a venture capital program and bought a share in a San Francisco venture capital fund with the understanding that its portfolio would include a large number of local projects.

Employ market incentives where feasible. In cases where government is required to redress a failure, for instance in firm upgrading or training schemes, employing market-type incentives is likely to lead to better allocation of resources. For example, the design of financing mechanisms is critical—whatever the subsidies the government provides, the *marginal* costs of training or extension policies should be paid by the beneficiaries so that the policy clearly fails if its beneficiaries do not subscribe. Several such mechanisms are discussed in more detail in the agencies section below.

Design to avoid capture. The likelihood of policy capture is also higher in countries with less established institutions, fledgling ability to monitor, and weaker autonomy so that mechanisms are necessary to prevent it. Science and technology ministries are often heavily lobbied by academic departments that lack a vision of how their research will help industry to achieve productivity growth. Countrywide training programs can become politically useful as "universities of the poor," but may be unaligned with private sector needs. Innovation support programs can often be captured by the same set of firms, some of which may be already performing R&D and innovation activities with little or no additionality from public funding. Having a broad set of actors supporting the design of such policies can be a mechanism for minimizing capture. For example, private sector participation on boards of directors or research institutions can help guide the overall direction toward industry collaboration.[7] Or, given that the academic community in many emerging countries is small and interconnected, research proposals may be vetted outside of the country. Market mechanisms in allocation aids in transparency and responsiveness.

The Need for Evaluating and Learning[8]

The previous discussion highlights the importance for policy design of a dynamic feedback loop, from design to implementation to evaluation and back to design. Building in an impact evaluation from the inception of the program, especially for policy instruments that are considered experimental or small-scale[9] pilot versions for informing future full-size or longer-term policies, will aid in programs design, and facilitate the termination of unsuccessful ones. Further, given that imported policies may function differently in the local context, monitoring and evaluation (M&E) also is important to tune up or locally test successful policies. For example, matching grants for innovative projects in Finland may have proved very successful in resolving the appropriation failure while encouraging collaboration among different agents in the system (Czarnitzki, Ebersberger, and Fier 2007). However, evaluations suggest that such approaches have not always been successful in developing countries (Campos et al. 2012) or in improving firm performance (see, for example, Becker 2015).

Evaluation can also provide a useful check on the political economy forces leading to the fragmentation and duplication of policies identified above, and helps instill a culture of justification and evaluation that encourages a more transparent and professional innovation policy.

Again, weak government capabilities can limit the impact of evaluations. First, they require high-level human capital to be implemented properly and specialized units to distill the main findings and integrate what is learned into policy design. Ideally evaluation departments should evolve to "perform six types of brokering activities: identifying knowledge users' needs, acquiring credible knowledge, feeding it to users, building networks between producers and users, accumulating knowledge over time and promoting an evidence-based culture" (Olejniczak, Raimondo, and Kupiec 2016; p. 1).[10] Hence, the evaluation function becomes tightly integrated with the design and information disseminations tasks. Partnering with external academia or multilateral agencies with installed capacity can help kick-start the evaluation agenda. Over time, the evolving network can offset the fact that, in practice, policy makers often cannot recognize the value of the feedback, and evaluation results are often underutilized in decision making.[11]

Critically, a greater embedding of evaluation can also ensure that policies are not only started but are also continued or terminated for solid empirical reasons (Teirlinck et al. 2013). Often, these decisions are driven more by ideological concerns, pressures from interest groups, or perceptions of program ineffectiveness than as the result of analytical performance assessment (Krause, Yi, and Feiock 2016). Programs survive for decades with no demonstration of efficacy. Proof of this can be found in the myriad instruments in many countries with budgets below US$100,000, a scale precluding any meaningful impact. Ongoing evaluation thus provides discipline in constructing and pruning the *policy mix*.

In sum, the design of the appropriate policies requires several elements (an example of design challenges facing even a good innovation policy performer is given in box 6.3). An empirical diagnostic can consider the possibility of false failures and show how inputs, activities, and outputs lead to outcomes and impacts, and affect specific stake-holders and audiences. Policy design also should reflect lessons from existing evidence and a consideration of the capabilities of the private and public sector agencies involved in executing the policy. A strategy for considering the views of targeted beneficiaries and procedures to minimizing capture are also necessary. Measurement and experimentation with iterative feedback should be used to modify the intervention in an ongoing fashion (see Dutz et al. 2014 for a description of learning and experimentation in innovation policy.) This is facilitated by having from the onset of the policy a clear, logical framework that lays out the problem to be solved, how the intervention is supposed to work, why it is preferred to plausible alternatives, how success will be measured, and how feedback from evaluations will alter design over time.

Implementing Innovation Policy Effectively

As is the case in the private sector, design and planning must be followed by effective implementation and this, too, tends to lag in developing countries. Many of the issues important for implementation are not specific to innovation but are rather

---

BOX 6.3

Challenges in Innovation Policy Design in Latin America

Evaluations using the PER methodology (see box 6.1 for a description) of STI policies implemented in a few Latin American countries suggest that design is the weakest element in innovation policy. Figure B6.3.1 summarizes the quality of design, implementation, and governance of the innovation policy mix in a good innovation policy performer. Each dimension is evaluated on a scale from 1 to 5, with 5 indicating the full adoption of a good practice. Although this country shows the highest innovation design quality in the region, two key weaknesses emerge in the design stage, which are common in most countries in the region:

- The design lacks a fully developed logical model and articulated theory of change for the different instruments. How the intervention is supposed to work is not fully articulated and there are no clear and measurable objectives, which makes monitoring difficult and evaluation of whether the policy is having the desired impact challenging.
- Some policies have ad hoc justifications and are not based on robust diagnostic exercises of the main market failures.

Another common weakness is the failure to consider alternative instruments and mechanisms of intervention. The typical procedure for design among program managers is to adopt existing

(Box continues on the following page.)

Challenges in Innovation Policy Design in Latin America *(continued)*

FIGURE B6.3.1 **Evaluation of the Quality of Innovation Policy Design, Implementation, and Governance**

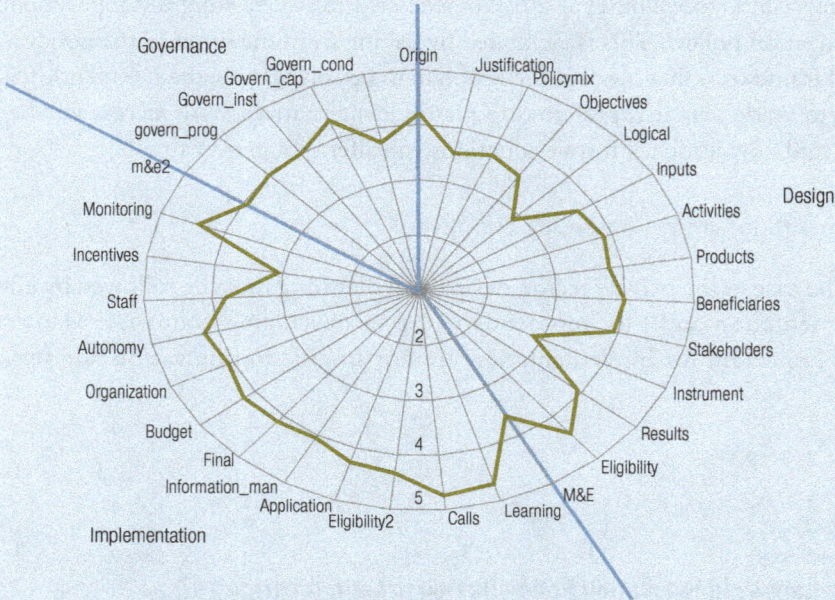

Source: Elaboration based on Public Expenditure Reviews analysis.

Note: 1 = low quality practice, 5 = good practice adopted. Figure shows average scores across all innovation programs and agencies.

mechanisms from other countries, especially in the Organisation for Economic Co-operation and Development (OECD), instead of looking at the local problem and assessing the different instrument possibilities.

The PER reveals that most mechanisms of intervention—up to 80 percent—used to support innovation projects are matching grants, highlighted in figure B6.3.2. It is very unlikely that matching grants are the mechanism of intervention to optimally address most innovation failures, especially if they are not tightly linked to technical assistance, given the large information asymmetry and lack of knowledge in SMEs to implement innovation projects.

A final important weakness in these countries is the lack of appropriate M&E frameworks and impact evaluations. Many innovation programs lack a well-defined, logical framework that could inform M&E efforts. In addition, impact evaluation in innovation programs is in a very early stage, with only a handful of evaluations available for the whole Latin American region.

(Box continues on the following page.)

Challenges in Innovation Policy Design in Latin America *(continued)*

FIGURE B6.3.2 **Distribution of Mechanism of Intervention in the Policy Mix**

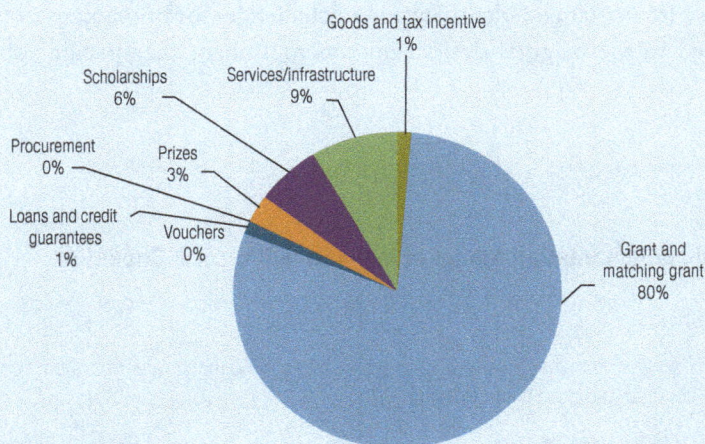

Goods and tax incentive
1%

Scholarships
6%

Services/infrastructure
9%

Procurement
0%

Prizes
3%

Loans and credit
guarantees
1%

Vouchers
0%

Grant and
matching grant
80%

Source: Elaboration based on Public Expenditure Reviews analysis.
Note: Percentages refer to main mechanism of intervention used across 140 innovation instruments in a Latin American country.

part of a larger agenda of improving public sector management, a topic too vast for this volume. However, the new public management strand of the public policy and administration literature has emphasized performance management, and in particular issues of measurement and tracking, as key for public policy implementation.[12] This is primarily because there is evidence that the application of good management practices in government can produce benefits. An early meta-analysis of 70 studies finds that the adoption of management by objectives, an early version of performance management, had a positive impact in public and private sectors (Rodgers and Hunter 1992). A more recent study supported the notion that proper implementation of performance management improves education outcomes (Sun and Van Ryzin 2014). Application in the context of developing countries has also showed positive results (Rasul and Rogger 2017).

The key practices that can improve the efficiency of policy management and contribute to effective implementation, and which are used to evaluate the quality of innovation policy management in PERs, can be divided into three main dimensions: (1) learning, (2) tools for implementation, and (3) quality of managerial practices (box 6.4).

Learning and Adaptation

As discussed earlier, measuring and evaluating are critical for designing effective innovation policy. However, an appropriate learning system is also key for verifying efficacy of implementation and ensuring that knowledge generated in M&E systems and impact evaluations is preserved and that policy lessons are learned. The key processes to ensure effective learning are documentation of experiences and decisions to adapt to new circumstances, identification of challenges for implementation that were not addressed in the original design, documentation of the specific solutions that

---

BOX 6.4

The Good Implementation Model of Innovation Policy: A Checklist

1. *Learning*

   a. *Knowledge management.* Clearly define knowledge management systems and provide codified and accessible information.

2. *Policy tool implementation*

   a. *Solicitations and project management.* When solicitations and calls for proposals are not originally planned, provide a good justification and explanation of how changes align to the original plan.

   b. *Participant selection practices.* Disseminate criteria for selection ex ante, define the appeal mechanism, and provide for evaluation by external experts.

   c. *Application procedures.* Requirements to apply should be easy to understand, and documentation requirements should be minimal, focusing on what is necessary for the program.

   d. *Program information management.* Digital database with all the information on applicants should be systematized and accessible.

   e. *Finalization of participation in the program.* Establish ex ante when a beneficiary's participation in a specific policy support program ends, and ensure that the end is connected to an assessment of the achievement of the policy's goals and that collection of outcome information continues during the life of the project.[a]

3. *Management Quality*

   a. *Budgeting.* Provide resources that are sufficient to implement a policy and support the desired level of beneficiaries, without cutting the quality of services.

   b. *Organization management.* Clearly define the management structure, with a small number of layers between decision making and implementation.

   c. *Role definition and autonomy.* Define clear roles for management and supervision positions, and ensure technical autonomy for design and implementation to limit political interference.

(Box continues on the following page.)

were adopted and of the problems that remain, and relevant data showing how the solution improved performance. This learning capability is especially important in many developing countries, where rotation of civil servants is the norm because of political changes and human resource policies, which severely constrains institutional memory and learning. Learning is not confined to the implementation of individual policy instruments, but rather is a component of the entire organization and a feature of its culture.

Tools for Implementation

Innovation policies are heavily dependent on grant funding schemes with a common basic structure. They involve the design and publication of a solicitation or request for proposals that contains basic information about the type of projects to be funded, level of funding, participant eligibility criteria, and application procedures and requirements. This needs to be done in a way that maximizes participation from the desired beneficiaries. Too often, however, application procedures require excessive documentation or cumbersome application forms, which imply significant costs for applicants and act as a deterrent to apply for government support. Thus, in some countries some consultants have specialized in filling applications, which can result in these programs being captured by those same firms that have developed a good understanding of the application processes or that have hired these consultants.

Avoiding this capture and reaching out to the main policy beneficiaries requires light application processes, with clear and transparent requirements that are evaluated by externally qualified evaluators with previously designed appeal mechanisms. Ensuring good quality evaluation of projects and applications is often challenging in developing countries because of a lack of local capacity. As suggested in the next section, cooperation with international partners can facilitate access to external experts for the evaluation process.

Management Quality

Effective management requires appropriate financial and human resources. Regarding the latter, human resource policy is key. Favero, Meier, and O'Toole (2016) show that best practices in internal management, namely, setting goals for staff, building trust with employees, meaningful feedback, and employee motivation, among others, have measurable effects on the outcomes of policies. Jacobson and Sowa (2015) show in the context of municipal governments how strategic human resource management (SHRM) has significant effects on performance.[13] Human resource practices signal management's commitment to employees and breed trust. Practices that focus on autonomy, compensation, communication, performance appraisal, and career development are associated with trust in public organizations (Cho and Poister 2013). More important, having good incentives is key for bringing innovation into the public sector (Borins 2008) in terms of process improvement and creating value in the services provided (Moore 2013).

This human resource management is often missing in developing countries (see Finan, Olken, and Pande 2015 for an overview), but it is critical for attracting staff with some degree of industry expertise. In most developing countries, poor human resource policies, significant wage differentials between the public and private sectors, and large turnover in public management positions severely constrain the recruitment of the talent needed to design and implement innovation policies. As we will see in the next section, some innovation agencies have addressed this challenge by having different governance status than line ministries, which enables them to pay higher wages and attract talent.

These weaknesses undermine innovation policy effectiveness (box 6.5 provides examples from Latin America) because, as Rasul and Rogger (2017) show in the case of Nigeria, good project management practices impact the quality of the outcomes achieved. The good news is that the evidence from PER exercises suggests great heterogeneity in policy quality within countries and even within agencies. There are good practices in many agencies, which therefore can be leveraged for improving worse-performing programs.

Weak Implementation in Latin America: Lessons from the PERs

Several challenges have been identified when evaluating the quality of implementation of innovation policies in Latin America.

- The lack of an M&E system in the early stages of policy formation cascades into a lack of implementation of monitoring both of implementation processes and of policy instrument performance. Impact evaluation is in its inception in most countries, and there are few specialized units of evaluation or formal learning processes. Evaluation is thought of mostly as an auditing or legitimizing tool applied at the tail end of policy implementation. Little attention is paid to the complementarity of external and internal evaluation to maximize learning and improvement, as opposed to final adjudication of effects and worthiness of the policy as a whole.
- The quality and use of documentation for improving instrument management is low. In general, documentation is formulaic rather than practical, and is rarely included systematically in internal reviews of performance progress. The use of information and communications technology is limited and below potential, given the availability of standard systems. It is often difficult to share information across programs and agencies.
- The appropriate management of human resources and accounting of administrative costs per intervention is another challenge. In general, incentives for staff are not aligned with the performance of the policy instruments they manage. Furthermore, the resources of an agency are pooled across many policy instruments with varying relations to each other and distributed in temporary patterns that respond to short-term bureaucratic priorities. Thus, the true administrative costs of each instrument are unknown, making it almost impossible to improve management efficiency.

Source: Elaboration based on Public Expenditure Reviews analysis.

Coherence

To say that policy is coherent is to say that policy solutions match the diagnosis of the problem, target populations and beneficiaries are clearly connected to the public good benefits that the policy is to address, the focus and resources pertaining to the instruments match policy objectives, and the elements of the policy mix reinforce rather than duplicate or offset each other. In practice, however, such coherence is often violated as policy instruments evolve by accretion in multiple interactions and budget negotiations or are driven by the political considerations discussed above.

Need for Effective Coordination

The need for coherence extends both horizontally across the government and vertically within ministries. Chapter 7 lays out a set of programs to support progressively more sophisticated capabilities, beginning with basic managerial extension and training programs, and moving up, for instance, to technology centers and institutes. Singapore's ladder of programs is a good example of a well-articulated and coherent set of programs seamlessly resolving the market failures facing progressively more sophisticated firms. The initial interface with the firms is a costless diagnostic of firm performance and approved consulting services work, up to S$20,000. This is intended to resolve the initial information market failures about own capability and the quality of providers. It also provides the government information on likely growth-potential firms. More specialized services are facilitated in subsequent stages, albeit with fewer subsidies. At the top of the pyramid are interactions with specialized government-supported research institutes.

However, in much of the developing world, policies are frequently balkanized, lacking coherence across ministries and alignment across instruments. Innovation policy is often formally relegated to a ministry of science and technology, which may focus resources on nonapplied academic research, with no coordination with the ministry of industry's policies focused on the private sector. Further, political economy considerations often lead to duplicative and fragmented policies allocated across industries, with different agencies tasked by distinct and conflicting laws with management of the NIS, leading to confusion within the private sector about who is responsible for providing support. As box 6.8 later in the chapter shows, governments often focus on, for instance, the supply of a particular kind of knowledge without concerning themselves with the demand. The section below on agencies discusses some of the mechanisms that may help in aligning both sides of the equation.

Coherence in Allocating Funds to Desired Objectives

The allocation of funds is the key mechanism to align objectives and link elements of the NIS, generate quality outputs, and provide competition, as opposed to establishing privileged actors in the system. This is often not the case. For instance, the evidence uncovered in the PER exercise reveals a major incongruity between policy statements and the actual budgets across instruments. The stated priorities of innovation policy often mention large-scale and long-term goals, such as diversification of the economy, establishment of a more entrepreneurial and innovative business culture, and strengthening the links between various sectors to create synergies. However, the actual expenditures allocated do not correspond to these priorities. Figure 6.1 shows previous allocations of STI expenditure by broad economic objective in a Latin American country. Although diversification of the economy was the main objective of innovation policy, most of the allocated budget did not support diversification.[14] The assessments suggest a lack of coherence of stated priorities and expenditure commitments, volatility in budget allocations that undermine medium- to long-term change and impact processes, disparity in budget sizes across programs that do not reflect expected efficacy of the instruments, and a lack of diversity in the menu of instruments despite the diversity of innovation policy problems, reflecting inertia from experience with a single instrument.

FIGURE 6.1 **Only a Small Share of Innovation Expenditures Support Diversification**

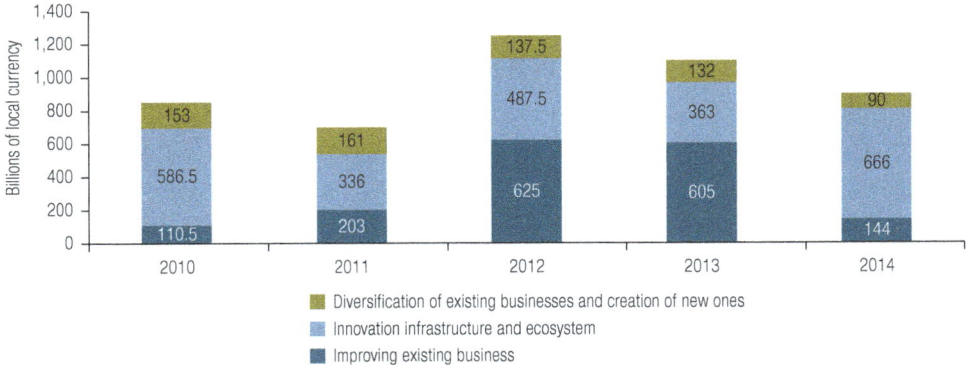

Source: Elaboration based on Public Expenditure Reviews analysis.

Preventing such mismatches occurs at the policy planning process stage, but then requires ongoing checking against the original objectives and how the program evolves. Appropriate logical frameworks and stated goals, as well as mid-term reviews of existing policies, can help to redirect financial resources toward stated policy goals. A systematic overview of instruments and how they fit together coherently is essential.

More generally, there is the challenge of broader oversight of the system and getting the various involved ministries to coordinate and enforce coherence. Often, high-level ministerial committees are established to this end. However, without a strong mandate from the public and the highest public officials, these committees can degenerate into ineffective zombie institutions attended by mid-level bureaucrats with no higher-level support.

A final coordination challenge occurs across different levels of government. Local governments are often less prepared to implement innovation policies and, except for highly developed regions, do not have a tradition of including innovation objectives among their policy targets. National policies in developing countries are starting to address the geographical concentration of innovation capabilities, but the application of this priority to the specifics of innovation policy design and implementation is still challenging and underdeveloped.

Policy Consistency over Time

Building a well-conceptualized, efficient, and coherent innovation system is a project of decades, if not centuries. The major research universities of the West have accumulated the human capital, interconnections, and links with the private sector that enable them to play the role they do over very long periods. Developing a dynamic private sector has taken the Koreas and Singapores of the world decades of deliberate policies. Establishing a business consulting industry that can facilitate firm upgrading and a reputation that firms will trust takes time and effort. Venture capital firms require both resources and ways of supporting managers with experience in high-tech and risky start-ups, which are available only when such an industry already exists. In sum, building national innovative capacity takes sustained effort and oversight over a long period.

This implies long-term and predictable financial and institutional commitment, which is difficult to obtain when policies and financing shift with the political cycle. In many developing countries, institutions experience frequent leadership changes with corresponding changes in innovation policies and strategies. Lack of isolation of even very modest STI budget funding from the business cycle implies large volatility of innovation budgets and often reductions to the point of inefficacy. Such volatility also limits the ability of policy managers to learn from existing instruments, which may have no calls for proposals for over a year or two, and then start from zero when the budget allocation is more favorable.

Measures such as ring-fencing budgets or financing from dedicated funds can help support consistency across time in innovation policy. However, at core, long-term cultivation and vigilance of the system require broad-based support across the political spectrum. Some countries are extremely deliberate about building a consensus around innovation policies. In Finland, all new parliamentarians are required to pass through a course on the "Finnish Model" to understand previous thinking and coherence. In the 1980s, Singapore developed a productivity strategy with the help of the Japanese Productivity Center meant to build public consciousness around the importance of productivity and innovation, spearheaded by high-profile institutions such as SPRING. Box 6.6 offers an example from Latin America about how consistent support in the political discourse, in this case, the state of the union addresses of the head of state, translates into higher innovation indexes and growth.

Agencies and Institutions to Support Innovation

Innovation policy is often implemented through institutions dedicated to such tasks as public research, firm support, or finance. The advantage of such specialized agencies, as

---

BOX 6.6

Innovation and Political Commitment

Political commitment is important for policy. Calvo-González, Eizmendi, and Reyes (2017) analyze political commitment in Latin American countries by looking at state of the nation speeches. The authors find that, in countries where there is more variance in topics across speeches, there is also less growth in income per capita (figure B6.6.1), suggesting little focus on and commitment to existing policies.

(Box continues on the following page.)

BOX 6.6

Innovation and Political Commitment *(continued)*

FIGURE B6.6.1   **Policy Discontinuity and Percent Change of U.S. GDP per Capita, Selected Latin American Countries, 1950–2010**

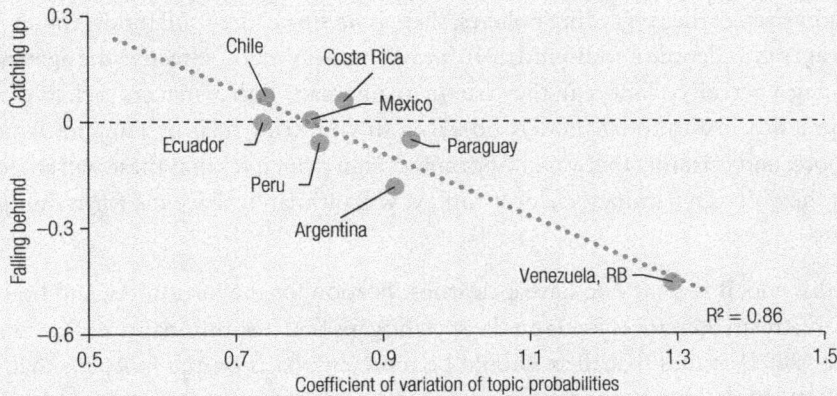

Source: Calvo-González, Eizmendi, and Reyes 2017.

FIGURE B6.6.2   **Correlation between Political Commitment on Innovation and Degree of Innovation Performance, Selected Latin American Countries**

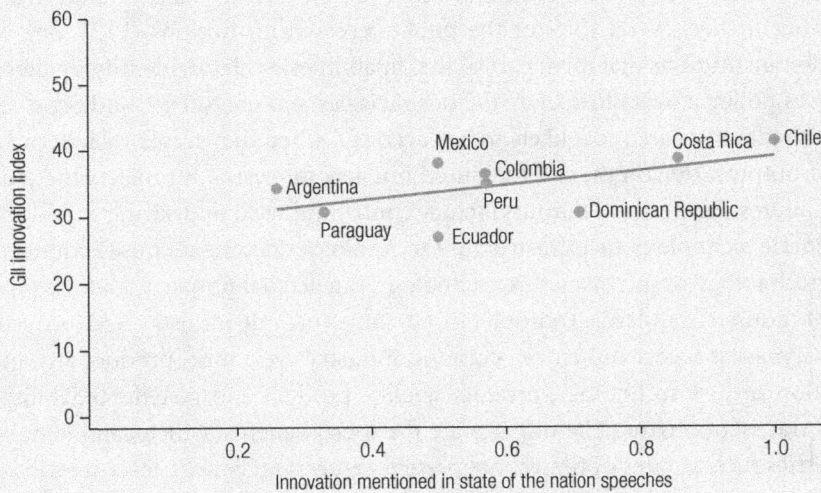

Source: Elaboration using data from Calvo-González, Eizmendi, and Reyes 2017.

One can use this data on political commitment and analyze how often "innovation" is a topic of the speech as a commitment to innovation policies. Figure B6.6.2 shows the correlation for selected Latin American countries of the share of "innovation" in these speeches in the 2010s and the Global Innovation Index. The results show a clear positive correlation between the proxy of political commitment and the degree of innovation of the country.

opposed to line ministries, is that they can have a clearer mission orientation to focus on fewer objectives and at the same time have more independent and flexible structures to hire and retain talent. The four dimensions highlighted in the previous section remain salient for these supporting institutions.

Rationale and Design: Defining Their Mission

As emphasized earlier regarding policies, there is *no single successful* model for an innovation agency (Glennie and Bound 2016); what matters is how effective the agency is in redressing a perceived failure in the system. Again, many policy makers seek to emulate good-practice institutional models observed in countries such as Finland, Israel, or Singapore; and certainly there are important design principles that these will share. But within these design parameters, local context will ultimately drive the form the agency will take.

To this end, it is central to have a clear justification for the institution, and both NIS and mainstream literatures focus on the specific gaps that institutions are designed to fill. Edquist (2004) argues that there should be more emphasis on the *functions* that these institutions provide in supporting the innovation ecosystem, such as supporting R&D, competence building, incubation, consultancy services, and financing of enterprises. The mainstream perspective will ask what market failures, such as appropriation externality, information asymmetry, or coordination problem need to be resolved in each case.

As an example, in box 6.7 Link and Scott (2009) identify failures underlying the motivation for the several roles of the public research institutions (PRI), one of the innovation institutions that form part of the capabilities escalator. Identifying these failures forces policy makers to specify the beneficiaries and goals. Link and Scott (2009) emphasize that PRIs are most likely to be successful when they frame their activities in terms of outputs, outcomes, and measured impacts for research projects that address market failures. Examples of outputs include contributions to underlying science, developed generic technology or infrastructure technology, documented use in industry of generic technology or infrastructure technology, intellectual property, and the promulgation of industry standards. Examples of outcomes include industry R&D investment decisions, market access and entry decisions, industry cycle time, productivity, market penetration of new technology, product quality, product and systems reliability, and reduced transaction costs. The impacts are the social benefits, which can be measured with metrics such as rates of return, net present values, and benefit-to-cost ratios.

The problem is that often rationale and success metrics are unclear. Link and Scott (2009) were surprised that none of their Latin American case studies seemed to think in terms of the outputs and outcomes from public research; hence, it was difficult to identify a public good aspect to their research. This is a common problem for this type of institution. Historical inertia from a period when PRIs in Eastern Europe served a preassigned client, such as a large state-owned enterprise, has made it difficult for some

The Rationale for Public Research Institutes

Public Research Institutes (PRIs) are prominent features in most NISs. Link and Scott (2009) identify several roles they play, addressing particular market failures:

1. *Advanced technical extension services.* PRIs can facilitate technology transfer in sectors such as light industry or agriculture when, for example, small firms face limited appropriability from their investments in new technologies that would provide large external benefits to the economy as a whole.

2. *Developing appropriate knowledge to transfer.* Institutions such as the U.S. National Institute of Standards and Technology (NIST) can foster the technology transfer provided by extension programs through their knowledge of the key technologies and working relationships with the industries supplying the technologies, and can assist the transfer of technologies without opportunistic exploitation of small firms, allowing them to grow as independent sources of initiative and growth.

3. *Coordination of research efforts.* PRIs can serve as honest brokers, helping to facilitate cooperative efforts by industry, universities, and government in research that is subsidized by the government (see Hall, Link, and Scott 2003). To play this role, the PRI needs to have a research capacity itself. For example, the Advanced Technology Program (ATP) at NIST relies on the research capability of NIST to ensure sound oversight of competitions for government research funds.

4. *Bridge from basic to applied science.* PRIs can facilitate the diffusion of advances from research, such as in biotechnology, chemistry, materials science, and pharmaceuticals. In many cases, government funds will have been used by universities to develop the basic science because the ideas have a strong public good component and there would not have been sufficient incentive to develop them without government funding. Once the basic science is available, the knowledgeable public research institution with expertise in both research and connections to industry can help to disseminate the information widely.

5. *Standards setting.* For more advanced countries, PRIs can participate in the development of standards, which helps to reduce the risk associated with adopting new technologies.

of them to evolve to supporting SMEs or start-ups. The tendency to import organograms can also imply misalignment of mission with sophistication of the economy. Without this clarity of mission and outputs, their research is likely to be irrelevant for the private sector. Further, as Nelson (2005) notes, innovation institutions also need to evolve over time, and design needs to facilitate the receipt of signals that change is needed and in which direction.

Ensuring Independence and Preventing Capture

As discussed earlier in this chapter, ensuring responsiveness to the target client and preventing capture remain central design challenges. Having diverse and, particularly, private sector participation on boards of directors contributes to maintaining the initial mission and the alignment of goals with the needs of business. For example, the 17-member board of Singapore's firm upgrading program SPRING comprises members from leading private sector companies as well as government officials. The Malaysian Technology Development Corporation includes three individuals from the private sector on its nine-member Board.

In addition, ensuring substantial independence from government bureaucracy can shield agencies from political considerations (Glennie and Bound 2016). Robust and transparent governance improves relevance and legitimacy and is an important component of accountability. Agency independence can be codified in many ways, including legislatively by an act of government, through its founding documents, governmental "ownership" structures and reporting lines, or the authority afforded to its advisory/management boards as well as the composition of its funding bodies.[15]

In small countries, the interlocked nature of the elites can undermine this strategy; hence, international review can buy additional measures of objectivity. Chile's research funding agencies often present scientific proposals to international experts for review. Finland's Tekes has its program funding externally reviewed every 3 years. Both are countries with above average levels of social capital and relatively transparent processes, yet they still rely on these additional guarantees of objectivity to prevent capture.

Financing Structures and Market Discipline

As with policy, the design of financing and exploiting market forces helps ensure that resources are aligned with intended beneficiaries, and encourages more transparent, efficient, and effective decision-making bodies sensitive to firm needs and longer-term market trends. For example, government support is often best allocated inframarginally whereas private sector contributions are best made at the margin: to offset standard externalities arising because worker mobility means firms are unable to capture the full value of their training investments, the Penang Skills Center in Malaysia receives government funding for equipment and infrastructure; but private firms pay the individual student fees. Thus, if the private sector does not value the services provided, the center will not survive. O'Connell et al. (2017) shows how a version of PRONATEC (a technical and vocational training program in Brazil, that explicitly takes input from firms in determining the location and skill content) has much larger employment effects than nondemand-driven programs. Colombia's National Training System (SENA) offers a contrasting model in which the government underwrites the full cost of government-designed training programs and firms cannot choose among providers with their mandatory training budgets. In the absence of market discipline, firms complain of poor alignment of training classes with corporate needs, and they have no recourse to alternate providers.

This also raises the issue of what the overall subsidy should be, particularly in applied research institutes. The appropriation externality—that a firm cannot fully recoup the benefits of research it may do because other firms can use the new ideas as well—is often resolved by having a publicly subsidized research institute undertake the provision of this public good. At one extreme, many public research institutions in developing countries enjoy full grant funding by the state, which, combined with unclear missions, offers little incentive to be relevant to the private sector or pressure for quality control. At the other extreme, the New Zealand Crown Research Institutes for a while had very little public sector financing, leading them to behave like a private sector consulting firm and generating insufficient public goods. The Technical Research Centre of Finland (VTT) occupies an intermediate position, where the state provides a third of basal financing, another third comes from competitive grants, and a third comes from private sector contracts. This helps to guarantee both the quality of public goods and alignment with industry needs.

Implementation: Attracting, Retaining, and Retraining Staff

After clarity of mission, attracting high-quality human capital and motivating it with well-aligned incentives are critical to meeting output and quality goals. Recruiting staff with the needed technical skills requires competitive salaries, insulation from political considerations, and incentive structures that demand excellence.

In keeping with the greater specialization of agencies that is part of their raison d'être, staff need to have particular skill sets: innovation agencies in Israel; Taiwan, China; and the United Kingdom recruit individuals from industry or with particular technical experience, typically eschewing policy generalists (Glennie and Bound 2016). At a minimum, front-line staff need to be able to identify private sector providers that can implement support programs. For example, most extension consultants in the Colombian National Productivity Center have experience in working with large Colombian firms or multinational enterprises. Recruiting such staff is more challenging in Africa, for instance, where there is less experience with either frontier local firms or multinational enterprises. As another example, clients of venture capital firms, while confirming the importance of the financing provided, also stress the importance of the experienced management support that accompanied it (De Carvalho, Calomiris, and De Matos 2008). Countries without experience in risky industries are unlikely to have many such managers. One alternative may be to draw on foreign talent embodied in multinationals, as discussed in chapter 5, or directly contract foreign specialists, including those from the diaspora. To attract international experts requires higher levels of compensation. To this end, some innovation agencies are established to be able to offer attractive recruitment packages.[16]

International partnerships can also help innovation agencies in emerging economies to develop capabilities, cultivate human capital, and use global funding and knowledge networks to design better programming that is aligned with ongoing global trends and good practice. As chapter 3 noted, fundamentally, the NIS must be international—that is where most knowledge, including how to run successful agencies, is found. In addition to attracting funds, agencies in small, nascent ecosystems can establish their credibility by affiliation with more reputable agencies and associations globally.

Collaboration and Alignment with Other Agencies and Actors

As with policy more generally, how a particular institution will interact with the rest of the system (or policy mix) is critical. This has been a focus of the NIS literature, which has extensively studied the importance and dynamic nature of links, for instance, among government institutions, the private sector, and universities. Successful agencies network with domestic and international partners and particularly with the private sector. For example, SPRING Singapore works closely with other agencies, such as the Economic Development Board, which focuses on economic development planning, attracting foreign direct investment, and facilitating industrial development. The Serbian innovation agency works with other national agencies, for example the Serbian Development Fund, which provides subsidized loans to businesses, and the Serbian Development Agency, which provides grants and technical assistance to businesses. Close collaboration among these agencies conserves resources and helps ensure that enterprises receive much needed support services (Kapil and Aridi 2017).

However, in developing countries this is often not the case. As one crude measure, figure 6.2 graphs the private sector's perceptions of the degree of collaboration between the scientific research institutions and the private sector. Clearly, collaboration is much higher in the more technologically advanced countries. Healthy interactions cannot be mandated by law; they are often driven by professional values of a nonmaterial nature that may take years to establish. However, the figure shows a high degree of correlation between the perceived quality of the scientific establishment and the degree of interaction, suggesting that firms may see no benefit in collaboration. Digging deeper, low-quality research may reflect political considerations distorting the mission and selection of agency personnel, or poor financial design as discussed in the previous section. On the other side of the NIS, weak firm capabilities may prevent firms from seeing the benefit of what research centers are producing. Box 6.8 shows an example of how to break the mismatch between the demand and supply of knowledge, and to provide the incentives to adapt programs to the objective of supporting research–industry collaboration.

Securing Long-Term Government Commitment

As with innovation policy in general, building effective institutions requires, in addition to establishing clear mission and effective design, government commitment over the medium to long term. As discussed above, over the long term, the optimal financing of agencies is likely to combine government and private sector funding to ensure alignment with objectives and quality. However, as Kapil and Aridi (2017) argue on the basis of their analysis of agencies in seven middle-income and two high-income countries,[17]

FIGURE 6.2 **Entrepreneurs' Perceived Quality of Scientific Institutions and Degree of Private Sector–University Collaboration Is Higher in Advanced Countries**

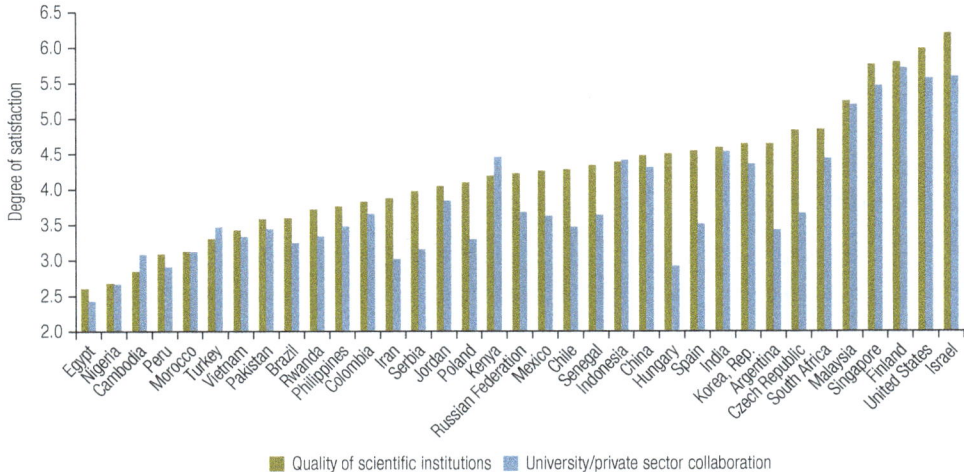

Quality of scientific institutions ■ University/private sector collaboration

Source: World Competitiveness Indicators 2017.

Note: The y axis measures the responses to the following questions: In your country, how do you assess the quality of scientific research institutions? [1 = extremely poor—among the worst in the world; 7 = extremely good—among the best in the world] In your country, to what extent do business and universities collaborate on research and development (R&D)? [1 = do not collaborate at all; 7 = collaborate extensively]

BOX 6.8

Matching the Supply and Demand for Knowledge in the Republic of Korea

Increasing firm capabilities is essential to adopt technologies from abroad or from multinational enterprises and to ensure the efficacy of government-sponsored research. As an example, Oh (1997) reports bottlenecks that impede the diffusion to firms of knowledge financed by the Korean government: 42 percent of public research institute and university respondents to a survey on research diffusion pointed to a lack of technological capacity on the part of firms to use their research. On the other side of the equation, the private sector felt that universities and PRIs did not produce appropriate knowledge.

Korea's Science and Technology Policy Institute concluded that direct technology transfer from PRIs and universities was the best approach to ensure better alignment of the supply and demand for new knowledge. Rotating personnel from the research sector into firms or having masters and doctoral students work in firms were sound forms of technology transfer. Similarly, in Finland, the highest ranked university–firm interactions were rotations of masters and PhD students through firms. At the same time, Korea developed its own system of firm upgrading analogous to those in Japan and Singapore.

in the "start-up" period policy makers are likely to need to secure financial resources for operations, capacity building, and rigorous piloting—that is, with sufficient resources to evaluate program efficiency and additionality.

Sustainability can be achieved only through precommitments to operational budgets or scale-up funding for successful pilots. Securing some precommitments for operational funds from the government for a 3–5-year horizon provides an agency with breathing room and the ability to raise funds for other programs, and to hire and retain capable staff. Over the longer term, the government's contribution to financing needs to be placed on a solid and predictable footing (see Kapil, Piatkowsi, and Navarrete 2014).[18]

Natural resource–rich countries, such as Colombia, set aside 10 percent of extractives revenues to support subnational innovation programs. Set-aside provisions based on a stated percentage of a larger budget can provide stability in medium to large countries. For example, funding for the U.S. Small Business Innovation Research program, a small business innovation support program administered by the 11 largest innovation agencies, is based on a set percentage (about 3 percent) of each agency's external R&D budget. Finally, programs might allow the transfer of unspent program funds across fiscal years, providing greater flexibility for funding decisions.

In some countries, government commitment also encourages agencies to build public-private partnerships for agenda setting, program design, and funding, where feasible. In Poland, for instance, the European Union's Smart Specialization fueled by a stable 7-year cycle of Structural Funds prompted the National Center for R&D to proactively engage the private sector to design specific instruments. Agency responsiveness to private sector needs is critical in bolstering its relevance and reputation with ecosystem stakeholders.

Concluding Remarks

Academic and policy discussions about innovation policy often omit the question of who actually implements it. The role public servants, ministries, and agencies play in ensuring or undermining the effectiveness of policy instruments is rarely considered. This is a critical part of the resolution of the innovation paradox: as the complexity and scope of the interventions necessary to resolve the failures that impede exploiting the gains from technological catch-up increase with distance from the frontier, the capabilities of governments to design and implement the interventions tend to diminish. Overall, the issue of capabilities in innovation policy making and how to improve them is probably one of the most pressing, yet unacknowledged agendas in innovation policy in developing countries.

In this chapter, we have offered a set of considerations and guidelines that can help to ensure effective design and implementation of innovation policies and agencies. The next chapter focuses particularly on policies and agencies dedicated to upgrading firm managerial and technological capabilities.

Notes

1. Asymmetric information triggers three problems that severely affect the ability of firms to finance innovation activities. *Adverse selection*—the inability of a party to observe the other agent's private information—can reduce innovation contracts between firms or bank financing for innovation activities, given the perceived risks. *Signaling and screening* problems arise as a response to asymmetric information. Firms with more information may face difficulties in signaling less-informed firms of their strong ability to conduct innovation activities. Less-informed firms may face difficulties in designing reliable mechanisms to determine which firms have the ability to carry out innovation projects. In both cases, multiple equilibria are possible, some of which result in good firms not engaging in any collaboration in innovation activities. *Principal–agent* problems/*moral hazard* problems arise when one of the parties to a transaction may be unable to monitor the performance of the other party. For example, financial institutions may lack the capacity to monitor compliance with an innovation finance contract, or one member of a research consortium may be unable to monitor research efforts by the other party. Again, this can limit innovation finance and impair cooperation in innovation contracts or in setting basic infrastructure and services.

2. The NIS has emphasized that the ability of firms to engage in innovation does not depend solely on the firm but is highly dependent on existing framework conditions—the range of markets, institutions, and policies that constitute the NIS. This approach adopts an evolutionary lens and sees the NIS as the historical development of a system that is path dependent (Fagerberg 2015) and where firms learn by interaction (Lundvall 1992), rejecting the notion of market failure and optimality.

3. There are several types of system failures identified by the literature that are relevant when building innovation capabilities. Firms may have insufficient access to human capital, infrastructure, or technology. For example, firms in developing countries can be trapped in markets with low technological development that lack the complementary factors important for innovation, such as research centers or quality certification. There is, therefore, a big infrastructure failure that cannot be addressed only by the market. Like coordination failures, links between firms and nonmarket institutions may be limited, reducing opportunities for learning and the creation of new products and new technologies. More important, there are systemic failures associated with weak institutions and inadequate regulations, which may distort and constrain firm innovation activities. For example, distortions that undermine capital investments also constrain investments in innovation activities, or a lack of research incentives in the university system may constrain science and R&D activity (BIS 2014). The role of innovation policy is, therefore, to make sure that all these different sources of knowledge and know-how are connected in the system (Dodgson et al. 2011).

4. In the NIS literature, Edquist (2004) stresses that institutions should be thought of in terms of the problem they are solving, rather than the institution per se.

5. Bleda and Del Río (2013, p. 1049), in trying to integrate both perspectives, suggest that "neoclassical market failures can be conceived within this framework as evolutionary market failures that take place at the last stage of the market formation function. Put simply, they are coordination failures that occur in an evolutionary market at its operational level." In other words, this "last stage" occurs when knowledge and technology have been formed but have not been diffused or adopted.

6. When fostering innovation capabilities in firms in low- and middle-income countries, not only systemic elements are important, but so is the extent to which information asymmetry is so large that firms do not know how to manage the learning process. Lee (2013) labels this as a *capability failure*, which implies that innovation policy needs to not only incentivize the accumulation of these capabilities but also directly support access to knowledge and help in the learning process.

7. This can help avoid, as one large Latin American firm said, that the innovation agency is "run by Bolsheviks who despise the private sector and just finances university research for art's sake."

8. The focus on experimentation fits well with a compatible strand in the literature on evidence-based policy (EBP). This strand is strongest in public health policy because of the influence of evidence-based medicine, which sought to systematize all the available evidence for specific treatments to recommend only those that had strong experimental evidence. Two approaches used in the health area have been adopted in policy: randomized controlled trials (RCT) as the gold standard for evidence, and systematic reviews of available studies that collate and rank all evidence produced on interventions of interest. These are the types of studies that are most relied on in chapter 4 to validate the efficacy of extension programs.

9. The idea of smaller-scale experiments to inform larger investments in a policy is attractive. However, studies have found that success requires careful design. Van der Heijden (2014) studied the use of experiments in policy design of new building sustainability policies in Australia, the Netherlands, and the United States. Two areas stood out for successful experimental design. First, defining the expected outcome of a successful experiment may be difficult. For example, the number of buildings using the sustainability recommendations is one measure of the success of the policy. However, attracting significant numbers of participants in the experiment is also a measure of success because it reveals buy-in. The conditions under which companies or individuals are motivated to join an experiment and follow through until completion are critical and difficult to achieve.

10. Gambi (2012) reviews the role of the centralized evaluation agency in Chile, which has carried out evaluations of several programs. The author concludes that the evaluations have not had any effect on decisions about these programs.

11. Teirlinck et al. (2013) argue that this arises from a lack of early involvement of stakeholders and an inadequate selection of indicators and methods that allow comparisons with other programs and previous versions of the one in question.

12. However, very little is devoted to specific practices that lead to high performance; most of the practices recommended in this perspective relate to the definition of performance indicators, data gathering, monitoring, and reporting of performance results.

13. Traditional human resource policies usually attempt to match candidates to a specific role and conditions of the job. SHRM, on the other hand, engages in a partnership with the workers to leverage their own talents to contribute to the strategic goals of the organization.

14. This mismatch between budget allocation and objectives is being addressed in the new innovation strategy of the country aimed at supporting innovation and productivity growth and aligning existing instruments to those goals.

15. An innovation agency can be part of a larger government ministry (for example, BICRO is part of the Croatian Ministry of Science, Education, and Sports), or it may be an independent organization owned primarily by the government (for example, SPRING Singapore) or a quasi-governmental institution (MTDC is owned by Khasanah Nasional Berhad, Malaysia's sovereign investment fund).

16. For example, Croatia's BICRO, Serbia's IF, Sri Lanka's SLINTEC, and Colombia's INNpulsa tend to pay higher wages that inline ministries.

17. The innovation agencies analyzed are BICRO in Croatia; BIRAC in India; EIF in Armenia; IF in Serbia; INNpulsa in Colombia; Kafalat in Lebanon; MTDC in Malaysia; and SPRING in Singapore.

18. Agencies often face budget challenges because either they are directly dependent on a region or country's tax income, which is difficult to predict, or they are at the whim of annual budgetary decisions, which may introduce uncertainties related to program deployment and sustainment. Given the uncertain nature of government funding, agencies have found creative ways to support

their operations. Kafalat presents itself as a platform for donor-funded projects with little money coming from its government. Serbia's IF is similarly funded by donors, including the European Union (EU) and World Bank, and the Serbian government has agreed to fund the program once donor commitments end. Poland's NCBIR and other European state agencies rely heavily on EU Structural Funds. Other countries, like Malaysia and Colombia, are not normally eligible for international development funds, so INNpulsa and MTDC have presented themselves as platforms for other domestic agencies to fund innovation-related projects.

References

Andrews, M. 2013. *The Limits of Institutional Reform in Development.* New York: Cambridge University Press.

Andrews, Matt. 2015. "Explaining Positive Deviance in Public Sector Reforms in Development." *World Development* 74: 197–208.

Andrews, Matt, and Lant Pritchett. 2013. "Escaping Capability Traps through Problem Driven Iterative Adaptation (PDIA)." *World Development* 51: 234–44.

Andrews, Matt, Lant Pritchett, and Michael Woolcock. 2013. "Looking Like a State: Techniques of Persistent Failure in State Capability for Implementation." *Journal of Development Studies* 49 (1): 1–18.

———. 2017. *Building State Capability: Evidence, Analysis.* Oxford, UK: Oxford University Press.

Arrow, Kenneth. 1962. "Economic Welfare and the Allocation of Resources for Invention." In *The Rate and Direction of Inventive Activity: Economic and Social Factors*, edited by National Bureau of Economic Research, 609–26. Princeton, NJ: Princeton University Press.

Becker, Bettina. 2015. "Public R&D Policies and Private R&D Investment: A Survey of the Empirical Evidence." *Journal of Economic Surveys* 29: 917–42.

BIS. 2014. "The Case for Public Support for Innovation." Report prepared by Technopolis.

Bleda, Mercedes, and Pablo del Río. 2013. "The Market Failure and the Systemic Failure Rationales in Technological Innovation Systems." *Research Policy* 42 (5): 1039–52.

Borins, Sandford, ed. 2008. *Innovations in Government Research, Recognition, and Replication.* Washington, DC: Brookings Institution Press/Ash Center.

Calvo-González, O, and A. Eizmendi, G. Reyes. 2017. "Winners Never Quit, Quitters Never Grow: Using Text Mining to Measure Policy Volatility and Its Link with Long-Term Growth in Latin America." Working Paper, World Bank, Washington, DC.

Camagni, Roberto, and Roberta Capello. 2013. "Regional Innovation Patterns and the EU Regional Policy Reform: Toward Smart Innovation Policies." *Growth and Change* 44 (2): 355–89.

Campos, Francisco, Aidan Coville, Ana M. Fernandes, Markus Goldstein, and David McKenzie. 2012. "Learning from the Experiments That Never Happened: Lessons from Trying to Conduct Randomized Evaluations of Matching Grant Programs in Africa." Policy Research Working Paper No. 6296, World Bank, Washington, DC.

Cho, Yoon Jik, and Theordore H. Poister. 2013. "Human Resource Management Practices and Trust in Public Organizations." *Public Management Review* 15 (6): 816–38.

Correa, Paulo. 2014. "Public Expenditure Reviews in Science, Technology, and Innovation: A Guidance Note." World Bank, Washington, DC.

Czarnitzki, Dirk, Bernd Ebersberger, and Andreas Fier. 2007. "The Relationship between R&D Collaboration, Subsidies and R&D Performance: Empirical Evidence from Finland and Germany." *Journal of Applied Economics* 22 (7): 1347–66.

De Carvalho, Antonio Gledson, Charles W. Calomiris, and João Amaro de Matos. 2008. "Venture Capital as Human Resource Management." *Journal of Economics and Business* 60 (3): 223–55.

Dodgson, Mark, Alan Hughes, John Foster, and Stan Metcalfe. 2011. "Systems Thinking, Market Failure, and the Development of Innovation Policy: The Case of Australia." *Research Policy* 40 (9): 1145–56.

Dutz, M.A., Y. Kuznetsov, E. Lasagabaster and D. Pilat (eds.), 2014. *Making Innovation Policy Work: Learning from Experimentation*, Paris: OECD and World Bank.

Edquist, Charles. 2004. "Final Remarks: Reflections on the Systems of Innovation Approach." *Science and Public Policy* 36 (6): 485–89.

Fagerberg, Jan. 2015. "Innovation Policy, National Innovation Systems and Economic Performance: In Search of a Useful Theoretical Framework." Working Papers on Innovation Studies 20150321, Centre for Technology, Innovation and Culture, University of Oslo, Norway.

Favero, Nathan, Kenneth J Meier, Laurence J. O'Toole, Jr. 2016. "Goals, Trust, Participation, and Feedback: Linking Internal Management with Performance Outcomes." *Journal of Public Administration Research and Theory* 26: 327–43.

Finan, Frederico, Benjamin A. Olken, and Rohini Pande. 2015. "The Personnel Economics of the State," NBER Working Papers 21825, National Bureau of Economic Research, Inc., Cambridge, MA.

Gambi, Mauricio Olavarría. 2012. "Evaluation of Programs in Chile: Analysis of a Sample of Evaluated Public Programs." *Revista CLAD Reforma y Democracia* 54: 143–64.

Glennie, Alex, and Kirsten Bound. 2016. "How Innovation Agencies Work: International Lessons to Inspire and Inform National Strategies." Nesta, London, UK. https://www.bl.uk/britishlibrary/~ /media/bl/global/social%20welfare/pdfs/non-secure/h/o/w/how-innovation-agencies-work -international-lessons-to-inspire-and-inform-national-strategies.pdf.

Hall, Bronwyn H., Albert N. Link, and John T. Scott. 2003. "Universities as Research Partners." *Review of Economics and Statistics* 85 (2): 485–91.

Jacobson, Willow S., and Jessica E. Sowa. 2015. "Strategic Human Capital Management in Municipal Government: An Assessment of Implementation Practices." *Public Personnel Management* 44: 317–39.

Kapil, Natasha, and Anwar Aridi. 2017. "Innovation Agencies: Takeaways from Emerging Innovation Systems." Unpublished Report, World Bank, Washington, DC.

Kapil, Natasha, Martin Piatkowski, and Cristina Navarrete. 2014. "Poland: Smart Growth Operational Program Review." World Bank, Washington, DC.

Krause, Rachel M., Hongtao Yi, and Richard C. Feiock. 2016. "Applying Policy Termination Theory to the Abandonment of Climate Protection Initiatives by US Local Governments." *Policy Studies Journal* 44: 176–95.

Lee, Keun. 2013. *Schumpeterian Analysis of Economic Catch-Up: Knowledge, Path-Creation, and the Middle-Income Trap.* Cambridge, UK: Cambridge University Press.

Link, A. N., and J. T. Scott. 2009. "The Role of Public Research Institutions in a National Innovation System: An Economic Perspective." Working Paper, World Bank, Washington, DC.

Lundvall, Bengt-Åke, ed. 1992. *National Systems of Innovation: Towards a Theory of Innovation and Interactive Learning.* London: Pinter.

Maloney, William F. 2017. "Revisiting the National Innovation System in Developing Countries." Working Paper, World Bank, Washington, DC.

Moore, Mark H. 2013. *Recognizing Public Value.* Cambridge, MA: Harvard University Press.

Nelson, Richard R. 1959. "The Economics of Invention: A Survey of the Literature." *Journal of Business* 32 (2): 101–27.

———. 2005. *Technology, Institutions, and Economic Growth.* Cambridge, MA: Harvard University Press.

Oh, Chai Kon. 1997. "A Study on the Promotion of the Effective Diffusion of National R&D Results." Science and Technology Policy Institute. (in Korean), Seoul.

O'Connell, Stephen D., Lucas Ferreira Mation, Joao Bevilaqua Teixeira Basto, and Mark Andrew Dutz. 2017. "Can Business Input Improve the Effectiveness of Worker Training? Evidence from Brazil's Pronatec-MDIC," Policy Research Working Paper Series 8155, The World Bank, Washington, DC.

Olejniczak, Karol, Estelle Raimondo, and Tomasz Kupiec. 2016. "Evaluation Units as Knowledge Brokers: Testing and Calibrating an Innovative Framework." *Evaluation* 22 (2): 168–89.

Rasul, I. and D. Rogger. 2017. "Management of Bureaucrats and Public Service Delivery: Evidence from the Nigerian Civil Service." *The Economic Journal* doi:10.1111/ecoj.12418.

Rodgers, Robert, and John E. Hunter. 1992. "A Foundation of Good Management Practice in Government Management by Objectives." *Public Administration Review* 52 (1): 27–39.

Rodrik, Dani. 2004. "Industrial Policy for the Twenty-First Century." John F. Kennedy School of Government, Harvard University, Cambridge, MA.

———. 2008. "Second-Best Institutions." *American Economic Review: Papers and Proceedings* 98 (2): 100–104.

Rogers, Juan. D. 2017. "'Good' Innovation Policy Making: Capabilities for Effectively Implementing Innovation Policy." Unpublished Report, Georgia Institute of Technology, Athens.

Sun, R., and G. Van Ryzin. 2014. "Are Performance Management Practices Associated with Better Outcomes? Empirical Evidence from New York Public Schools." *American Review of Public Administration* 44 (3): 324–38.

Teirlinck, Peter, Henri Delanghe, Pierre Padilla, and Arnold Verbeek. 2013. "Closing the Policy Cycle: Increasing the Utilization of Evaluation Findings in Research, Technological Development and Innovation Policy Design." *Science and Public Policy* 40 (3): 366–77.

U.S. National Science Foundation. 2016. *General Grant Terms and Conditions.* https://www.nsf.gov/pubs/policydocs/gc1/july16.pdf.

Van der Heijden, Jeroen. 2014. "Experimentation in Policy Design: Insights from the Building Sector." *Policy Sciences* 47: 249–66.

World Competitiveness Indicators. 2017. World Economic Forum http://www3.weforum.org/docs/GCR2016-2017/05FullReport/TheGlobalCompetitivenessReport2016-2017_FINAL.pdf.

Wu, Xun, and M. Ramesh. 2014. "Market Imperfections, Government Imperfections, and Policy Mixes: Policy Innovations in Singapore." *Policy Sciences* 47 (3): 305–20.

7. Instruments to Support Firm Capabilities for Innovation

Introduction

Resolving the innovation policy dilemma requires choosing the appropriate combination of innovation policy instruments—the *policy mix*. This is likely to differ and evolve in complexity as capabilities are accumulated and firms transition from technology adoption/absorption toward technology and product generation, as described in chapter 2. In this chapter, we describe the different stages of the capabilities escalator and the set of instruments that are both critical to firm needs at each stage and feasible given government capacity to design and implement policy.

The Instruments of the Innovation Policy Space

The policy response to the set of failures described above needs to consider a combination of instruments, the *policy mix*.[1] Commonly, policy makers use this term to refer to the set of instruments being implemented under the umbrella of science, technology, and innovation (STI) policy. However, as discussed in chapter 4, the definition needs to be broader, both in terms of relevant instruments and in terms of reflecting the complementarities among instruments.

To frame the subsequent discussion, figure 7.1 shows a schematic diagram of the different policy instruments populating the *policy space*. On the vertical axis, we move from outcomes related to the supply of knowledge and research to outcomes related to firms' demand for research and development (R&D) and non-R&D innovation activities. Along the horizontal axis, we present a range of government measures, including indirect and direct financial support, other services, and requirements or recommendations for firm behavior. Along this axis, we also divide the type of support into categories of market-based incentives such as tax exemptions and subsidies, nonmarket incentives such as prizes and awards, the direct provision of services and infrastructure, voluntary measures to improve collaboration and firm conduct, and regulations.

Figure 7.1 is meant to illustrate the breadth and complexity of the instruments that can support firm innovation, as well as the potential for complementarities between instruments.[2] At the same time, it is a snapshot of a mature *policy mix*, and represents the final destination of the capabilities escalator, rather than the beginning.

FIGURE 7.1 **The Innovation Policy Space**

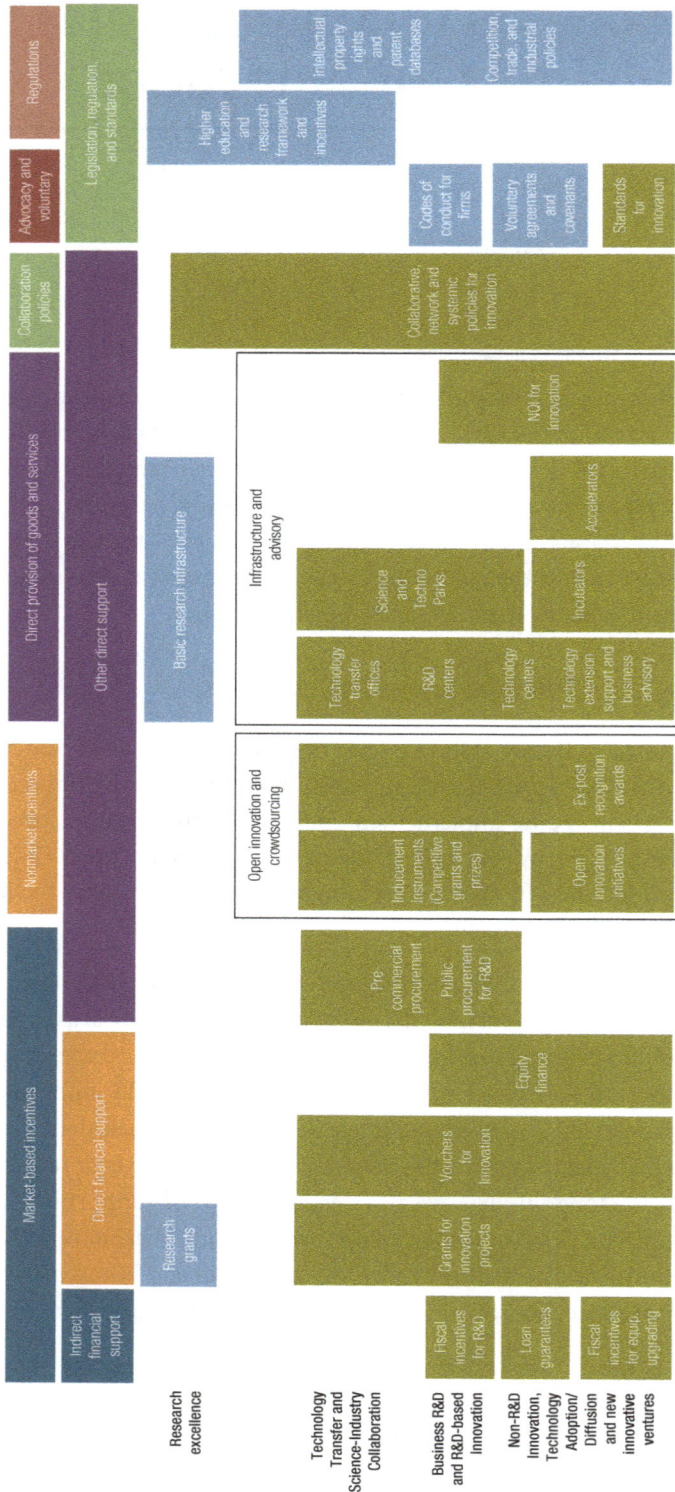

Source: World Bank 2017.

Note: NQI = national quality infrastructure; R&D = research and development.

Many developing countries strain their governance capabilities for implementation and coordination trying to occupy the policy space all at once, and imitate the National Innovation System (NIS) of more advanced countries. This can result in a misalignment of the *policy mix* with the present need of industry, in particular, to build innovation capabilities, and lead to a fragmented and undirected set of instruments. The next section proposes a gradual path of expanding the mix that is aligned with the capabilities of both the private sector and of policy makers and institutions.

Supporting the Capabilities Escalator: Innovation Policy Mixes and Convergence to the Technological Frontier

Countries at similar stages of development share common challenges related to the nature of innovation activities, implementation capacity, and framework conditions, and these constraints dictate the *policy mix*. Although the combinations of instruments vary over a continuum of capabilities building, in this section, for simplicity, we highlight three key stages of this capabilities escalator: (1) production and management capabilities, (2) technological capabilities, and (3) invention and technology-generation capabilities. In the background, as discussed in chapter 4 with respect to the expanded NIS, across all stages, governments need to remove barriers to the accumulation of all types of capital—human, physical, and knowledge—and this will entail structural reforms to improve education and training, ensure access to financial markets, open trade, and establish a supportive business climate and competition framework.

The demands for public support differ by stage (figure 7.2), reflecting the innovation trajectories described in chapter 2 and the typologies of capabilities summarized in chapter 4 and represented in Figure 1.2. In stage 1, most firms in developing countries are on the lower end of this path (Bell and Pavitt 1993; Lundvall et al. 2009; Bell and Figueiredo 2012; Zanello et al. 2013). Innovation involves ad hoc efforts that include the adoption of basic managerial and organizational practices, machinery upgrading, and basic process improvement, but little formal R&D. Innovation activities are usually dispersed and less systematic than in advanced countries, and tend to be more incremental because of the lack of complementary factors, and the fact that demand for novel local goods in these markets may be low or innovations may be difficult to protect. Under these conditions, policy needs to ensure that technology is accessible, to help strengthen firm capabilities to absorb technology from advanced countries.

As countries move toward the technological frontier in stage 2, the intensity of R&D increases, and the types of innovation introduced by leading firms (particularly those in trade-exposed sectors) tend to increase in sophistication and quality to meet increasing internal demand and standards for participation in export markets. In this transition, instruments that support business R&D projects and, in some cases, collaboration between researchers and industry become more relevant. However, broader policies to support

FIGURE 7.2   **The Capabilities Escalator: Innovation Policy Needs**

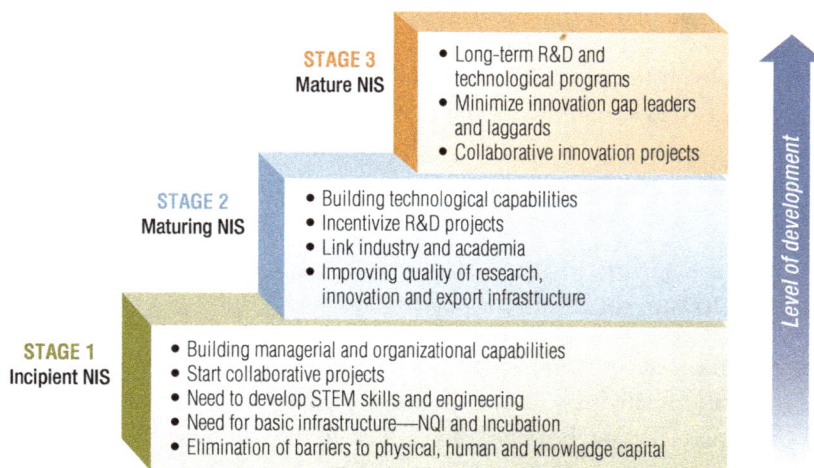

STAGE 3
Mature NIS
- Long-term R&D and technological programs
- Minimize innovation gap leaders and laggards
- Collaborative innovation projects

STAGE 2
Maturing NIS
- Building technological capabilities
- Incentivize R&D projects
- Link industry and academia
- Improving quality of research, innovation and export infrastructure

STAGE 1
Incipient NIS
- Building managerial and organizational capabilities
- Start collaborative projects
- Need to develop STEM skills and engineering
- Need for basic infrastructure—NQI and Incubation
- Elimination of barriers to physical, human and knowledge capital

Level of development

Note: NIS = National Innovation System; NQI = national quality infrastructure; R&D = research and development; STEM = science, technology, engineering, and mathematics.

firm capabilities remain important because the ability to innovate is not uniform across the economy and most sectors are still dominated by basic innovation activities.

Finally, in countries where a significant number of firms have reached the technological frontier and with a more mature NIS, innovation policies focus on promoting the generation of new technologies and supporting increasingly complex innovative projects, while continuing to build absorptive capacity in laggard small and medium enterprises (SMEs). It is important to highlight that the institutions appropriate to this stage take decades to build. Though we have stressed basic capability building as the priority in the early stages, laying the groundwork for an advanced science and technology (S&T) capability must also begin at this stage.

Table 7.1 profiles these development stages, describing symptoms that may warrant policy intervention, with probable causes, ecosystem conditions, and combinations of instruments that could be used in response. A graphic illustration of these stages and the implication for the *policy mix* is shown in figure 7.3. The important message of the figure is that the *policy mix* of innovation policy instruments is cumulative and evolves from little to more sophistication, as firms advance in the capabilities escalator. In line with the significant capabilities failure described in the first section of chapter 6, the *policy mix* starts with building basic managerial and organizational capabilities via management extension that bridges large information asymmetries and supports learning. It also combines incentivizing collaboration between firms, via for example vouchers for innovation (see box 7.1 for a description of this instrument), and focusing on developing key complementary factors such as science, technology, engineering, and mathematics (STEM) skills and early stage infrastructure.

TABLE 7.1 The Policy Mix in Different Stages of the National Innovation System

	Causes		Enabling conditions		
Symptoms	Absorptive capacity in firms	Knowledge generation and collaboration capacity	Ecosystem conditions	Complementary public goods for STI[1]	Illustrative policy mix of instruments
Stage 1: Incipient NIS (Long distance of firms to the technological frontier) Building managerial and organizational practices. Prevalent in low- and lower-middle-income countries.	Low absorptive capacity to transfer technology from advanced to developing economies. ■ **Inputs:** firms present basic managerial and organizational practices, and conduct little formal R&D activity. **Outputs:** Very low quality of innovation. Patenting is nonexistent. Lack of entry in export markets, and exports primarily based on commodities.	■ Basic research capacity remains deficient and unaligned with needs of industry. ■ Applied R&D capacity from firms is minimum. Knowledge inflows from FDI remain low. ■ Mechanisms for science-industry exchange and collaboration are weak. ■ Lack of cooperation between firms, innovations developed informally and in isolation; absence of firm clusters. ■ Low research capacity in universities and absence of industry–university collaboration.	■ Lack of export orientation reduces incentives for local firms to innovate. ■ Environmental, consumer protection, and social regulations are often either weak or not properly enforced. ■ FDI penetration is usually low, and existing investments are extractive, with minimal spillovers to the local economy. ■ Large rates of business informality hinder adoption of technology and innovation. ■ Significant distortions reduce competition and increase misallocation.	■ Absent or obsolete innovation infrastructure makes innovation costly for firms. ■ Low availability of laboratories, testing facilities, and other NQI systems reduces incentives for firms to acquire new innovations ■ STEM education and postsecondary technical programs remain basic. Academic competencies for research remain low. ■ Essential technological and science infrastructure is lacking. ■ Weak IP rights framework slows investments in R&D.	Focus on employing instruments that support absorptive capacity and management and production capabilities: ■ Management extension programs ■ Early stage infrastructure and advisory (incubators) ■ Foster collaboration and simple innovation projects such as vouchers for collaboration and direct grants for business innovation (with embedded advisory services) ■ Standards and basic NQI infrastructure for innovation ■ Strengthen research quality

(Table continues on the following page.)

TABLE 7.1 The Policy Mix in Different Stages of the National Innovation System *(continued)*

Symptoms	Causes		Enabling conditions		Illustrative policy mix of instruments
	Absorptive capacity in firms	Knowledge generation and collaboration capacity	Ecosystem conditions	Complementary public goods for STI[1]	
Stage 2: Maturing NIS Building innovation capabilities and accelerating technology transfer. Prevalent in middle- and upper-middle-income countries.	Incremental innovation remains prevalent, and isolated cases of radical innovation are seen. The generation of new technologies and more complex innovative projects is incipient. **Inputs:** Intensity of R&D and the level of sophistication of knowledge inputs increase. **Outputs:** Firms start participating in technology sector, with increased presence of manufacturing and services exports, and incipient participation in GVCs. A few university spin-offs and patenting applications.	▪ Firms' investments in knowledge activities are modest. ▪ Most learning remains informal, but firms start developing more sophisticated competencies, particularly around quality. ▪ Some learning through GVCs and participation in international markets.	▪ Specific sectors and multinational companies conduct formal R&D activities in country. R&D activities remain incipient. ▪ Collaboration between firms, and between firms and universities to conduct joint innovation activities exist, but are underdeveloped. ▪ A few clusters of high-quality and applied research in universities appear. ▪ As more publicly funded resources become available, universities start getting involved in R&D, for example, through competitive research funding. ▪ Knowledge inflows from international research partnerships are more visible.	▪ Increasing internal demand and participation in export markets raise performance standards for products. ▪ Stricter consumer standards and safety regulations increase demand for quality infrastructure. ▪ Increased export orientation and sophistication of exports intensify competitive pressures facing domestic firms. ▪ Improved enabling environment for firms, but some distortions remain and competition is limited in some sectors. ▪ FDI commitments are stronger, and there are signals of local content development, with modest knowledge spillovers. ▪ Business informality exists, but is not prevalent.	▪ Deficit of STEM skills raises firms' costs because skills are unavailable or must be imported from abroad. ▪ Technological and science infrastructure is more available. However, testing infrastructure and R&D facilities are not sophisticated. ▪ Competitive scientific research funding is more available. ▪ The IP rights framework is inadequate.	In addition to continue building absorptive capacity, support technology extension projects and starting university-industry collaboration becomes more important in certain clusters: ▪ Technology extension and business advisory programs ▪ Local supply chain development and export programs ▪ Grants for innovative projects to finance prototyping, testing, and commercialization activities and technical assistance ▪ Early stage infrastructure and advisory programs (incubators) and some accelerators ▪ Innovation vouchers and grants for collaborative projects. ▪ Focus on research quality and STEM

(Table continues on the following page.)

TABLE 7.1 **The Policy Mix in Different Stages of the National Innovation System** *(continued)*

	Symptoms	Causes		Enabling conditions		Illustrative policy mix of instruments
		Absorptive capacity in firms	Knowledge generation and collaboration capacity	Ecosystem conditions	Complementary public goods for STI[1]	
Stage 3: Mature NIS Technology generation and supporting capabilities. Building in laggard firms. Prevalent in higher-income economies.	**Inputs:** Presence of radical inventions. Significant R&D intensity in some sectors, but less so in the SME sector. **Outputs:** A few technology-intensive sectors generate new technologies, but a significant part of the SME sector lags behind. Significant number of university spin-offs. Large number of export firms and widespread import of inputs and participation in GVCs. Developed tech sector.	■ Firms show more developed competencies, and are generally more inclined to innovate. Some market failures persist—externalities in the case of tech sectors and asymmetric information for SMEs. ■ Good-quality services to support technology absorption, and other complementary factors.	■ Strong university research with high contractual R&D activity in universities and patenting activities. ■ Consolidated clusters and substantial collaboration in innovation between larger companies. ■ Public funding is widely available, and several knowledge providers (including universities) remain highly engaged in conducting diverse R&D activities. ■ Knowledge partnerships between domestic providers and international research agencies are well established.	■ Business regulation promotes a relatively friendly and competitive business climate. ■ Market requirement levels are high because of high export orientation and strong consumer protection mechanisms. ■ The macro context is stable, and labor market rigidities are few. ■ FDI intensity remains high, and of high quality, with positive knowledge spillovers to the local economy. ■ The depth of credit and capital markets ensures promising ventures enjoy funding.	■ IP rights and regulation are relatively developed. ■ Knowledge institutions offer advanced degree scholarships at a high rate, ensuring the availability of specialized human capital. ■ Universities and innovation agencies have advanced talent acquisition strategies, promoting knowledge exchanges, from both international and domestic sources of specialized skills. ■ Modern R&D infrastructure and well-developed quality and standards infrastructure ensure low transaction costs for innovative firms. ■ Skill base is more developed, although gaps may still exist, particularly in specific STEM skills.	The *policy mix* combines instruments to support frontier technology generation and high R&D intensive projects, with a variety of instruments for SMEs to ignite innovation. These include: ■ Tax incentives for R&D ■ Grants to large complex, long-term and collaborative R&D projects ■ Procurement for innovation ■ Equity finance for innovation and early stage capital ■ Collaborative, network, and systemic policies for innovation ■ loan guarantees with accompanying firm-level capacity building and advisory programs ■ Open innovation initiatives ■ Technology extension and-business advisory services

Source: (1) World Bank 2017; Crespi, Fernández-Arias, and Stein 2014; '(2) Maloney 2017b.

Note: FDI = foreign direct investment; GVC = global value chain; IP = intellectual property, R&D = research and development; SME = small and medium enterprise; STEM = science, technology, engineering, and mathematics; STI = science, technology, and innovation.

FIGURE 7.3 **The Capabilities Escalator: The Policy Mix Evolves from Less to More Sophistication**

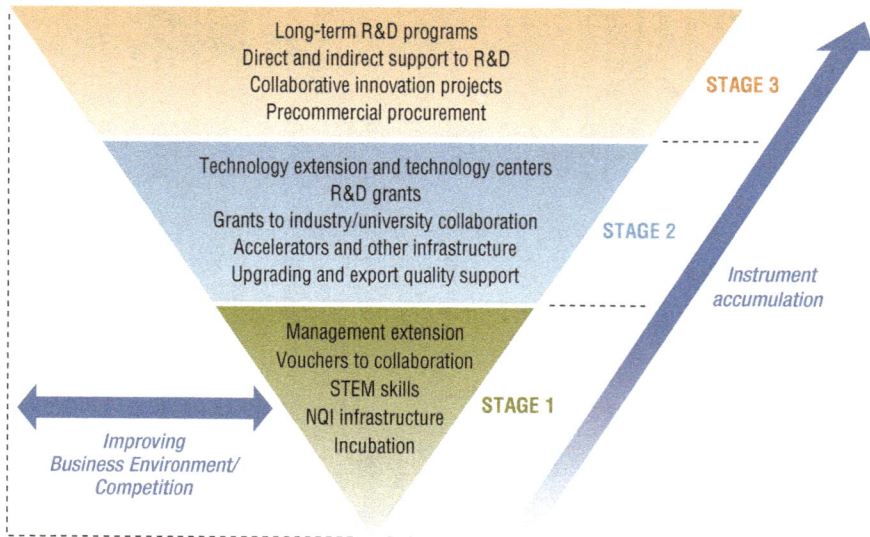

Long-term R&D programs
Direct and indirect support to R&D
Collaborative innovation projects
Precommercial procurement

STAGE 3

Technology extension and technology centers
R&D grants
Grants to industry/university collaboration
Accelerators and other infrastructure
Upgrading and export quality support

STAGE 2

Instrument accumulation

Management extension
Vouchers to collaboration
STEM skills
NQI infrastructure
Incubation

STAGE 1

Improving Business Environment/ Competition

Note: NQI = national quality infrastructure; R&D = research and development; STEM = science, technology, engineering, and mathematics.

BOX 7.1

Innovation Vouchers to Foster Innovation Activities and Collaboration

One pervasive failure in low-capabilities countries is the lack of collaboration between firms and between firms and knowledge providers. Innovation vouchers are one way of addressing this failure. Vouchers are small grants allocated to SMEs to purchase services from external knowledge providers. The main objective is usually to entice non-innovator SMEs to start collaborating with knowledge organizations and providers. Vouchers also can be used for SMEs already innovating, to encourage them to enter new areas. Through voucher schemes, non-innovative SMEs or SMEs engaged in simple forms of innovation are expected to start engaging in innovation activities and increase the sophistication of their activities.

Unlike grants, voucher schemes are often entitlement-based rather than competition-based, which means that applicants can receive vouchers as long as they meet the eligibility requirements. This reduces administrative costs for applicants and the government. Also, vouchers often involve smaller amounts than matching grants because they aim to provide an incentive to start collaborating and to develop small projects. The advantages of vouchers can be summarized as follows: simplicity in their management, flexibility in the type of collaboration incentivized, and demand orientation.

On the other hand, innovation vouchers present several potential risks. First, it is difficult to ensure that collaboration is not a one-off transaction, and, in some cases, the incentive provided is too small to attract the intended target group of noninnovators. More important are the risks associated with lock-in to a small number of knowledge providers and fraudulent use of

(Box continues on the following page.)

schemes, whereby BDS providers search for partner SMEs with no intention of developing cooperative projects.

Despite the recent popularity of voucher programs in many developed countries, very few of them have been formally evaluated. Little solid evidence on effectiveness is available from developing countries. However, evidence from evaluations in developed countries suggests significant additionality in the number of innovation projects in the short run. A randomized control trial of the Creative Credits program in the United Kingdom finds a positive impact on additional projects being conducted in the short run; recipients were statistically more likely than nonrecipients to have introduced product/process innovations (72.4 percent versus 55.9 percent for product innovation; 63.8 percent versus 47.2 percent for process innovation). However, the difference was not statistically significant after 12 months. There was also a significant, positive impact on firm performance equal to short-term additional sales of approximately £3,430 per voucher.

Voucher schemes require some minimal competencies from SMEs to identify their challenges that can be addressed by external knowledge providers. Also, the schemes require program managers who can facilitate the matching between firms and knowledge providers and act as brokers. This requires dedicated staff who can ensure professional delivery and avoid conflicts of interest, which is often challenging in some lower-income countries.

Source: World Bank 2017.

The second stage focuses on strengthening technological capabilities via technological extension or technology centers, and direct and indirect support to R&D projects, while continuing to strengthen existing complementary factors and infrastructure for innovation. In the final stage, the focus is on facilitating advanced technological development capabilities and invention, while supporting basic innovation capabilities in laggard firms. So, in this final stage the *policy mix* has matured to resemble the broad scope of figure 7.1.

In what follows, we focus in more detail on some of these key innovation policy instruments that are required to build these capabilities.[3]

Building Managerial and Organizational Practices for Innovation

Policies supporting management and organizational capabilities need to be at the center of innovation policy in stage 1. Supporting these capabilities is particularly important at an early stage of technological development. However, the quality of these practices varies enormously within and between countries. In this section, we focus on some successful experiences of management extension programs, as well as describing some of the key challenges when implementing these programs.

Addressing the Capabilities Gap

As discussed in chapter 4, there are several reasons why firms do not invest more in innovation. Low capabilities prevent firms from identifying productive opportunities, evaluating their feasibility, managing their risk, and allocating human resources effectively. This explains the ubiquity of business advisory services, originating in the agricultural sector and now very popular in, for example, Europe, Japan, Singapore, and the United States (see Ezell and Atkinson 2011; Maloney 2017a). Typically, these comprise a group of consultants that:

- Benchmark firm management along some of the dimensions already discussed in the World Management Survey, including operations, financial management, planning, and human resource policy.
- Design an improvement plan over the next year or 18 months, typically done jointly with management on the basis of the diagnostic and the areas that are most critical to improving firm performance.
- Accompany management in the implementation of the plan.

In the process, there is learning by the firm, and by the consultants about the firm, that can subsequently be used to tailor support in other areas. For instance, once the foundations in terms of core capabilities are in place, the firm can be directed toward more sophisticated innovation support, such as developing R&D projects. A key characteristic of this type of instrument, *management extension*, as opposed to more traditional business advisory services, is the more proactive role of the industry specialist or "extensionist" in engaging with the firm and guiding it though the learning process.

The Origins of Management Extension

Extension systems enjoy a long pedigree. The Morrill Land Grant College program that established many of the great U.S. universities was established partly to redress the fact that the United States had no systems of agricultural or mechanical extension such as were found in Europe at the time. In both regions—Europe and the United States—productivity and quality studies would advance throughout the nineteenth century.

Extension services would play a central role in the recoveries of the post–World War II period. Japan during the war had established the Japan Management Association in 1942 to upgrade industry quality and develop new methods to promote technological coordination between large and small firms. After the war, the awareness of an almost tenfold lag in productivity relative to the United States, a lag exceeding that faced by most contemporary middle-income countries, highlighted the need for a concerted effort to adopt labor management, training, and quality control (QC) techniques (see box 7.2), especially from the United States, which was then recognized as the world leader. The U.S. government also used the Marshall Plan as part of a goal of worldwide dissemination of U.S. managerial techniques. In conjunction with local

Post–World War II Recovery and Firm Upgrading in Japan

Exiting World War II, not only did Japan have a tenth of the productivity of the United States and a third of Germany, but its exports also had a reputation for poor quality. In recent years, the government's emphasis has shifted somewhat from catch-up to one of supporting firms with high innovation potential. However, for the second half of the 20th century, programs were focused on narrowing the productivity and quality gap of firms with their larger counterparts in Japan and with peers in the advanced world.

The Japanese government approached this task with several instruments. In 1948, the Small and Medium Enterprise Agency was established under the Ministry of International Trade and Industry (MITI). The Export Inspections Act of 1957 established inspections by government organizations to improve quality, which helped all Japanese firms by improving the reputation of Japanese products. The Industrial Standardization Law introduced a special JIS (Japanese Industrial Standards) mark that certified the standards of quality control. This signal appears especially important in helping SMEs secure contracts (Kikuchi 2009). Public research organizations (*Kosetsushi*, presently about 600 in the country) were set up to conduct public testing and research to meet the industrial needs of local communities (Wada 2009).

Of great importance was the establishment of the system of publicly registered SME management diagnosticians/consultants (*chusho kigyo shindan-shi* or *Shindan Shi* where *shindan* means "diagnostic") that evaluate SMEs' business performance and provide them with advice and consultation. The *Shindan Shi* system was adopted by MITI's regional and prefectural offices—10,000 consultations were provided to companies in 1950 alone (Wada 2009). In addition, a system of direct financial support and guarantees for private sector lending was established. Three private institutions, the most well known being the Japanese Productivity Center, were critical to capabilities formation.

Japan has had particular success in promoting these programs on the operational side, and terms like "5s" and "Kaizen" are now used around the world. The 5s methodology consists of five steps—*seiri, seiton, seiso, seiketsu, and shitsuke* broadly translated as "sort," "set in order," "shine," "standardize," and "sustain"—which are considered basic building blocks for just-in-time management systems. They begin with extremely basic issues, such as organization of tools and eliminating distractions on the work floor, and work up to standardizing practices and maintaining high quality in production. The *Kaizen* or "continuous improvement" approach sees productivity as improving processes and flow in a continuous fashion, interspersed with occasional bursts of innovation.

Source: Maloney 2017a.

executives, this would result in what was called the "productivity movement" and the creation in 1953 of the Japan Productivity Center, a public-private partnership with the goal of dissemination of new technologies and managerial ideas to Japanese industry. The statistical techniques for QC developed by the American W. Edwards Deming were also propagated in person in conjunction with the Japan Union of Scientists and Engineers and Japan Management Association. They became the basis for subsequent QC techniques that Japan became famous for in subsequent decades (Morris-Suzuki 1994; Kikuchi 2011).

Similar efforts were important to Europe's recovery. Bureau of Labor Statistics Chief of Productivity and Technology Development James Silberman claimed that inefficiencies in management were a more severe problem than war damages (Giorcelli 2016). Between 1952 and 1958, as in Japan, the U.S. Productivity Program organized study trips of European managers to U.S. plants, followed by consulting sessions of U.S. experts in European firms. Giorcelli offers perhaps the most systematic study of how the program rolled out in Italy, combined with part of the Marshall Plan, where, as in Japan, European managers were invited to learn modern management skills through study trips to the United States. The program gave visiting Italian managers the opportunity to participate in formal training and internships in U.S. firms, as well as providing equipment loans.

These techniques would be unevenly disseminated throughout the developing world in the next decades. Most notably, in the 1980s, Singapore had become disappointed with the productivity gains arising from its growth model. In particular, the country had been successful in attracting multinational enterprises (MNEs), but local firms had not yet been able to link into these value chains. Singapore contracted with the Japanese Productivity Center to set up what is now known as SPRING (the Standards, Productivity and Innovation Board), which now delivers a menu of firm capability support programs. SPRING offers a wide array of programs, ranging from basic to advanced, including incentivizing the private sector through awards and prizes, making equity investments or co-investments, and building capacity in the entire ecosystem through multiple national and international partnerships (see box 7.3 and annex 7A). The Republic of Korea, also faced with a lagging SME sector in a very dualistic economy, has developed its own Korea Productivity Center. Below, we discuss several other more recent interventions in emerging economies.

BOX 7.3

National Quality Infrastructure

The national quality infrastructure (NQI) is part of a country's framework conditions for innovation. As such, the government can play two main roles. The first is developing an NQI and guaranteeing a minimum level of functionality and service provision from it. The second is supporting the development of local standards, or at least participation in the development of international standards, and then potentially their uptake by industry where relevant.

The NQI comprises public and private parties that deliver specific functions to determine whether a product, process, or service meets a defined set of requirements. These functions are delivered through a group of services that support standardization, including measurement, inspection, certification, accreditation, and conformity assessments. The use of standards for innovation is a central element of the NQI system. The NQI represents a system of interrelated institutions that facilitate the diffusion of standards in the economy.

(Box continues on the following page.)

National Quality Infrastructure *(continued)*

Conformity assessment is the group of procedures to evaluate whether a product, process, or service fulfills certain standards, linking the standards with the product, processes, and services themselves. These procedures include some—and sometimes all—of the following:

1. *Testing and inspection.* Measures to evaluate a product, process, or service, according to a specified procedure
2. *Calibration.* Determines the relationship between instrument inputs and the magnitude of response in its outputs
3. *Certification.* Provides independent assurance that a certain product or service complies with a certain standard, and can help manufacturing and service firms to differentiate from less reputable suppliers.

Standards specify characteristics or performance, convey information, or provide means of communication. In their most general definition, they can be regarded as a reference that has been established by some form of authority, custom, or general consent (Guasch et al. 2007). Standards codify know-how and market requirements, enable interoperability between products and processes, set a minimum level of quality, and reduce variety, enabling economies of learning and scale (Guasch et al. 2007). See for Eastern Europe, Racine (2010).

Source: Guasch et al. 2007; World Bank 2017.

The Returns to Management Extension

Recent studies find that management extension services tend to generate very high rates of return. For the United States, Jarmin (1999) finds that firms that participated in manufacturing extension partnership (MEP) programs in the United States experienced between 3.4 and 16 percent higher labor productivity growth between 1987 and 1992 than nonparticipating firms. In addition, Ehlen (2001) finds that Illinois MEP-affiliated centers generated US$10 million in revenues in 1999: while the cost to the state was US$6 million, or US$1.66 in tax revenue for each public dollar invested. The Georgia MEP-affiliated centers reported US$4.44 in tax revenue per dollar spent in public support.

Although a prime disseminator of such techniques, Japan has published no public studies of their efficacy. However, Giorcelli (2016) has studied the analogous policies in postwar Italy. Using archive data, she finds that businesses participating in the productivity program increased sales and productivity and stayed in business longer than comparable companies that were not part of the program. Management practices had larger and more persistent effects than machinery purchases or technology and had a compounding effect on business success, with impacts increasing over time and persisting even 15 years after the program ended. The key channel through which these new capabilities impacted firm performance was by helping managers make better investment decisions—investing in new plants or new machines, for example—which made their production more efficient.

In a randomized control trial in India where textile firms were provided extension services, Bloom et al. (2013) find a dramatic increase in the adoption of good management practices by treated plants (figure 7.4). The control group, which received only the diagnostic, also improved substantially, suggesting, again, that limited access to information is a major barrier. The rate of productivity growth was 11 percentage points higher in the treatment group (firms that adopted these new practices) than in the control group, enough to afford the full cost of expensive consulting for one year.

A similar study by Iacovone, McKenzie, and Maloney (2017) finds that locally provided consulting services—provided by the National Productivity Center in Cali, Colombia—have a positive impact on management practices in Colombia. Panel b of figure 7.4 shows a dramatic difference between those firms accompanied by in-firm consultants (in green) and those who were given only a diagnostic (blue).

The positive returns of management extension do not only apply to more established SMEs. For micro and small enterprises in Mexico, Bruhn, Karlan, and Schoar (2016) find that productivity more than doubled after one year of local consulting services. McKenzie and Puerto (2017) look at the impact of providing management training on innovation to a large sample of rural women microentrepreneurs in Kenya.

FIGURE 7.4 **Management Extension Improved Management Practices in India and Colombia**

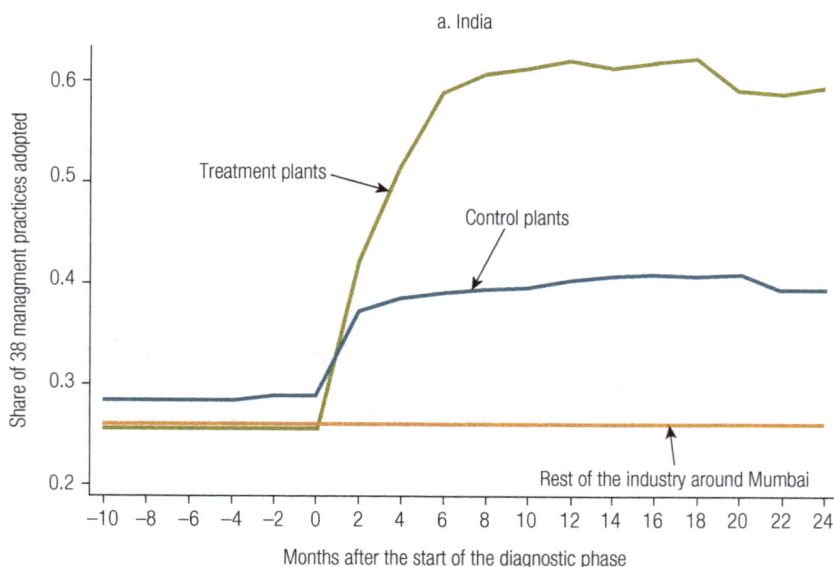

a. India

(Figure continues on the following page.)

The Innovation Paradox

FIGURE 7.4 **Management Extension Improved Management Practices in India and Colombia *(continued)***

b. Colombia

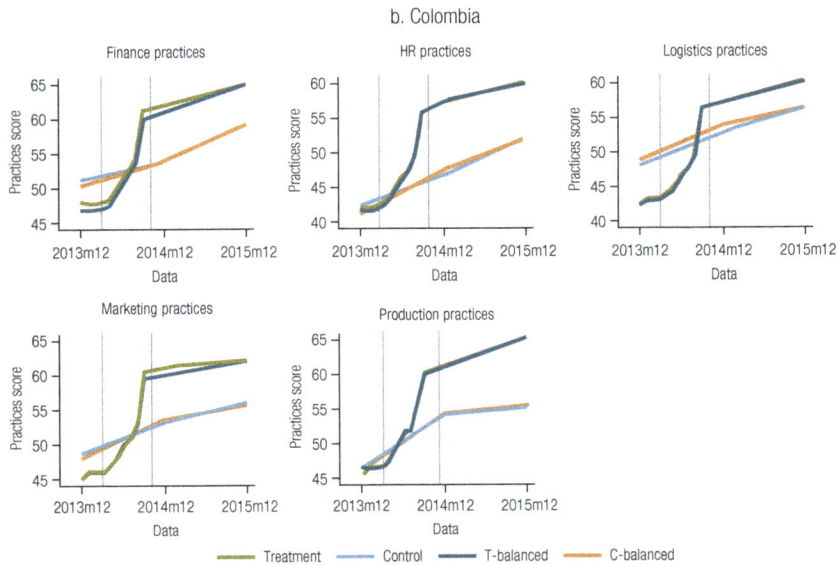

Finance practices

HR practices

Logistics practices

Marketing practices

Production practices

Treatment — Control — T-balanced — C-balanced

Source: Bloom et al. 2013 (panel a); Iacovone, McKenzie, and Maloney 2017 (panel b).

Note: In panel b, Treatment and Control lines are for the full sample for which data are available, with the sample size changing over time due to attrition. Balanced show the changes over time for the balanced panel of 67 firms for which management practices data are available for both preintervention and postintervention. Vertical lines bracket the intervention period for the individual treatment. HR = human resources.

They show that the women who receive the services are 8–11 percent more likely to introduce a new product than the control group.[4]

The type of intervention appears to matter as well. Anderson-Macdonald et al. (2017) offered marketing or finance training to microfirms in South Africa. After a year, the finance group saw profits increase 41 percent relative to those with no training, mostly through efficiency gains; the marketing group saw profits increase 61 percent by adopting a growth focus on higher sales, greater investments in stock and materials, and hiring more employees. With a slightly different take, Brooks, Donovan, and Johnson (2017) show that profits of inexperienced female microenterprise owners in a Kenyan slum grew by 20 percent with mentorship by an experienced entrepreneur in the same community focusing on localized specific information (like finding suppliers) rather than on abstract general information (how to keep books).

In general, the small but incipient evidence related to management extension and business advisory, much of it randomized control trials and hence the gold standard, appears to be positive across different types of firms.

Another type of intervention supporting business upgrading is the provision of quality-enhancing programs oriented to the adoption of existing quality standards (see box 7.3 for a description of the national quality infrastructure). The available evidence of the impact of quality enhancement programs and standards setting is less solid but also positive. Guasch et al. (2007) cites a United Kingdom's DTI 2005 study showing a significant long-run contribution of standards to economic growth in the United Kingdom: from 1948 and 2002, standards contributed to 13 percent of the growth in labor productivity. A similar, but older, study in Germany indicates that standards contributed 0.9 percentage points of an average overall growth rate of 3.3 percent. Other European studies show that standards are as important as patents for productivity, but the impact differs across sectors, suggesting that standards have greater impact in mature sectors than in R&D-intensive industries where patents proved more important. Using firm-level surveys, Escribano and Guasch (2005) find that standards (proxied by International Organization for Standardization certification) increased productivity by some 2.4–17.6 percent in four Central American countries, less than 1 percent in four Southeast Asian countries, and 4.5 percent in China.

If Extension Programs Yield Such Positive Rates of Return, Why Don't Firms Pay for Them Themselves?

The logical question is why, if returns are so high, firms do not upgrade themselves. The NIS literature argues for a systemic failure in inducing firms to learn, and the neoclassical tradition offers specifics on how. For example, the European Commission's Study of Business Support Services and Market Failure offers several reasons, two of which find increasing support in the recent empirical literature.

Firms Don't Know What They Don't Know

First, consistent with biased self-evaluations found by Bloom and Van Reenen (2007), firms may not know what they do not know and hence do not perceive the value of investing in themselves. As figure 7.5 shows, not only do entrepreneurs in most countries overestimate their abilities, but the magnitude of their overconfidence also increases with distance from the managerial frontier.[5]

McKenzie and Woodruff (2013) examine several additional hypotheses to understand the lack of investments in managerial and organizational practices, ranging from deficient information to credit and insurance market failures. If true, these explanations, again, suggest the need to avoid false diagnoses in designing policy: if innovation in managerial practices is limited by a lack of credit, then creating a government institution to train managers is unlikely to be the efficient solution.

However, although such failures are presumably less important in advanced countries, subsidies to support introductory advisory services nonetheless remain huge: 100 percent in Korea, Singapore, and Scotland, or 60 percent in Japan. This is suggestive

FIGURE 7.5   **Managers Tend to Overrate Their Abilities (Measured versus Self-Evaluated Management Practices Score)**

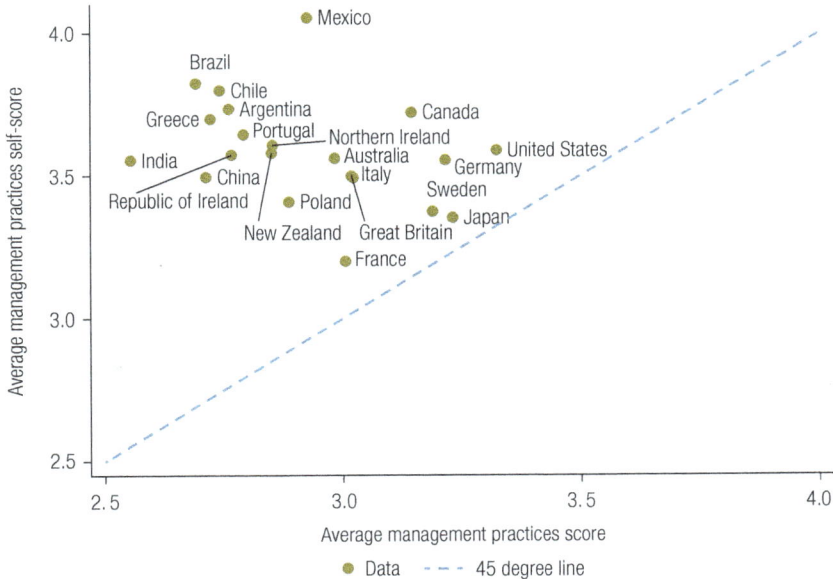

Source: World Management Survey; Bloom and Van Reenen 2007; and Maloney 2017b.

of an important role for information asymmetries about the true managerial quality and the potential for improvement, which could explain the lack of willingness to pay for these services. The heavily subsidized initial consultations provide a benchmark of firm managerial quality and areas of potential improvement, and then serve as a gateway to a broader set of firm support programs of progressively higher technological sophistication.[6]

They also reveal information about potential high-performing firms and firms that are less likely to succeed; indeed, in both Japan and Singapore (see box 7.4) gaining such intelligence is a deliberate part of the escalator infrastructure. This role is especially important in developing countries, where significant distortions may prevent allocative efficiency, allowing some less-productive firms to remain in the market (Hsieh and Klenow 2009). Indeed, it may be asked whether it would be better to just encourage the entry of better new firms than trying to upgrade existing firms with expensive consulting services. There is no ready answer here, except that about half of productivity gains in advanced countries appear to occur within incumbent firms, and the measured rates of return discussed above appear to justify the intervention. On the basis of the India evaluation above, if we imagine that firms pay a 20 percent tax rate, then a 100 percent subsidy of consulting services could easily be recouped from the productivity gains in under five years. The U.S. studies suggest the return in taxes to range from 60 percent to 400 percent. Further, to the degree that government gains

The Capabilities Escalator in Singapore

The National Productivity Board (NPB) was established in 1972 to improve productivity in all sectors and levels of the economy. The NPB followed a *total productivity* approach, which emphasized productivity measurement, product quality, a flexible wage system, worker training, and assistance to small- and medium-sized enterprises.

To promote productivity in both the public and the private sectors, the board used mass media publicity, seminars, conventions, and publications to remind Singaporeans that productivity must be a permanent pillar of the economy. The board sponsored a productivity campaign each year with such slogans as this one for 1988: "Train Up—Be the Best You Can Be."

A critical motivation for Singapore's support was related to better leveraging of MNEs' presence in the country. Singapore has relied to a great extent on large inflows of foreign MNEs rather than on indigenous companies. Into the 1990s, about 75 percent of its manufacturing output and 80 percent of exports came from foreign MNEs, with large parts of the services sector, such as financial services, hotels, and transport, foreign owned. The realization in the 1980s that spillovers from MNEs to domestic SMEs were weak, and that the domestic SME sector was badly lagging, gave new impetus to the productivity focus.

Prime Minister Lee Kuan Yew asked the Japanese Productivity Center directly for support to bolster this sector, which they did from 1983 to 2000. As in Japan, his goal was to change not only behavior but also the mindset of the managers, workers, and general population. Unlike in Japan, the core organizations were established by the government, and what became known as the Productivity Movement was introduced not only to the business but also the public sector. The success of the program is attributed to the prime minister's strong personal commitment. Further, the establishment of technological extension services was accompanied by a massive public awareness campaign. As in Japan, the program was undertaken with tripartite cooperation among government, industry, and labor unions.

SME Centers, formerly Enterprise Development Centers, offer one-stop information, advice, and assistance from relevant government agencies, in particular SPRING (the Standards, Productivity, and Innovation Board) and private sector organizations. SPRING, the descendent of the original 1990s National Productivity Board, sits under the Ministry of Trade and Industry, and is broadly in charge of supporting firms, both SMEs and larger. More generally, as in Japan, the government underwrites consultancy and other services to resolve progressively more sophisticated problems. This allows flexibility and tailoring to individual firm needs.

The first step is for the firm to go to the SME Center, which is generally run by the trade association (chamber of commerce). SPRING underwrites the costs of outreach services the SMEs undertake. The business advisor visits the firm and recommends what needs to be done and then may suggest a private sector consultant. As firms grow more sophisticated, they may be matched with an account manager in SPRING. This may occur because the trade association thinks the firm has potential and calls it to the attention of SPRING but also because the SPRING account manager is always scoping his sector for potential.

(Box continues on the following page.)

The Capabilities Escalator in Singapore *(continued)*

The key element of Singapore's approach is that policy support is aligned to the position of the firm in the escalator, ensuring that the SME has available a broad menu of policy instruments tailored to its needs to support and finance upgrading. At a higher level of sophistication, once the first step of the escalator has been climbed, SMEs can access A*STAR (Agency for Science Technology and Research), which provides a broad range of instruments to support technological upgrading. Annex 7A describes the full menu of instruments for upgrading management and technology in SPRING and A*STAR.

Source: Maloney 2017a.

information on the barriers to potential high-growth firms, it also increases the likelihood that new industries and sectors emerge. This said, efficiency considerations when selecting the beneficiaries of these programs in terms of merits and ability to upgrade need to be seriously considered, and the information gained also informs which firms not to offer subsidies to in subsequent stages of the escalator. For instance, the family-managed firms discussed in chapter 5 may be structurally handicapped in ways that are revealed in the initial diagnostics.

Supply-Side Constraints

The second barrier may emerge on the service supply side. SMEs may lack the scale to assess the value of these services or the quality of providers, which in turn prevents the emergence of a support industry even if firms desire to upgrade. There is, thus, both a coordination and information asymmetry in the market for management and extension services. In all advanced countries, the government has had a role in creating the market for these services. The various agencies appear central to the story of postwar recovery in Italy, as well as the subsequent Asian miracles. Japan still supports this market, posting the rankings of service providers on the Internet, for instance, precisely to resolve the information asymmetry surrounding quality.

Other countries have also experimented with extension programs, many on the Japanese Productivity Center model, with greater or lesser success (see Ezell and Atkinson 2011 and Racine 2004 for descriptions of country experiences). The Japanese Productivity Center set up several productivity centers in Latin America, although they for the most part have not received political backing nor did they occur in the context of a larger productivity movement found in the cases discussed above. Others have been stymied by the limited availability and poor quality of management extension specialists and service providers. The most successful extensionists have experience in best-practice companies, usually large national or multinational enterprises. In poor countries, there will be few such companies and even fewer employees willing to leave them to work as consultants. Yet the quality of extensionists is absolutely central to the success of such programs; they cannot be replaced by recent business school graduates as is the case in some countries or, by career government staff.[7] Training and extension programs are better implemented by a network of competitive private providers who face incentives to provide services most aligned with the changing needs of the private sector across all levels of firm sophistication. Hence, extension programs need to help potential private sector providers expand their competencies through training and quality certification of their technical skills.

Subsequent Steps on the Capabilities Escalator

Technological Transfer and Extension

As firms master basic competencies, adoption of existing technologies from abroad becomes a priority. However, such dissemination is subject to the usual appropriation externalities. Hence, there is an argument for government to redress this market failure. This is often done by technological transfer extension. Because it is often necessary to adapt foreign technologies to the local context, such extension systems are frequently paired with technology centers or Public Research Institutes. There has been a long tradition of technology extension in agriculture, most famously with the U.S. land-grant universities, continuing to the present day. As box 7.5 shows for the case of EMBRAPA, the Brazilian Agricultural Research Corporation in Brazil, these services can have significant effects on upgrading in agriculture.

A similar phenomenon exists in the industrial realm, where technology centers can support technological upgrading in SMEs. Some of these centers offer both management extension and more specialized technology extension. One example is the U.S. MEPs, which, while focusing on constant improvement in management and production processes, can also direct SMEs toward more specialized technological support. A different model of technology extension was developed during the 1980s and 1990s in some European regions specializing in specific sectoral clusters (see box 7.6 for a description of a technology center in Catalonia). These responded to the technological upgrading needs of important sector clusters.

There are two key lessons of these models of technology extension. First, they often are the result of public-private partnerships. This ensures both industry knowledge and alignment with specific needs of industry, and addresses coordination failures. Second, they tend to be subnational and close to specific sector clusters, ensuring proximity and engagement with local firms. This implies some degree of capabilities maturity in the sectors to organize themselves in clusters that may be hard to find in stage 1 of the escalator process.

Agriculture Extension: The Case of EMBRAPA

EMBRAPA generates and transfers new technologies and techniques tailored to Brazil's climate and soil conditions. The use of these technologies by Brazilian farmers facilitated the expansion of Brazilian agriculture and increased exports at internationally competitive prices—first, by expanding the supply of arable land and, second, by improving the productivity of selected crops. New techniques to improve the quality of the otherwise inhospitable Cerrado soil opened a vast tract of newly arable land, keeping marginal agricultural costs down and enabling an increase in agricultural production, while improvements in the cultivars of soybeans and cotton ultimately yielded biannual harvests. Both activities increased the productivity of land.

Why did EMBRAPA succeed where other research organizations failed? EMBRAPA's mission orientation, focusing from the outset on the improvement of agricultural productivity rather than the production of scientific work, was a key driver of its success. Integration into the international flow of knowledge increased research efficiency and accelerated training. An open intellectual property rights policy—and a network of offices spread throughout the country—facilitated the dissemination of EMBRAPA's discoveries. Funding was kept at adequate levels for more than two decades. Investments in human capital were highly prioritized. A meritocratic culture was actively promoted by the organization. As a result, research dealt with the practical problems of agriculture, and farmers quickly deployed technology and innovations sourced through EMBRAPA. By reacting to market signals and focusing on activities for which demand was increasing in international markets, EMBRAPA avoided the usual challenges of purely "supply-push" technology transfer policies.

Source: Correa and Smith 2014.

Supporting Links and Trade Upgrading

The correlation between interaction with world markets and productivity and quality is long established. Exporters and firms participating in global value chains (GVCs) tend to perform better across a range of dimensions. The direction of causality is probably bidirectional. As discussed in chapter 5, trade links are important sources of capabilities for innovation through access to inputs and markets, competition, and technology transfer (see, for example, Eslava et al. 2013). However, benefiting from this channel also requires capabilities to compete and manage the risk inherent in entering new markets. Firms need to upgrade their capabilities to introduce a new export product (Cirera, Marin, and Markwald 2015) and, as the case studies in Chandra (2006) document, these include financial, management, and technical skills that are often difficult to acquire. The same is true for non-exporting firms facing new competition from imports in the context of free trade agreements. Interviews with Colombian auto parts firms reveal that many lacked the ability to develop a strategy to manage the lower-priced Asian products entering their markets. Hence, increasing international exposure and upgrading capabilities are complementary agendas.

Technology Centers: The Case of ASCAMM

The Association of Enterprises Mould-Makers and Die-Makers (ASCAMM) is a design and industrial production technology center set up in 1987 by the Catalan Association of Mould and Die Manufacturers. In 1997, it became an independent entity and has the form of a private nonprofit foundation. ASCAMM Foundation is located in the Vallès Technological Park and stretches over an area of 11,000 square miles. It has 130 employees, most of whom are technical staff.

ASCAMM's objectives are as follows:

- To generate, through their own research and development activities, technological knowledge in the production technologies field; and
- To transfer this knowledge to the industry and facilitate its usage.

Annually, more than 200 companies are involved in over 70 ongoing, collaborative research, technology development, and innovation projects, in which ASCAMM is the leader or a technical partner. To date, the center has generated 8 patents of industrial application, 4 technology-based start-ups, and 12 innovative technological products. Most of ASCAMM's know-how focuses on design and production technologies, in particular those related to polymers and metals (ferrous materials and light alloys), and composites.

The second objective of knowledge transfer is accomplished through contract R&D projects, technological services, advisory services, training, and the dissemination of knowledge through conferences, publications, and other means.

ASCAMM Foundation actively collaborates with more than 500 companies in transport (in the automotive, aeronautics, and railway sectors), industrial equipment, energy, biomedical and health care (devices and equipment), packaging, consumer goods, plastic and metal transformers, and other sectors. It collaborates with many industrial, technological, and training organizations throughout Europe and the rest of the world.

ASCAMM has evolved independently from the mould makers' industry and has become one of the leading technology centers in Europe. Originally it specialized in plastic injection and molding, but later the center enlarged its interest into new areas, such as business creation.

The ability of the management to obtain funding and the good results of their services and research projects paved the way to financial self-sufficiency (60 percent from services and 40 percent from competitive research), and eventually to recognition as an Advanced Technological Center (CTA) by the Catalan government. This made it eligible for an annual noncompetitive subsidy covering about 12 percent of its budget. In exchange, ASCAMM committed to promote technologically based ventures, which it did until transforming into a venture capitalist firm.

Source: The Cluster Competitiveness Group 2011.

Finally, as discussed in chapter 5, for local firms to benefit from links to MNEs requires meeting price, quality, and timeliness targets achievable only with advanced firm capabilities. As the discussions of Singapore above and the Czech Republic in box 7.7 suggest, not having these capabilities can lead to a dualistic market structure where low-capability local firms remain entirely separate from developing linkages to MNEs.

Czech Supplier Development Program

The Czech Republic had been one of the most successful locations in attracting foreign direct investment (FDI) following the fall of communism in the 1990s, but relatively little of the benefits potentially connected with FDI had been felt in the local economy. MNEs drew few of their inputs from Czech suppliers. An effective mechanism was required to widen FDI benefits to the local economy. There was a need to strengthen local suppliers' capacities so that they could cope with European Union single market forces and succeed in becoming internationally competitive, following enterprises' isolation from world markets and comparative advantages under central planning.

The Czech government implemented a pilot National Supplier Development Program (SDP) in 2000–02. The program focused on developing and promoting links between MNE inward investors and local SMEs. The program was demand driven and aimed at improving the competitiveness of Czech SMEs to the level required to enter GVCs by becoming suppliers to MNEs. A related objective was to develop a local world-class supplier base. A dozen MNEs were involved throughout the project, and 45 SMEs received targeted training based on needs revealed during business reviews.

The SDP was implemented by CzechInvest, the Czech investment promotion agency. It was designed by the World Bank Foreign Investment Advisory Services and funded by the European Union preaccession PHARE Program. The program built on the United Kingdom and Irish experience. A team of two U.K. advisors joined the CzechInvest team for the pilot phase to ensure transfer of experience and build implementation capacity.

The Czech SDP strengthened local companies' skills and enhanced the benefits of FDI to the local economy. Process and product upgrading have been evident at the supplier level. Business reviews showed an increase in company performance in areas required to meet MNE requirements. An evaluation undertaken 18 months after the end of the 2000–02 period, surveying all 45 companies participating in the pilot (with 42 responding), showed that 15 companies had gained new business, which they attributed to the program, with these contracts worth US$46 million for the period 2000–03. Four companies had also found new customers abroad, and three companies had obtained contracts for higher-value-added content. The share of components sourced from Czech companies by the MNEs participating in the program correspondingly increased, from a rate of 0–5 percent at the start to 2.5–30 percent by 2004.

Following the success of the pilot SDP in electronics, the program was replicated in three other sectors. This expansion led to an increased focus on the local benefits of FDI in national policy making, with CzechInvest playing a key policy advocacy role. The program also informed the development of the follow-on Czech national cluster policy.

Driven by supply-side improvements in export performance, the Czech Republic experienced significant gains in global market shares in the late 2000s. Export growth was driven by motor vehicles and machinery and electrical equipment sectors. Both have grown at double-digit rates over the last decade, and have shown continuous improvement in product quality, although clearly there is room for further progress.

Source: Mariscal and Taglioni 2017.

Developing these capabilities is plagued by information asymmetries and coordination failures. As with any other type of knowledge, there are important externalities associated with the gathering of foreign market information related to consumer preferences, business opportunities, quality and technical requirements, and so on. Private firms alone will not undertake this research if competitors can free ride. The same applies to pioneer exporters, who make a considerable investment in attempts to open foreign markets, cultivating contacts, establishing distribution chains, and undertaking other costly activities that can be used by their rivals. Hence, there is a role for a dynamic export promotion effort that addresses these issues (see, for example, Lederman, Olarreaga, and Payton 2010; Lederman, Olarreaga, and Zavala 2013; Eaton et al. 2007).

There are also more tailored skills involved in exporting. In the 1960s, after the liberalization of the Irish economy, the export promotion board in Ireland started a program to help domestic firms face tougher competition and enter export markets. The program provided a highly subsidized service, with two days of support services in market research, which included working with the companies on how to use market information. Artopoulos, Friel, and Hallak (2013) analyze case studies of successful Argentinean exporters and find evidence that exporters to developed country markets adopt a new set of business practices that are very different from those used in the domestic market. The authors argue that export pioneers absorb the tacit knowledge about foreign markets by interacting with the business community of the export market. Exports then emerge as this tacit knowledge is disseminated throughout the sector.

As discussed previously, developing an NQI (see box 7.2) involves not only helping firms improving their quality but also signaling this quality with standards compliance. This requires domestic infrastructure for testing and certification; otherwise, firms are forced to be certified in third countries, increasing significantly the sunk costs of exporting.

Many of the programs to raise capabilities for trade and participation in GVCs are similar to those discussed earlier. Some MNEs provide an initial diagnostic of management and production functions, and then work with suppliers in upgrading their capabilities with more emphasis on quality and value chain issues. These programs have proliferated primarily around the automotive sector (see box 7.7) and electronics, and are currently implemented in most high- and middle-income countries. In other cases, technological centers such as those described above have focused on upgrading within existing linkages. These linkage programs offer powerful incentives for SMEs to invest in upgrading their production and technology, given the lower risk of efforts associated with a significant increase in demand combined with reliable upgrading services.

Other Instruments to Support Innovation

One final set of instruments pertains to the last stage of the capabilities escalator: supporting more complex R&D projects and the development of new technologies. Throughout this report we have documented the lack of formal R&D activities in most firms in developing countries, and we have argued that much of the policy debate has focused on how to increase R&D, without acknowledging that such activities require complementary management capabilities. Firms must walk before they can run. It is nonetheless the case that there are firms that have climbed the escalator and are ready to undertake sophisticated R&D projects, and policy makers need to explore how best to support them.

Three instruments have traditionally been used to offset the externalities associated with R&D: (1) tax incentives, (2) direct grants, and (3) research centers. Tax incentives (see box 7.8) are pervasive in middle- and high-income countries. Although there is some

---

BOX 7.8

Tax Incentives to R&D Projects

R&D tax incentives reduce the tax burden of firms that invest in eligible R&D activities, representing an indirect way of supporting investments in R&D. On the basis of R&D tax incentive database definitions of the Organisation for Economic Co-operation and Development (OECD),[a] we can differentiate between the following two main types of tax incentives for R&D:

1. *Tax incentives based on expenditures in R&D.* This is the most common type of tax support for R&D, including corporate tax income benefits, social security withholding tax incentives, reductions in tariffs for imported research equipment, and reimbursements of value added tax.
2. *Tax incentives based on results from R&D or related innovation activities.* This type of tax support is generally applied to income generated from R&D activities and intellectual property (that is, income-based provisions). These schemes grant a lower corporate tax rate to firms on profits generated from patents, licensing, or asset liquidation linked to R&D. Although the state of implementation of this type of instrument is incipient and its impacts have not been extensively evaluated, its popularity is increasing, particularly among OECD member states.

Policy makers have used both narrow and broad approaches to the scope of support and eligibility of R&D expenditure.[b] Most schemes have taken into consideration the definitions of R&D expenditures under the OECD *Frascati Manual*, the 2015 edition of which provides guidelines on the measurement of government tax relief for R&D (OECD 2015). Considering the implementation experience from OECD countries, policy makers have shown a preference for granting eligibility to R&D labor, subcontracted and collaborative R&D, and materials and overhead. The rationale appears to be the potential loss of embedded knowledge when physical assets are subsequently disposed of, and the fact that investments in R&D personnel can facilitate knowledge diffusion in the domestic economy. Although evidence suggests that generic and early-stage research is often more risky than applied research, only a few schemes reward basic over applied research. Designing these differentiated schemes is complex. Success depends, among other factors, on whether the implementing agency can manage the increasing complexities of schemes that rely on differentiation of spending by type of R&D or beneficiary, and on tying incentives closely to R&D spending.

(Box continues on the following page.)

---

evidence of additionality in generating more R&D investment, these incentives tend to concentrate in larger firms and, especially, in those firms that already carry out R&D. In addition, the first two instruments do not tend to encourage interactions among actors in the system, with the exception of grants that are designed for collaborative projects.

The institutions that design and implement tax incentives require certain capabilities. The first requirement is a mature and agile tax system. If firms can avoid scrutiny by the tax authorities as to how the resources are really being spent, the impact will be minimal. In addition, some schemes require coordination between a line agency with R&D responsibilities and a tax authority that can process applications through the tax collection system. Sophisticated designs, such as those that differentiate between spending categories and beneficiaries, will increase the complexity of implementation and thus pose challenges for policy makers.

Grants and matching grants have always been the most common type of direct support instrument used to increase business R&D and non-R&D innovation activities (figure 7.6).

FIGURE 7.6 Grants for Innovation Projects

Definition	Evidence of impact
Grants represent direct allocation of funding from public agencies to innovation actors to finance all or part of an innovation project. Modalities of grants are primarily defined by dimensions such as the selection mechanism, size, duration, eligible activities, payment procedures, and delivery mechanisms.	• *Overall:* Positive impact of grants schemes on business innovation, especially regarding input and behavioral additionality. The literature rejects full crowding-out effects, while confirming crowding-in effects, especially in emerging countries (Özçelik and Taymaz 2008). • *Output additionality:* Studies of output additionality of grants schemes are less common than for input additionality. Selected studies find increases in employment: 4.6–6.4%; sales: 11.5–39.6%; TFP: 31.4%; and labor productivity: 6–10%. • *Behavioral additionality:* A program found increased firm probability of innovating by 19.3%, and probability to initiate new collaborations by about 27%

Market and system failure addressed

The policy justification for the application of grants for innovation is based on the following situations:
- Externalities and spillovers   • Capability failure
- Information asymmetry
- Coordination failure

Key "must have" for replicability

- Capability needs to design and implement policy instruments: government: design and monitoring; industry and independent expertise; M&E and learning; beneficiaries: lack of complementary factors in terms of infrastructure but also, in terms of managerial competencies, absorptive capacity, such as openess, and learning behavior.

Target group

Individual firms, and among them, SMEs. A second type of target group is collaboration between firms or between firms and other organizations

Strengths	Potential drawbacks & risks	Dos	DON'Ts
• Selectivity of goals, and directionality of policy • Ease of implementation, relative to other instruments • Flexibility and control in the definition of conditions for support • Signaling power for accreditation of firms capabilities	• Managerially, more intensive than indirect mechanisms • Require monetary stability to ensure continuity • Susceptible to government failure • Inability to address broader policy issues • Can crowd out private funding	Consider alternatives Evaluate the extent of market failure and potential additionality of beneficiaries Ensure political commitment, predictability, and policy continuity Design agile and simple application processes	Don't simply assume that grant is the right instrument. Don't select the participants on the merit of proposals only, as they are likely to find private funding sources independently. Don't treat all firms within the same broad target group

Source: World Bank 2017.

Note: M&E = monitoring and evaluation; SME = small and medium enterprise; TFP = total factor productivity.

They usually finance specific expenditures of innovation projects, including proof of concept, prototyping, testing, machinery, technical assistance, and so on. In the case of matching grants, public agencies match a percentage contribution of the project made by the applicant. Grant schemes can vary from very simplistic, one-off funding allocations to complex strategic programs built on formal public-private partnerships. Very often grants function jointly with other types of instruments to achieve particular policy objectives. In theory, matching grants foment partnerships and the densification of innovation networks in the NIS. However, again, they require capable partners in the private sector, and these have often been scarce in developing countries. Grants not delivered in conjunction with mentoring or technical assistance are effective only if firms can design good innovation projects but lack financing.

The evidence on these schemes is mixed, although a significant number of studies find a positive impact of grant schemes on business innovation, especially regarding input and behavioral additionality. The evidence regarding output and outcome additionality is positive, although scarce, especially in developing countries. Syntheses/meta-analyses, such as García-Quevedo (2004), Zúñiga-Vicente et al. (2014), and Becker (2015), all conclude that most of the evidence focuses on input additionalities—impact on innovation expenditure—and hardly any evidence focuses on innovation outcomes and firm performance. Some evaluations of grants in the OECD suggest that these can be more effective in supporting R&D projects than tax incentives (Arqué-Castells and Mohnen 2015). A recent evaluation by Bruhn and McKenzie (2017) of Poland's In-Tech program, a grant to projects that are carried out by consortia of firms and research entities, shows that the program leads to more science–industry collaboration, higher probability of applying for a patent or publishing a research paper related to the project, and positive effects on commercialization of products related to the proposed project. However, more evidence is needed given the huge popularity of these instruments in supporting innovation to establish its effectiveness in supporting innovation.

Public research institutes constitute a final instrument used to support both applied and basic R&D. As we discussed above in the case of EMBRAPA in agriculture, these tend to be sector specific and perform contract R&D on demand. Perhaps the most well-known centers are the Fraunhofer Institutes in Germany, which function as a complex network that helps firms develop technological capabilities as well as perform R&D projects of different complexity. This model is difficult to replicate, given the very large in-house technological capabilities required, but a significant number of applied R&D centers have been implemented in developing countries. Evidence is thin on their impact, although Link and Scott (2009), looking at Latin American case studies of similar models discussed in the previous chapter, show unclear mission orientation and poor design, suggesting that in many cases the impact is likely to be limited.

Lack of impact of these instruments is exacerbated when countries mimic the organograms of advanced countries but do not design institutions with an idea of resolving a local problem. For this reason, this report has proposed a gradual building up of innovation instruments with adherence to a framework that focuses on failures to be redressed and the appropriate accompanying incentives system. Only following this gradual approach can these institutions generate quality knowledge relevant to the needs of the private sector.

While the focus of the report is primarily on existing firms, ideally, the *policy mix* would offer support across all stages of the firm life and innovation cycle, including start-ups (see figure 7.7), given that productivity growth is driven both by upgrading within existing sectors as well as by start-ups. However, two key issues should be kept in mind in allocating resources between incumbents and new entrants. First, the potential impact of these early-stage instruments, such as incubators and accelerators, or equity instruments that target start-ups in the tech sector is constrained by the limited contribution of this sector to the overall economy, in terms of both employment and firm growth. Second, the most important support is often missing in the most difficult phase of firm growth, the scale-up phase after the firm has been established (Isenberg 2012).

FIGURE 7.7 Early-Stage Infrastructure and Advisory

Definition	Evidence of impact
Incubators and accelerators host innovative companies, sometimes linked to universities, to support the commercialization of knowledge. They exploit the benefits of networking and spillover effects arising from co-location, but vary on the extent and duration of advisory services provided. Unlike incubators, accelerators tend to be cohort-based, provide links to potential investors, and span through shorter periods, usually 3–6 months (versus years).	• Output additionality: Treated firms did not perform significantly different than nontreated in terms of patenting (Colombo and Delmastro, 2002). In Turkey, employment generation (including R&D personnel) and sales growth, on-incubator firms significantly outperform off-incubator firms. Other incubation programs report job creation in Maryland (RTI 2007), and California (Chabin 2009). Accelerator programs in the United Kingdom were found to increase the level of company survivorship by 10% to 15% by the fifth year following the exit (Birdsall 2013) • Roberts et al., 2016 found that revenue grew more in ventures of entrepreneurs accepted in selected accelerators than in the ventures of rejected entrepreneurs. Entrepreneurship schooling leads to significant increases in venture fundraising and scale (Gonzalez Uribe 2016).

Market and system failure addressed

The policy justification for the provision of early stage infrastructure and advisory rests on the following issues:
- Capability failure
- Information asymmetry
- Network and infrastructure failure

Key "must have" for replicability

- Conduct a feasibility study for setting up an incubator to understand the current landscape of the entrepreneurial ecosystem, target market, and strategic direction.
- Financial commitments: incubation takes time to achieve results
- Competent, innovative, and knowledgeable management is a factor that is critical to an incubator or accelerator success.

Target group

Incubators and accelerators target start-ups and early-stage entrepreneurs (sometimes idea stage entrepreneurs), often in technology sectors.

Strengths	Potential drawbacks & risks
• Network effects, technology transfer, and spillover effect • Economies of scale in fixed costs and service provision • Dedicated advisory assistance • Signaling and enabling high-risk investment at early stages	• High cost of running programs and limited outreach • Lack of clear policy on selection criteria • Proliferation of incubation and acceleration programs • Limited focus on scaling up and growth stages

Dos	DON'Ts
Be demand driven and focus on measuring Plan governance structure carefully Enable accessible physical location Ensure mentors are seasoned business professionals. Develop linkages and networks	Don't use incubators, accelerators and science parks as the same instrument Don't set up unrealistic targets, and milestones Don't ignore the financial sustainability strategy of the instrument

Source: World Bank 2017.
Note: R&D = research and development.

Concluding Remarks

This chapter has highlighted the set of policy instruments that can support the building of innovation capabilities. As discussed in the previous chapter, innovation policy in developing countries is more challenging and complex than in advanced countries because the market failures and missing complementarities are likely to be more acute. A way of reducing the demands on government capabilities is to engage in a gradual process of accumulating instruments. This results in an inverted pyramid (as suggested in figure 7.3), where the instruments available increase as both firm capabilities for innovation and government capabilities for design and implementation increase.

Dividing the capabilities escalator—the process of transition to the technological frontier—in three stages offers heuristic help in defining the set of instruments that should be prioritized. Economies at the base of the escalator benefit more from support to management and production capabilities, and then evolve toward technology extension and support to R&D projects as knowledge and capabilities are accumulated. While there is heterogeneity in sophistication of firms so that the stages may not be so clearly defined, the approach that has been traditionally followed by many countries of jumping right to the final stage and focusing primarily on R&D is unlikely to be effective.

Although this report has focused on a subset of instruments deemed to be more important for capabilities accumulation, clearly there is a much broader range of innovation support instruments. A detailed overview of such instruments highlighted in figure 7.1, with a description of the conditions of implementation and evidence on impact, is provided in a parallel volume to this report: *Instruments to Support Business Innovation: A Guide for Policy Makers and Practitioners.* Further, in the background remains the broader agenda of removing the barriers to all necessary complementary factors—human and physical capital—through an ongoing process of structural reform.

One final priority for innovation policy is closing the evidence gap. The evaluation agenda in innovation policy is still in its inception and tends to be focused primarily in OECD countries and on a few instruments, such as R&D tax incentives or grants for innovation. To date, there is very little evidence on innovation programs in developing countries. It is thus critical to systematize impact evaluations of innovation policies in innovation agencies and even coordinate in a global overall knowledge strategy perhaps through international organizations, so lessons can be shared across the practitioner community.

Annex 7A The Capabilities Escalator in Singapore: The Menu of Instruments

Singapore provides a suite of instruments to SMEs that want to upgrade their capabilities. SMEs start the engagement at the SME Centre, which is generally run by the trade association (chamber of commerce), where SPRING covers the costs of the business development services that they undertake. As a first step, a business advisor visits the firm and provides a diagnostic suggesting the upgrading area and matching the SME to a local private sector consultant. As firms grow more sophisticated, they may be matched with an account manager in SPRING who acts as their "general practitioner" doctor.

Singapore provides a broad menu of instruments to support upgrading though SPRING and A*STAR, depending of the sophistication of the SME's capabilities. The former provides support to management upgrading to those firms primarily at the bottom of the escalator, whereas the latter combines instruments for upgrading technology in firms with more sophisticated capabilities.

Specifically, SPRING offers the following schemes to support and finance upgrading Maloney (2017a):

- *Support and Toolkit Online*. EnterpriseOne is a Single Window portal that helps firms navigate the government's programs. Further, SPRING has an online Toolkit that includes Self-help guides on Customer Service, Financial Management, Human Resource Capability, Marketing, and Productivity.
- *Innovation and Capability Voucher (ICV)*: The entryway to government programs is a S$5,000 voucher to upgrade and strengthen core business operations through consultancy projects in innovation, productivity, human resources, and financial management.
- *Loans*. These include the Micro Loan Program, Local Enterprise Fund Scheme, and Loan Insurance Scheme—the government pays 50 percent of the cost of insurance through a third party for trade credit or working capital. The Local Enterprise Finance Scheme (LEFS) helps SMEs secure financing for productive assets, working with a partner financial firm to get SMEs loans of up to S$15 million, with tenure of up to 10 years.
- *Capability and Development Grant (CDG)*. This program covers from 0 to 70 percent of costs—up to S$100,000—for technical upgrading. Eligible activities include consultancy, manpower, training, certification, upgrading productivity and developing business capabilities for process improvement, product development, and market access. There are 10 areas: (1) Brand Development, (2) Business Innovation and Design, (3) Business Strategy Development, (4) Quality and Standards Enhancement, (5) Financial Management, (6) Human Capital Development, (7) Intellectual Property, (8) Franchising and Productivity Improvement,

(9) Services Excellence, and (10) Technology. Firms may apply to SPRING, and may be recruited by SPRING directly or through the chambers of commerce, which are on the lookout for promising firms.

- *Productivity and Innovation Credit scheme (PIC)*. Firms may either deduct 40 percent of investment or receive a cash payout of 60 percent up to S$100,000 for each year in all six qualifying activities of investment, including acquisition of information technology and automation equipment, training of employees, registration of patents, trade market designs and plant varieties, acquisition and in-licensing of intellectual property rights, project design, and R&D.

At a higher level of sophistication, A*STAR provides a range of products to support technological upgrading:

- *Growing Enterprises with Technological Upgrade*. GET-Up is an industry program managed by the Science and Engineering Research Council (SERC) that seeks to upgrade technological capabilities of local SMEs to enhance global competitiveness. It involves numerous agencies that together provide a holistic and concerted assistance. T-Up (Technology for Enterprise Capability) seconds research scientists to companies to build in-house R&D/technical capabilities through projects defined and managed by the companies. This can include new products and processes, setting up a new technical department, or technological transfer from oversees.
- *Operational and Technology Roadmapping (OTR)*. Firms can hire experts from A*STAR to help create operations and technology roadmaps, through five half-day sessions that seek to align firm technology acquisition with business goals. Payment can be with the ICV.
- *Technology Adoption Program (TAP)*. This program seeks to match firm needs with existing technologies. A*STAR works with firms to pilot new technologies and adapt them to the business needs of the local SMEs.
- *SIMTech, the Singapore Institute of Manufacturing Technology*. This institution operates within A*STAR and offers a basic lean implementation program through lean techniques and continuous improvement (Kaizen). It includes a 4.5-day classroom session and an 8.5-day mentoring session onsite in basic lean techniques such as 6S workplace organization, plant-re-layout, SMED (Single-Minute Exchange of Die) and TPM (Total Productive Maintenance). SIMTECH predicts that completion of the program can help achieve a 30–50 percent reduction in inventories, a 20–50 percent reduction in cycle times, a 20–40 percent reduction in delivery lead times, a 10–40 percent increase in labor productivity, a 20–40 percent reduction in space use, and a 20–50 percent reduction in defects. The total cost is estimated to be S$12,000. SPRING finances 70 percent, and an additional PIC cash payout reduces it even further to S$2,280, for roughly an 80 percent subsidy.

Other resources available for upgrading and innovation:

- *Centers of Innovation.* These offer technical advice in six areas. There have been efforts to make them self-sustaining, although in practice they are heavily financed by matching grants.
- *Local Enterprise and Association Development Programme (LEAD).* This is a multiagency effort to enhance industry and enterprise competitiveness via trade associations and chambers of commerce (TACs). The TACs drive initiatives to upgrade capabilities and lead internationalization efforts.
- *Partnership for Capability Transformation (PACT).* This program fosters collaboration between SMEs and large enterprises (defined as >S$100 million). The state underwrites up to 60 percent of approved projects in knowledge transfer from the large organization, capability upgrading of the large firm's new or existing suppliers, development, and testing of innovative solutions between large firms and at least one SME.
- The PACT now encompasses an earlier program that created incentives for MNEs to mentor local firms into world-class suppliers, especially for technologically intensive industries. As part of this effort in 1986 the Economic Development Board (EDB) implemented the *Local Industry Upgrading Program (LIUP).* In this program the EDB enters remunerative contractual relationships with MNEs to second experienced engineers to work with the EDB as an LIUP manager. The LIUP manager works with engineering and technical employees of a local firm to create necessary technology and skills for the local firm to become a supplier to the mentoring MNE.
- *Programs for building SME human capital.* Singapore has a variety of other programs for building future SME leaders, strengthening existing management, and strengthening middle management and promising executives.
- Several financial and technical assistance schemes were set up. The Local Industry Finance Scheme (LEFS) described above gave loans to buy machinery and equipment. The *Local Enterprise Technical Assistance Scheme (LETAS)* gave grants to engage external experts to upgrade operations and management.
- *Human capital upgrading.* EDB also worked with MNEs to set up training centers for skills that could be of use across many industries, thus promoting interindustry spillovers. Government finances the project but decided to leave the training to the MNEs rather than setting up public sector training centers and schools (Blomström, Kokko, and Sjöholm 2002). The Skills Development Fund (SDF) shared the costs of investing in skills upgrading of the workforce.
- *Cluster Policy.* The government identified and supported 14 clusters, many cross-cutting, including commodity trading, shipping, precision engineering, electronics, information technology, petroleum and petrochemical, construction, heavy engineering, finance, insurance, general supporting industries, and tourism. Each cluster was subjected to the market test for efficiency and

competitiveness, and each has some common core comparative advantage in terms of natural advantages, created competitive advantages, or industry structure. These clusters undertook higher-end tasks, while assembly work was progressively off-shored. A*STAR also sponsored 12 research institutes that undertake R&D related to industry needs.

Notes

1. The term "policy mix" was traditionally used in the macroeconomics literature (Flanagan, Uyarra, and Laranja 2011). The use of different instruments has been an important element of public policy for many decades. A good example is Tinbergen's well-known rule that there must be as many policy instruments as policy goals (Tinbergen 1952). The use of the term "policy mix" in innovation policy gained traction especially after the emergence of the National Innovation System literature in the 1980s and 1990s (Cunningham et al. 2013), and has become a dominant part of the innovation policy jargon.

2. At a higher level of aggregation and given that constraints to any type of investment will also discourage investments in firm capabilities and innovation, policies to spur innovation need to include policies to improve the investment climate. Thus, as chapter 2 stressed, innovation policies need to be coordinated with policies governing education, competition, macroeconomic stability, and labor market institutions (see Aghion, David, and Foray 2009). At the policy instrument level, complementarities are also important. Instruments that finance early-stage product development often will not be effective without instruments that finance commercialization. Inducing more research–industry collaboration can be supported by demand-side measures, for instance using vouchers that encourage firms to collaborate with universities. Supply-side measures, such as setting up technology transfer offices or placement programs for researchers, can also be used. Moreover, overall success may require policies to reward researchers for working with industry or perhaps for participating in business ventures, as well as an intellectual property system that rewards commercialization.

3. A more detailed description of these instruments and practical considerations for their implementation can be found in the parallel document to this report, the innovation policy guide (World Bank 2017).

4. The literature focusing on informal microenterprises also has looked at the impact of changing entrepreneurial traits. In an experiment looking at supporting personal initiative traits in a sample of 109 Ugandan businesses, Campos et al. (2017) show that firms that went through training to instill a mindset of greater personal initiative have introduced more new products than a control group.

5. The subjective scale ranges from 1 to 10 and the objective from 1 to 5. We have simply divided the former by two and this may lead to a misalignment of means. Nevertheless, the downward slope would remain however we center the data.

6. As Petar Stojic, the former Director of Business Support Policy for Britain's Department for Business, Innovation and Skills (BIS), which oversees the Manufacturing Advisory Service, comments: "After they have worked with MAS, they understand the value of lean principles and/or better innovation practices and the value of external expertise in general, so when they have to pay the full rate in the future, they now know what to look for and have greater confidence in approaching the market. In reality, far from supplanting private market advisory services, countries' manufacturing extension services tend to help SME manufacturers understand their value." Cited in Ezell and Atkinson (2011).

7. For example, Suzuki and Igei (2017) show how an intervention in Thailand aimed at improving the efficiency and quality of BDS providers, by creating and supporting a network of providers, had positive impacts on both BDS providers and SME performance.

References

Aghion Philippe, Paul A. David, and Dominique Foray. 2009. "Science, Technology and Innovation for Economic Growth: Linking Policy Research and Practice in 'STIG Systems.'" *Research Policy* 38 (4): 681–93.

Anderson-Macdonald, Stephen Joseph, Rajesh Chandy, and Bilal Husnain Zia. 2017. *Pathways to Profits: Identifying Separate Channels of Business Growth through Business Training.* Finance & PSD Impact Evaluation Note No. 41. Washington, DC: World Bank.

Appelt, S., M. Bajgar, C. Criscuolo, and F. Galindo-Rueda. 2016. "R&D Tax Incentives: Evidence on Design, Incidence and Impacts." OECD Science, Technology and Industry Policy Papers No. 32, Organisation for Economic Co-operation and Development, Paris.

Arqué-Castells, Pere, and Pierre Mohnen. 2015. "Sunk Costs, Extensive R&D Subsidies and Permanent Inducement Effects." *Journal of Industrial Economics* 63 (3): 458–94.

Artopoulos, Alejandro, Daniel Friel, and Juan Carlos Hallak. 2013. "Export Emergence of Differentiated Goods from Developing Countries: Export Pioneers and Business Practices in Argentina." *Journal of Development Economics* 105 (C): 19–35.

Becker, B. 2015. "Public R&D Policies and Private R&D Investment: A Survey of the Empirical Evidence." *Journal of Economic Surveys* 29: 917–42.

Bell, Martin, and Paulo N. Figueiredo. 2012. "Innovation Capability Building and Learning Mechanisms in Latecomer Firms: Recent Empirical Contributions and Implications for Research." *Revue Canadienne d'Études du Développement* 33 (1): 14–40.

Bell, M., and K. Pavitt. 1993. "Accumulating Technology Captivity in Developing Countries." *Industrial and Corporate Change* 2 (2): 157–210.

Blomström, M., A. Kokko, and F. Sjöholm. 2002. "Growth and Innovation Policies for a Knowledge Economy: Experiences from Finland, Sweden, and Singapore." Background Paper for the LAC Flagship Report, World Bank, Washington, DC.

Bloom, N., B. Eifert, A. Mahajan, D. McKenzie, and J. Roberts. 2013. "Does Management Matter? Evidence from India." *Quarterly Journal of Economics* 128 (1): 1–51.

Bloom, N., and J. Van Reenen. 2007. "Measuring and Explaining Management Practices across Firms and Countries." *Quarterly Journal of Economics* 122 (4): 1351–1408.

Brooks, Wyatt, Kevin Donovan, and Terence R. Johnson. 2017. "Mentors or Teachers? Microenterprise Training in Kenya." Working Paper. http://kevindonovan.weebly.com/uploads/8/7/0/2/8702484/dandora_web_current.pdf.

Bruhn, M., D. Karlan, and A. Schoar. 2016. "The Impact of Consulting Services on Small and Medium Enterprises: Evidence from a Randomized Trial in Mexico." Policy Research Working Paper No. 6508, World Bank, Washington, DC.

Bruhn, M., and D. J. McKenzie. 2017. "Can Grants to Consortia Spur Innovation and Science-Industry Collaboration?: Regression-Discontinuity Evidence from Poland." World Bank Policy Research Working Paper No. 7934, World Bank, Washington, DC.

Busom, Isabel, Beatriz Corchuelo, and Ester Martínez-Ros. 2014. "Tax Incentives … or Subsidies for Business R&D?" *Small Business Economics* 43 (3): 571–96.

Campos, Francisco, Michael Frese, Markus Goldstein, Leonardo Iacovone, Hillary Johnson, David McKenzie, Mona Mensmann. 2017. "Teaching Personal Initiative Beats Traditional Business Trainingin Boosting Small Business Growth." Unpublished, World Bank, Washington, DC.

Chandra, Vandana. 2006. *Technology, Adaptation, and Exports: How Some Developing Countries Got It Right.* Washington, DC: World Bank.

Cirera, Xavier, Anabel Marin, and Ricardo Markwald. 2015. "Explaining Export Diversification through Firm Innovation Decisions: The Case of Brazil." *Research Policy* 44 (10): 1962–73.

Cluster Competitiveness Group. 2011. Cluster Competitiveness Group. 2011. "Public-Private Dialogue for Sector Competitiveness and Local Economic Development: Lessons from the Mediterranean Region." A report for the Public-Private Dialogue program of the Investment Climate Department of the World Bank Group, and funded through the Catalonia (COPCA) / IFC Technical Assistance Trust Fund.

Cohen, W., and D. Levinthal. 1990. "Absorptive Capacity: A New Perspective on Learning and Innovation." *Administrative Science Quarterly* 35 (1): 128–52.

Colombo, Massimo G., and Marco Delmastro. 2002. "How Effective Are Technology Incubators? Evidence from Italy." *Research Policy* 31 (7): 1103–122.

Correa, Paulo, and Cristiane Schmidt. 2014. "Public Research Organizations and Agricultural Development in Brazil: How Did Embrapa Get It Right." Economic premise, no. 145. World Bank, Washington, DC.

Crespi, G., E. Fernandez-Arias, and E. Stein. 2014. *Rethinking Productive Development*. New York: Palgrave Macmillan for the Inter-American Development Bank.

Cunningham, Paul, Jacob Edler, Kieron Flanagan, and Philippe Laredo. 2013. "Innovation Policy Mix and Instrument Interaction: A Review." Nesta Working Paper No. 13/20, Nesta, London.

Eaton, Jonathan, Marcela Eslava, Maurice Kugler, and Samuel Kortum. 2007. "Export Dynamics in Colombia: Firm-Level Evidence." NBER Working Paper No. 13531, National Bureau of Economic Research, Cambridge, MA.

Ehlen, M. 2001. "The Economic Impact of Manufacturing Extension Centers." *Economic Development Quarterly* 15 (1): 36–44.

Escribano, A., and J. L. Guasch. 2005. "Assessing the Impact of the Investment Climate on Productivity Using Firm-Level Data: Methodology and the Cases of Guatemala, Honduras, and Nicaragua." Policy Research Working Paper WPS3621, World Bank, Washington, DC.

Eslava, Marcela, John Haltiwanger, Adriana Kugler, and Maurice Kugler. 2013. "Trade, Technical Change and Market Selection: Evidence from Manufacturing Plants in Colombia." *Review of Economic Dynamics* 16 (1): 135–58.

Ezell, S., and R. Atkinson. 2011. "The Case for a National Manufacturing Strategy." *Information Technology and Innovation Foundation*, April 26. https://itif.org/publications/2011/04/26/case-national-manufacturing-strategy.

Flanagan, K., E. Uyarra, and M. Laranja. 2011. "Reconceptualising the 'Policy Mix' for Innovation." *Research Policy* 40 (5): 702–13.

García-Quevedo, J. 2004. "Do Public Subsidies Complement Business R&D? A Metaanalysis of the Econometric Evidence. *Kyklos* 57, 87–102.

Giorcelli, M. 2016. "The Long-Term Effects of Management and Technology Transfer: Evidence from the US Productivity Program." SIEPR Discussion Paper No. 16-010, Stanford Institute for Economic Policy Research, Stanford University.

Guasch, J. L., S.-L. Racine, I. Sánchez, and M. Diop. 2007. *Quality Systems and Standards for a Competitive Edge*. Washington, DC: World Bank.

Hsieh, C. T., and P. J. Klenow. 2009. "Misallocation and Manufacturing TFP in China and India." *Quarterly Journal of Economics* 124 (4): 1403–48.

Iacovone, L., D. McKenzie, and William F. Maloney. 2017. "Management Upgrading in Colombia." Working Paper, World Bank, Washington, DC.

Isenberg, Daniel. 2012. "Focus Entrepreneurship Policy on Scale-Up, Not Start-Up." *Harvard Business Review*, November 30.

Jarmin, R. 1999. "Evaluating the Impact of Manufacturing Extension on Productivity Growth." *Journal of Policy Analysis and Management* 18 (1): 99–119.

Kasahara, Hiroyuki, Katsumi Shimotsu, and Michio Suzuki. 2014. "Does an R&D Tax Credit Affect R&D Expenditure? The Japanese R&D Tax Credit Reform in 2003." *Journal of the Japanese and International Economies* 34: 72–97.

Kikuchi, Tsuyoshi. 2009. "JICA-Supported Project for Quality and Productivity Improvement in Tunisia." In *Introducing KAIZEN in Africa*, edited by GRIPS Development Forum, 39–54. Tokyo: GRIPS Development Forum.

———. 2011. "The Role of Private Organization in the Introduction, Development and Diffusion of Production Management Technology in Japan." In *The Bulletin of the Graduate School of International Cooperation Studies* No. 4, Takushoku University, Japan.

Lederman, Daniel, M. Olarreaga, and L. Payton. 2010. "Export Promotion Agencies: Do They Work?" *Journal of Development Economics* 91: 257–65.

Lederman, Daniel, Marcelo Olarreaga, and Lucas Zavala. 2013. "The Effectiveness of Export Promotion Services in Promoting Firm Entry and Survival in World Markets." Policy Research Working Paper No. 73400, World Bank, Washington, DC.

Link, A. N., and J. T. Scott. 2009. "The Role of Public Research Institutions in a National Innovation System: An Economic Perspective." Working Paper, World Bank, Washington, DC.

Lokshin, B., and P. Mohnen. 2013. "Do R&D Tax Incentives Lead to Higher Wages for R&D Workers? Evidence from the Netherlands." *Research Policy* 42 (3): 823–30.

Lundvall, Bengt-Åke, K. J. Joseph, Cristina Chaminade, and Jan Vang, eds. 2009. *Handbook of Innovation Systems and Developing Countries: Building Domestic Capabilities in a Global Setting.* Cheltenham, UK: Edward Elgar.

Maloney, William F. 2017a. "Policies to Increase Firm Capabilities: Lessons from Japan and Singapore." Working Paper, World Bank, Washington, DC.

Maloney, William F. 2017b. "Revisiting the National Innovation System in Developing Countries." Working Paper, World Bank, Washington, DC.

Mariscal, A., and D. Taglioni. 2017. "GVCs as Source of Firm Capabilities." Unpublished Report, World Bank, Washington, DC.

McKenzie, D., and S. Puerto. 2017. "Business Training for Female Microenterprise Owners in Kenya Grew Their Firms without Harming Their Competitors." Brief, World Bank, Washington, DC.

McKenzie, D., & C. Woodruff. 2013. "What Are We Learning from Business Training and Entrepreneurship Evaluations around the Developing World?" *The World Bank Research Observer* 29 (1): 48–82.

Morris-Suzuki, T. 1994. *The Technological Transformation of Japan: From the Seventeenth to the Twenty-First Century.* Cambridge, UK: Cambridge University Press.

OECD (Organisation for Economic Co-operation and Development). 2015. OECD *Frascati Manual.* 2015 edition. Paris: OECD.

Özçelik, Emre, and Erol Taymaz. 2008. "R&D Support Programs in Developing Countries: The Turkish Experience." *Research Policy* 37 (2): 258–75.

Racine, J. L. 2004. Using Industrial Extension to Enhance the Technological Capabilities of Small and Medium Enterprises in Vietnam. Prepared for the United Nations Industrial Development Organization, Vietnam, and the National Institute for Science and Technology Policy and Strategy Studies, Ministry of Science and Technology, Vietnam.

———. 2010. "Harnessing Quality for Global Competitiveness." World Bank, Washington, DC.

Suzuki, A., and K. Igei. 2017. "Can Efficient Provision of Business Development Services Bring Better Results for SMEs? Evidence from a Networking Project in Thailand." JICA Research Institute Working Paper 147, JICA Research Institute, Tokyo.

Tinbergen, Jan. 1952. *On the Theory of Economic Policy*. Amsterdam: North-Holland Publishing Co.

Wada, M. 2009. "Sengo Nihon no Chusho Kigyo Seisaku, Nihon no Chusho Kigyo no ijutsu Suijun no Takasa no Gensen [Japanese SME Policies in the Postwar Period: Origin of the Japanese SME's High-Level Technology]." *The Teikyo University Economic Review* 42 (2).

World Bank. 2017. *Instruments to Support Business Innovation: A Guide for Policy Makers and Practitioners*. Washington, DC: World Bank.

Zanello, Giacomo, Xiaolan Fu, Pierre Mohnen, and Marc Ventresca. 2013. "The Diffusion of Innovation in the Private Sectors in Low-Income Countries (LICs): A Systematic Literature Review." TMD Working Paper 62, University of Oxford.

Zúñiga-Vicente, José Ángel, César Alonso-Borrego, Francisco J. Forcadell, and José I. Galán. 2014. "Assessing the Effect of Public Subsidies on Firm R&D Investment: A Survey." *Journal of Economic Surveys* 28 (1): 36–67.

8. The Continuing Challenge of Innovation and Capability Building in Developing Countries

The adoption of new processes and products by firms constitutes a central dimension of productivity growth and hence of economic development. The fruits of innovation—Mokyr's (2002) "Gifts of Athena"—have powered the advanced countries to levels of prosperity unimaginable even a century ago. And, as Schumpeter noted, the ability of lagging countries to tap into a now massive stock of global know-how and technical knowledge—to be able to adopt what has already been invented—is a potential transfer of wealth from rich to poor of historic proportions.

Yet relatively few developing countries have proven able to leverage this stock of knowledge to achieve sustained catch-up with advanced countries. This report begins by offering novel and detailed evidence on innovation patterns across developing countries. Although many firms report innovating in some way, more standardized measures, such as novel innovations and licensing or research and development (R&D), suggest very little is done by poor countries. These low rates of technological adoption represent a missed opportunity for reducing global poverty and inequality of equally historic proportions. Indeed, the apparent reluctance of firms and governments to pursue these opportunities in an aggressive and sustained manner poses an "innovation paradox": low investment in projects that by some measures would yield returns exceeding any other investment that poor countries could consider.

The report argues that this is not due to some irrationality on the part of developing country firms and governments. Nor is it simply a question of remedying the commonly articulated knowledge-related market failures. Rather, innovation in the developing world faces barriers that are orders of magnitude more challenging than those found in the advanced world along three key dimensions.

First, the dimensionality of the innovation problem is much greater. The advanced country literature can focus on appropriation externalities and other market failures affecting the accumulation of knowledge as a justification for a relatively narrow set of interventions because it can assume that most other markets function well and the necessary complementary factors are available. This is emphatically not the case in developing countries, which implies that the scope of the National Innovation System that policy makers must keep in their heads is much larger than in advanced countries and must include everything that affects the accumulation of all types of capital—physical, human, and knowledge assets—such as the business climate, the trade regime, labor regulations, tax regimes, or macroeconomic volatility.

It also implies that what looks like an innovation problem, such as a low rate of investment in R&D, may not be so, but rather reflect barriers to accumulating other factors, including physical and human capital. A firm may not invest in R&D because it is unable to import or finance the necessary machinery or to staff the project with the right technicians. Either shortage will depress the return on investment in R&D and thus validate the low rates of investment we see. Therefore, in determining the appropriate rate of innovation activities for an economy, it is important to consider the availability of other types of capital and complementary factors. For example, the common comparisons of gross domestic expenditure on R&D, under the assumption that more is better, are not justified.

Second, firm capabilities ranging from basic managerial skills to engineering capacity constitute a key missing complementary factor. They are critical ingredients of the absorptive capacity needed to facilitate technological adoption and to manage more complex innovation and R&D. The report shows that basic firm capabilities, too, diminish with distance from the frontier; hence, constructing the entire capabilities escalator is a central goal of developing country innovation policy. As the cover painting by Remedios Varo "The Creation of Birds" captures, metaphorically we need to teach firms how to fly. As we show, interventions in this realm are a standard part of the policy tool kit in the advanced world, and the upgrading of firm capabilities is the central ingredient of the Asian miracle in many narratives.

Third, weak capabilities on the government side compound the difficulties involved in constructing a functional National Innovation System (NIS) and building private sector capability. That is, the complexity and depth of the problems involved in innovation are greater in developing countries, while government capabilities to manage them are weaker. Innovation policy thus requires an honest balancing of capabilities with tasks, which demands working on a selective set of issues at a given moment rather than trying to import a full set of institutions and policies. More important, the common policy bias toward focusing mostly or exclusively on supporting R&D in low- and middle-income countries is likely to be misplaced. R&D is an important input for innovation, but it requires a set of capabilities that are unlikely to be met by many firms in developing countries. The report attempts to take a systematic look at how policy should be formulated across the different stages of the capabilities escalator.

To this end, it also, implicitly, makes a plea for more accurate measurement to help policy makers understand innovation in their economies and better benchmark performance of firms and the NIS. The analytical work here brings to light important shortcomings in the way statistical agencies are collecting and interpreting data. The lack of consistency in how firms interpret product and process innovation leads to poorer countries often appearing to be more innovative than more advanced countries, when other measures, such as the low productivity growth associated with innovation, suggest that the measurement of innovation needs to be revisited regarding both survey design and implementation.[1] In addition, although the World Management Survey employed here has been central to generating comparisons of capabilities across countries, we lack measures of higher-order technological capabilities. Even basic measures, such as presence of engineers in firms, are scarce, let alone measures of practices that support more sophisticated innovation.

Both better analytical frameworks and better data are necessary as developing countries face the dramatic and unpredictable evolution of the world economy. Numerous authors highlight rapid automation, a shift away from manufacturing and more toward services, and a less sure path of following the flying geese that the Asian miracles followed with such success (see, for example, Brynjolfsson and McAfee 2011, 2014; Rodrik 2016; Maloney and Molina 2016; Hallward-Driemeier and Nayyar 2017).

Some see a shift in technological paradigm to industry 4.0—characterized by the integration of big data with production processes (see OECD 2017)—that may change the parameters on how innovation is implemented, potentially allowing leapfrogging by developing countries (see also Lee 2016). It is still too early to identify what changes to production structures will become predominant, although some important changes are already occurring. The move from fixed and mass production to more flexible and mass customization production will require different sets of skills but also strong organizational and managerial practices to process and use data integration, manage leaner stocks and logistics systems, or coordinate production processes. Similarly, more flexible production systems are likely to require additional capabilities for information technology engineers, as well as new business models and customer relationships.

The shift toward services will also require a different set of capabilities in some dimensions from those required in manufacturing. Specifically, the literature on innovation in services suggests a more important role for human, design, and organizational factors than in manufacturing, and less reliance on R&D and scientific knowledge, because innovation in services is often more employee led than technology driven. Managerial and organizational practices are thus at least as important for services as they are for manufacturing.

Much of this literature is necessarily speculative beyond the general consensus that the rate of change appears to be accelerating. We cannot know with assurance which sectors will offer rapid routes to prosperity or what technologies will drive them. However, Pasteur's counsel that "fortune favors the prepared mind" remains as vitally relevant for countries as for people, and we have attempted to provide a map of areas where policy makers need to ensure they are ready. Raising the capabilities of firms to manage this uncertainty and chart their way forward, ensuring that the innovation system provides necessary complementary inputs and flows of knowledge, and strengthening government capabilities to manage a large and expanding set of challenges are all keys to resolving the innovation paradox and preparing countries for the opportunities ahead.

Note

1. In this regard, current efforts in the new edition of the *Oslo Manual* to better measure innovation through innovation surveys are very important and should be treated as a global public good, especially in relation to improve the way innovation is measured in developing countries.

References

Brynjolfsson, Erik, and Andrew McAfee. 2011. *Race against the Machine: How the Digital Revolution Is Accelerating Innovation, Driving Productivity, and Irreversibly Transforming Employment and the Economy.* Lexington, MA: Digital Frontier Press.

———. 2014. *The Second Machine Age: Work Progress and Prosperity in a Time of Brilliant Technologies.* New York: Norton.

Hallward-Driemeier, Mary, and Gaurav Nayyar. 2017. *Trouble in the Making? The Future of Manufacturing-Led Development.* Washington, DC: World Bank.

Lee, Keun. 2016. *Economic Catch-Up and Technological Leapfrogging: The Path to Development and Macroeconomic Stability in Korea.* London: Edward Elgar.

Maloney, William F., and Carlos Molina. 2016. "Are Automation and Trade Polarizing Developing Country Labor Markets, Too?" World Bank Policy Working Paper No. 7922, World Bank, Washington, DC.

Mokyr, Joel. 2002. *The Gifts of Athena: Historical Origins of the Knowledge Economy.* Princeton, NJ: Princeton University Press.

OECD (Organisation for Economic Co-operation and Development). 2017. *The Next Production Revolution: Implications for Governments and Business.* Paris: OECD.

Rodrik, Dani. 2016. "Premature Deindustrialization." *Journal of Economic Growth* 21 (1): 1–33.

www.ingramcontent.com/pod-product-compliance
Lightning Source LLC
Chambersburg PA
CBHW080421270326
41929CB00018B/3109